A Conflict of Loyalties

THE CASE FOR SELECTIVE CONSCIENTIOUS OBJECTION

Edited by JAMES FINN

PEGASUS / NEW YORK

Copyright © 1968 by Western Publishing, Inc.
All rights reserved. This book, or parts thereof,
may not be reproduced in any form without
permission of the publishers.
Printed in the United States of America.
Library of Congress Catalogue Card Number 68-21043

Contributors to *A Conflict of Loyalties*

JAMES FINN is editor of *worldview* and director of publications for the Council on Religion and International Affairs. Previously an editor of *Commonweal*, he has taught at the University of Nebraska, the University of Chicago and New York University. Author of *Protest: Pacifism and Politics*, his articles have appeared widely in national magazines and journals.

The late JOHN COURTNEY MURRAY, one of the leading theologians of the Catholic Church, was largely responsible for the form of the significant "Declaration on Religious Freedom" that emerged from Vatican Council II. Father Murray served on the National Advisory Commission on Selective Service.

PAUL RAMSEY, who is Harrington Spear Paine Professor at Princeton University, has written extensively on questions of politics and morality. Among his many books are *War and the Christian Conscience*, *Who Speaks for the Church?* and, most recently, *The Just War: Force and Political Responsibility*.

EVERETT E. GENDLER, rabbi of the Jewish Center in Princeton, is a member of the Fellowship of Reconciliation, the War Resisters League, and the Jewish Peace Fellowship.

MULFORD Q. SIBLEY, a professor of political science, is the co-author of *Conscription of Conscience*, a study of American conscientious objectors in World War II and the editor of *The Quiet Battle*, writings on the theory and practice of nonviolent resistance.

WILLIAM V. O'BRIEN is chairman of the Institute of World Polity and professor of government at Georgetown University. He is the editor of *World Polity: A Yearbook of Studies in International Law and Organization* and the author of *Nuclear War, Deterrence and Morality*.

QUENTIN L. QUADE, a member of the political science department at Marquette University, has written and lectured widely on political questions.

MICHAEL HARRINGTON is the author of *The Other America*, *The Accidental Century* and, most recently, *Toward a Democratic Left*.

ARNOLD S. KAUFMAN, associate professor of philosophy at the University of Michigan, is the author of *The Radical Liberal: New Man in American Politics*.

JEROME M. SEGAL, who graduated *magna cum laude* from the City College of New York, is now a graduate student in philosophy at the University of Michigan, where he was awarded the 1966 Hopwood Award for his writing.

TO MOLLY
WHOM I LOVE

Introduction

JAMES FINN

SELECTIVE conscientious objection has been called "a potentially explosive principle." That it is potentially explosive is the one judgment that invites general agreement. Beyond that point we enter into a morass of disputed action, of acrimony, suspicion, and accusation—and a measure of reasoned discussion.

We should not be surprised that this is so, for the principle of conscientious objection to war on a selective basis—objection not to all war, but to particular wars—touches deeply the rights and obligations of the individual person and the communities to which he belongs. It places a special burden on religious communities, the churches and synagogues that have taught him not only that he has political responsibilities but also that he must follow his conscience where it leads. It places a special burden on a political community that wishes to honor the individual conscience, but which cannot grant it an absolute right. As John Courtney Murray suggests, the whole relation of the person to society must be considered if our response is to be adequate to the challenge. The profound issues raised by the principle of selective conscientious objection (SCO) are likely to be with us for some time; this book is addressed to the demanding task of raising the level of public argument about those issues.

Some few people had considered the problem of the selective conscientious objector before the United States engaged itself militarily in Vietnam, but it is undoubtedly the war in Vietnam that has precipitated the problem into the national consciousness. Once raised, however, with the intensity and force they now command, the issues will not readily be brushed aside, for they transcend particular circumstances and will remain with us even when the war in Vietnam is, hopefully, brought to an end.

At least initially, the problem can be stated quite simply. The Universal Military Training and Service Act of the United States provides that a person can be granted legal status as a conscientious objector if he meets three criteria, if he is a person "who, *by reason of religious training and belief*, is *conscientiously opposed* to participation in *war in any form*. (My italics.) There is an increasing number of people who judge that formulation to be prejudicial to the person who, by reason of religious training and belief, is conscientiously opposed not to all war but to a particular war, for example, the war in Vietnam. And they are joined by others who would also jettison the first criterion. The burden of the present law is felt not only by the young man who believes that his conscience brings him into conflict with this law but also by those who would support him. For the National Selective Service Act declares that anyone "who knowingly counsels, aids, or abets another to refuse or evade registration or service in the armed forces . . . shall be liable to imprisonment for not more than five years or a fine of $10,000, or both."

In spite of these penalties, a number of young men who are not pacifists have judged the war in Vietnam to be unjust and have declared that they cannot in conscience participate in it. They have frequently been supported and in some instances persuaded by their peers and their elders. The late Martin Luther King, Jr., for example, said that "Every young man who believes this war [in Vietnam] is abominable and unjust should file as a conscientious objector." A group of over 1,000 students at Catholic, Protestant, and Jewish seminaries sent to the Secretary of Defense a letter endorsing selective objection. The United Presbyterian Church and the American Baptist Church have supported such policy. The General Board of the National Council of Churches has passed a resolution making support of selective conscientious objection the official policy of the Council. After a study that was initiated in November 1965, the General Synod of the United Church of Christ produced in June 1967 a pronouncement on selective objection that might serve as a model of the usual formulations. It reads in part:

> "Therefore be it resolved that the General Synod of the United Church of Christ recognize the right of conscientious objection to participation in a particular war or in war waged under particular circumstances, as well as the right of conscientious objection to participation in war as such; and
>
> "Be it further resolved that the General Synod remind those who are disposed to take this position that they ought not to do so lightly but only after careful examination and weighing of their own motives, the moral issues at stake including their proper obligations to the nation as an instrument of justice and order, the social as well as personal consequences of their decision, and their readiness to accept military or civilian service of equivalent time, risk, and personal inconvenience if afforded them, or else such penalties as may be legally imposed; and
>
> "Be it further resolved that the General Synod call upon pastors, congregations, Conferences, officers, and instrumentalities of the Church, and specifically upon the Council for Christian Social Action, to provide information, assistance, and counsel for those who take this position in order that they may both maintain integrity of conscience and find suitable alternative means for discharging their obligation as citizens in a time of national emergency or danger; and
>
> "Be it further resolved that the General Synod urge the Congress of the United States to amend the Selective Service Act to provide suitable alternatives of military or civilian service for those who on grounds of conscience object to participation in a particular war."

Recently, too, The Synagogue Council of America, representing the Orthodox, Conservative, and Reform branches of Judaism in the United States, has prepared for serious consideration a statement that would support the position of the selective objector. In addition to these religious groups, there are various political organizations, *ad hoc* committees, and an increasing number of responsible journals that vigorously support this principle.

The position of the selective conscientious objector was given, perhaps, its greatest support just as this book was going to press. Meeting in Uppsala, Sweden during the summer of 1968, the delegates to the World Council of Churches voted almost unanimously that "the churches should give spiritual care and support . . . to those who, especially in the light of the nature of modern warfare, object to participation in particular wars they feel bound in conscience to oppose. . . ." To translate this moral support into legal support is, of course, another matter. There are very few countries in the world that provide for the absolute pacifist the legal exemption that is available in the United States. However, since the World Council of Churches represents most major Protestant and Eastern Orthodox churches throughout the world, its position is not lightly to be dismissed.

But if support for the position is strong—and much more could be produced—so is opposition to it. When the House Armed Services Committee met to consider the draft law in May 1967, some members fulminated at those who counseled conscientious objection, mentioning Martin Luther King specifically. Representative F. Edward Hébert, Democrat of Louisiana, is reported to have urged prosecution, saying, "Let's forget the First Amendment. . . . It would show the American people that the Justice Department and Congress were trying to clean up this rat-infested area." After a young man of seventeen tried to explain to the Committee how one could be patriotic, not a pacifist, and yet object conscientiously to a particular war, one committee member said, "You make me sick." When some students questioned Hubert Humphrey in September 1967 about selective objection he said, "I don't think you can leave it up to individuals as to which wars they want to fight." To allow draftees to decide which wars are moral and which are not would, he added, "give a man God-like powers." A noted Chicago columnist expressed the same judgment in less hyperbolic terms when he said this would be "a helluva way to run a railroad." *The New York Times* considered the issue more soberly and responsibly and came to the same practical conclusion—the draftee could not pick and choose the war he chose to fight in.

These judgments probably represent the views of the majority of citizens and must be taken seriously. Nevertheless it must be said that few of the statements about the problem of the selective CO, pro or con, have been fully considered and well developed. On both sides it seems too often that the proponents of a particular position had the goal in mind and had only to chart the best path to get there. In so doing they bypassed or eluded basic issues and failed to draw upon those resources that will best enable us to cope with them. As Quentin Quade writes, "The result has been an often irrelevant argument, true to the American tradition of non-political discourses about politics."

The essays in this book are intended to point to and at least partially develop the relevant resources of our religious, political, and cultural traditions. They are also intended to show that these traditions are themselves subject to significant modification. To give but one example: the Catholic Church has always taught that one must follow his conscience, that "we must obey God rather than men" (Acts 5:29). But for many centuries that teaching was overshadowed by an emphasis on the difficulty of properly informing one's conscience and by an accompanying emphasis on the need to "be subject to the governing authorities for they are ordained of God" (Romans 13:1). In practical terms this left room for the Catholic pacifist—but very little. Some of the consequences of this attitude are evident in a Christmas message which Pius XII gave in 1956, stressing the obligations of the citizen in a time of war:

> "If, therefore, a body representative of the people and a Government—both having been chosen by free election—in a moment of extreme danger decide, by legitimate instruments of internal and external policy, on defensive precautions, and carry out the plans which they consider necessary, they do not act immorally; *so that a Catholic citizen cannot invoke his own conscience in order to refuse to serve and fulfill those duties the law imposes.*"

The portion that I have italicized may represent what most people still understand "the Catholic position" to be. That position was always subject to pressures exerted by the overarching political theory of which it was a part and by particular historical circumstances. Nevertheless, it gave little comfort to the person whose conscience brought him, in time of war, into principled opposition to the policies of the state. But the deliberations of Vatican Council II have given official support to such a person. One of the major documents of the Council, the *Pastoral Constitution on the Church in the Modern World,* states that "it seems right that laws make humane provisions for the case of those who for reasons of conscience refuse to bear arms, provided, however, that they agree to serve the human community in some other way." And when the Catholic bishops of the United States issued a statement on the war in Vietnam they said, "While we cannot resolve all the issues involved in the Vietnam conflict, it is clearly our duty to insist that they be kept under constant moral scrutiny. No one is free to evade his personal responsibility by leaving it entirely to others to make moral judgments."

This emphasis upon the individual's rights and responsibilities is simply supporting evidence for the view that our society generally has an increasing understanding of and sensitivity to the individual conscience. It is reflected in other religious and political institutions. This new perception helps to right a previous unbalance but it cannot dissolve, as some would like to have it, the tension that must always exist between the individual and his society and should not be thought to do so.

This volume is subtitled "The Case for Selective Conscientious Objection." A fair title, but if it did not sound too much like Erle Stanley Gardner, "The Case of the Selective Conscientious Objector" might have been better. For most of the contributors to this volume are intent less on making an argument for the controverted principle—although a few do—than on considering the politico-moral framework within which it should be discussed.

John Courtney Murray, Paul Ramsey, and Everett Gendler

show in different ways how religious traditions bear on political thought about the problem. Mulford Sibley shows how this immediate problem is related to the political tradition of dissent in this country and, incidentally, how much political and social enlightenment is provided by the struggle for what history has finally recorded as lost causes. William O'Brien examines the relevance of the Nuremberg principles—so often invoked—to this issue. Both Quentin Quade and Michael Harrington address themselves to the question of whether it is possible to distinguish moral objection to a war from political opposition and, indeed, the dangerous confusion that results if that distinction is not rightly considered. Arnold Kaufman examines not only the report made by the President's Commission on Selective Service, which rejected selective conscientious objection as an option, but the possibility of a system of raising an army that would largely bypass the most severe problems posed by selective conscientious objection. Finally, Jerome Segal presents his own ongoing attempt to receive exemption on other than a pacifist position. In doing so, he illustrates the very real difficulties that similar cases would present to the draft boards. Not every claimant for such an exemption would present such a complicated and involved position, but even the simplest and most direct might challenge the draft board's competence and, possibly, patience.

The war in Vietnam has raised the issue of the selective conscientious objector as an urgent question. But if the question subsides with the end of that war it will rise again. As Robert McNamara wrote when he was Secretary of Defense, "The greatest contribution Vietnam is making—right or wrong beside the point—is that it is developing an ability in the U.S. to fight a limited war, to go to war without the necessity of arousing the public ire. In that sense, Vietnam is almost a necessity in our history because that is the kind of war we'll most likely be facing for the next fifty years." It is too much to expect that we will cease to have, during the next fifty years, selective conscientious objectors, whether they are granted legal exemption or not.

A penultimate word. With one exception, all of the essays

here are original essays written expressly for this volume. The exception is that of the late Father John Courtney Murray. One of the last things he wrote, this text was originally delivered as a commencement address at Western Maryland College and is printed here with the kind permission of the authorities of that college. Finally, I would like to thank Susan Woolfson for her assistance at almost every stage of the manuscript.

Contents

INTRODUCTION BY JAMES FINN vii

War and Conscience 19
    JOHN COURTNEY MURRAY, S.J.

Selective Conscientious Objection:
Warrants and Reservations 31
    PAUL RAMSEY

War and the Jewish Tradition 78
    EVERETT E. GENDLER

Dissent: The Tradition and Its Implications 103
    MULFORD Q. SIBLEY

The Nuremberg Principles 140
    WILLIAM V. O'BRIEN

Selective Conscientious Objection
and Political Obligation 195
    QUENTIN L. QUADE

Politics, Morality, and Selective Dissent 219
    MICHAEL HARRINGTON

The Selective Service System: Actualities and Alternatives 240
    ARNOLD S. KAUFMAN

Conscientious Objection and Moral Agency 263
    JEROME M. SEGAL

APPENDIX 284

A Conflict of Loyalties

War and Conscience

JOHN COURTNEY MURRAY, S.J.

THE nation is confronted today with the issue of selective conscientious objection, conscientious objection to particular wars or, as it is sometimes called, discretionary armed service.

The theoretical implications of the issue are complex and subtle. The issue raises the whole question of war as a political act and the means whereby it should be confined within the moral universe. The issue also raises the question of the status of the private conscience in the face of public law and national policy. In fact, the whole relation of the person to society is involved in this issue. Moreover, the practical implications of the issue are far reaching. Selective conscientious objection, as Gordon Zahn has pointed out, is an "explosive principle." If once admitted with regard to the issue of war, the consequences of the principle might run to great lengths in the civil community.

My brief comments on this far-reaching principle are here directed, for reasons that will appear, both to the academic community, especially the student community, and to the political community and its representatives.

A personal note may be permissible here. During the deliberations of the President's Advisory Commission on Selective Service, on which I was privileged to serve, I undertook to advocate that the revised statute should extend the provisions of the present statute to include not only the absolute pacifist but also the relative pacifist; that the grounds for the status of conscientious objector should be not only religiously or non-religiously motivated opposition to participation in war in all forms, but also to similarly motivated opposition to participation in particular wars.

This position was rejected by the majority of the Commission. No Presidential recommendation was made to the Congress on the issue. There is evidence that the Congress is not sympathetic to the position of the selective objector and is not inclined to accept it. This does not mean that the issue has been satisfactorily settled. The public argument goes on and must go on. It is much too late in the day to defend the theory of General Hershey that "the conscientious objector by my theory is best handled if no one hears of him." The issue is before the country and it must be kept there.

It is true that the issue has been raised by a small number of people, chiefly in the academic community—students, seminarians, professors, not to speak of ministers of religion. But this group of citizens is socially significant. It must be heard and it must be talked to. I recognize that in many respects the issue has been raised rather badly, in ways that betray misunderstandings. Moreover, mistakes have been made about the mode of handling the issue. Nevertheless, the student community is to be praised for having raised a profound moral issue that has been too long disregarded in American life.

The American attitude toward war has tended to oscillate between absolute pacifism in peacetime and extremes of ferocity in wartime. Prevalent in American society has been an abstract ethic, conceived either in religious or in secularized terms, which condemns all war as immoral. No nation has the *jus ad bellum*. On the other hand, when a concrete historical situation creates the necessity for war, no ethic governs its conduct. There are no moral criteria operative to control the uses of force. There is no *jus in bello*. One may pursue hostilities to the military objective of unconditional surrender, and the nation may escalate the use of force to the paroxysm of violence of which Hiroshima and Nagasaki are forever the symbols, even though they were prepared for by the fire-bomb raids on Tokyo and by the saturation bombing of German cities. And all this use of violence can somehow be justified by slogans that were as simplistic as the principles of absolute pacifism.

These extreme alternatives are no longer tolerable. Our nation must make its way to some discriminating doctrine—moral, political, and military—on the uses of force. Perhaps the contemporary agitation in the academic community over selective conscientious objection may help in this direction. It has contributed to a revival of the traditional doctrine of the just war, whose origins were in Augustine and which was elaborated by the medieval Schoolmen and furthered by international jurists in the Scholastic tradition and by others in the later tradition of Grotius.

This doctrine has long been neglected, even by the churches; now we begin to witness its revival. We are also beginning to realize that it is not a sectarian doctrine. It is not exclusively Roman Catholic; in certain forms of its presentation, it is not even Christian. It emerges in the minds of all men of reason and good will when they face two inevitable questions. First, what are the norms that govern recourse to the violence of war? Second, what are the norms that govern the measure of violence to be used in war? In other words, when is war rightful, and what is rightful in war? One may indeed refuse the questions, but this is a form of moral abdication, which would likewise be fatal to civilization. If one does face the questions, one must arrive at the just war doctrine in its classical form, or at some analogue or surrogate, conceived in other terms.

The essential significance of the traditional doctrine is that it insists, first, that military decisions are a species of political decisions, and second, that political decisions must be viewed, not simply in the perspectives of politics as an exercise of power, but of morality and theology in some valid sense. If military and political decisions are not so viewed, the result is the degradation of those who make them and the destruction of the human community.

My conclusion here is that we all owe some debt of gratitude to those who, by raising the issue of selective conscientious objection, have undertaken to transform the tragic conflict in South Vietnam into an issue, not simply of political decision and military strategy, but of moral judgment as well.

The mention of South Vietnam leads me to my second point. The issue of selective conscientious objection has been raised in the midst of the war in Southeast Asia. Therefore, there is danger lest the issue be muddled and confused, or even misused and abused. In South Vietnam we see war stripped of all the false sanctities with which we managed to invest World War I and World War II, and to a lesser extent even Korea. The South Vietnamese war is not a crusade. There is not even a villain of the piece, as the Kaiser was, or Hitler, or Hirohito. Not even Ho Chi Minh or Mao Tse-tung can be cast in the role of the man in the black hat. We have no easy justifying slogans. We cannot cry, "On to Hanoi," as we cried "On to Berlin" and "On to Tokyo." This war does not raise the massive issue of national survival. It is a limited military action for limited political aims. As we view it in the press or on television it almost seems to fulfill Hobbes's vision of human life in the state of pure nature, "nasty, brutish, and short" except that the war in South Vietnam will not be short. In the face of the reality of it, all our ancient simplisms fail us. The American people are uncomfortable, baffled, and even resentful and angry.

To state the problem quite coldly, the war in South Vietnam is subject to opposition on political and military grounds, and also on grounds of national interest. This opposition has been voiced, and voiced in passionate terms. It has evoked a response in the name of patriotism that is also passionate. Consequently, in this context, it is difficult to raise the moral issue of selective conscientious objection. There are even some to whom it seems dangerous to let the issue be raised at all.

At this juncture I venture to make a recommendation in the common interest of good public argument. The issue of selective conscientious objection must be distinguished from the issue of the justice of the South Vietnam war. If this distinction is not made and enforced in argument, the result will be confusion and the clash of passions. The necessary public argument will degenerate into a useless and harmful quarrel. The distinction can be made. I make it myself. I advocate selective conscientious objection in the name of the traditional moral doctrine on war and also in the name of traditional American political doctrine on the rights of conscience. I am also prepared to make the case for the American military presence and action in South Vietnam.

I hasten to add that I can just about make the moral case. But so it always is. The morality of war can never be more than marginal. The issue of war can never be portrayed in black and white. Moral judgment on the issue must be reached by a balance of many factors. To argue about the morality of war inevitably leads one into gray areas. This is the point that was excellently made by Mr. Secretary Vance in his thoughtful address to the Annual Convention of the Episcopal Diocese of West Virginia on May 6th, 1967. It is evident here that our national tradition of confused moral thought on the uses of force does us a great disservice. It results in a polarization of opinion that makes communication among citizens difficult or even impossible. As Mr. Vance said, "In America today one of the greatest barriers to understanding is the very nature of the dialogue which has developed over the issue of Vietnam. It is heated and intolerant. The lines on both sides are too sharply drawn." I agree.

By the same token rational argument about selective conscientious objection will be impossible if public opinion is polarized by all the passions that have been aroused by the South Vietnam war. The two issues, I repeat, can and must be separated.

Another difficulty confronts us here. The issue about conscientious objection seems to have been drawn between the academic community and the political community—if you will, between poets and politicians, between scientists and statesmen, between humanists and men of affairs, between the churches and the secular world. It is, therefore, no accident that the dialogue at the present moment is in a miserable state. One may seek the reason for the fact in the differences in the climate of thought and feeling that prevail in the two distinct communities, academic and political. In consequence of this difference in climate each community, in a different way, can become the victim of the intellectual and moral vice that is known as the selective perception of reality.

It has been observed that the commitment of the intellectual today is not simply to the search for truth, but also to the betterment of the world—to the eradication of evil and to the creation of conditions of human dignity, first among which is peace. One might say that he has assumed a prophetic role, not unlike that of the churches. This is most laudable. The danger is lest the very strength of the moral commitment—to peace and against war—may foreclose inquiry into the military and political facts of the contemporary world—the naked facts of power situations and the requirements of law and order in an imperfect world, which may justify recourse to the arbitrament of arms. The problem is compounded if the so-called "norms of nonconformism" begin to operate. In that case opposition to war becomes the test of commitment to the ideals of the academic community.

On the other hand, the politician is no prophet. He may and should wish to shape the world unto the common desire of the heart of man which is peace with freedom and justice. But he is obliged to regard the world as an arena in which historical alternatives are always limited. He must face enduring problems, which may seem intractable, and which demand continuing decisions and acts. His actions cannot be based on absolute certainties or on considerations of the ideal, but on a careful balancing and choosing between the relativities that are before him.

In a word, for the prophets and for the intellectual, war is simply evil. For the politician it may well appear to be the lesser evil. This too is a conscientious position, but it is very different from the prophetic position, even though the choice of the lesser evil is part of the human pursuit of the good. In any event, it is not surprising that the politician and the prophet fail to communicate. It must also be remembered that the politician creates the situation within which the prophetic voice may be safely heard. There is much wisdom in the statement of Paul Ramsey: "The right of pacifist conscientious objection can be granted for the fostering of the consciences of free men, only because in national emergencies there are a sufficient number of individuals whose political discretion has been instructed in the need to repel, and the justice of repelling, injury to the common good."

I might add a practical point. The intellectual, whether he be student or professor, sets a premium on being provocative. His task is to challenge all certainties, especially easy certainties, and therefore to challenge the authorities on which certainties may depend. He wants evidence, not authority, and he sets a high value on dissent. All this is excellent and necessary. But there is danger in thrusting this scale of evaluation into the political community. It is not merely that the intellectual provokes reaction; he provokes an over-reaction on the part of the representatives of the political community, and thus he may easily defeat his own cause.

The advocacy of selective conscientious objection in the midst of the South Vietnamese war is provocative, and the political response to it has been an over-reaction. If you want the evidence you need only read the record of the hearings in the Congress, both Senate and House, on the revision of the Selective Service Act, when the issue of conscientious objection was brought up. The claim that the selective objector should be recognized was met with the response that all conscientious objection should be abolished.

All this amounts simply to saying that we face a most difficult issue. It might be of some value to try to locate some of the sources of the difficulty. Strictly on grounds of moral argument, the right conscientiously to object to participation in a particular war is incontestable. I shall not argue this issue. The practical question before all of us is how to get the moral validity of this right understood and how to get the right itself legally recognized, declared in statutory law. (I leave aside the question whether the right is a human right, which ought to receive sanction in the Bill of Rights as a constitutional right.)

I have made one practical suggestion already. The issue of selective conscientious objection must be argued on its own merits. It is not a question of whether one is for or against the war in Vietnam, for or against selective service, much less for or against killing other people. The worst thing that could happen would be to use the issue of conscientious objection as a tactical weapon for political opposition to the war in Vietnam or to the general course of American foreign policy. This would not be good morality and it would be worse politics. Perhaps the central practical question might be put in this way: Do the conditions exist which make possible the responsible exercise of a right of selective conscientious objection? The existence of these conditions is the prerequisite for granting legal status to the right itself.

There are two major conditions. The first is an exact understanding of the just-war doctrine, and the second is respect for what Socrates called "the conscience of the laws." I offer two examples, from among many, where these conditions were not observed.

Not long ago a young man in an anti-Vietnam protest on television declared that he would be willing to fight in Vietnam if he knew that the war there was just, but since he did not know, he was obliged to protest its immorality. This young man clearly did not understand the just-war doctrine and he did not understand what Socrates meant by the "conscience of the laws."

Similarly, in a statement issued by a Seminarians' Conference on the Draft held not long ago in Cambridge, there appears this statement: "The spirit of these principles [of the just-war doctrine] demands that every war be opposed until or unless it can be morally justified in relation to these principles." Socrates would not have agreed with this statement nor do I. The dear seminarians have got it backward.

The root of the error here may be simply described as a failure to understand that provision of the just-war doctrine which requires that a war should be "declared." This is not simply a nice piece of legalism, the prescription of a sheer technicality. Behind the provision lies a whole philosophy of the State as a moral and political agent. The provision implies the recognition of the authority of the political community by established political processes to make decisions about the course of its action in history, to muster behind these decisions the united efforts of the community, and to publicize these decisions before the world.

If there is to be a political community, capable of being a moral agent in the international community, there must be some way of publicly identifying the nation's decisions. These decisions must be declared to be the decisions of the community. Therefore, if the decision is for war, the war must be declared. This declaration is a moral and political act. It states a decision conscientiously arrived at in the interests of the international common good. It submits the decision to the judgment of mankind. Moreover, when the decision-making processes of the community have been employed and a decision has been reached, at least a preliminary measure of internal authority must be conceded by the citizens to this decision, even by those citizens who dissent from it. This, at least in part, is what Socrates meant by respect for the "conscience of the laws." This is why in the just-war theory it has always been maintained that the presumption stands for the decision of the community as officially declared. He who dissents from the decision must accept the burden of proof.

The truth, therefore, is contrary to the statement of the seminarians. The citizen is to concede the justness of the common political decision, made in behalf of the nation, unless and until he is sure in his own mind that the decision is unjust, for reasons that he in turn must be ready convincingly to declare. The burden of proof is on him, not on the government or the administration or the nation as a whole. He does not and may not resign his conscience into the keeping of the State, but he must recognize that the State too has its conscience which informs its laws and decisions. When his personal conscience clashes with the conscience of the laws, his personal decision is his alone. It is valid for him, and he must follow it. But in doing so he still stands within the community and is subject to its judgment as already declared.

Only if conceived in these terms can the inevitable tension between the person and the community be properly a tension of the moral order. Otherwise, it will degenerate into a mere power struggle between arbitrary authority and an aggregate of individuals, each of whom claims to be the final arbiter of right and wrong.

This is the line of reasoning which led me to argue before the National Advisory Commission on Selective Service that one who applies for the status of selective conscientious objector should be obliged to state his case before a competent panel of judges. I was also following the suggestion of Ralph Potter that the concession of status to the selective objector might help to upgrade the level of moral and political discourse in this country. It is presently lamentably low. On the other hand, Paul Ramsey has recently suggested that the matter works the other way round. "A considerable upgrading of the level of political discourse in America is among the conditions of the possibility of granting selective conscientious objection. At least the two things can and may and must go together." He adds rather sadly: "The signs of the times are not propitious for either." I agree.

Those who urge the just-war doctrine as the ground for selective conscientious objection must understand the doctrine itself. They may not naïvely or cynically employ it as a device for opting out from under the legitimate decisions of the political community, or as a tactic for political opposition to particular wars. Rightly understood, this doctrine is not an invitation to pacifism, and still less to civil disobedience. There is a further requisite for legal recognition of selective conscientious objection. It is the prior recognition of the difference between moral objection to a particular war and political opposition to a particular war. This seems to be the sticking point for the political community. It brings into question the whole ethos of our society in the matter of the uses of force.

Historically, we have been disposed to regard the intuitive verdict of the absolute pacifist that all wars are wrong as having the force of a moral imperative. The same moral force is not conceded to the judgment of the conscientious man, religious or not, who makes a reflective and discriminating judgment on the war in front of him. The general disposition is to say that objection to particular wars is and can only be political and, therefore, cannot entitle anyone to the status of conscientious objector.

Here again there is a misunderstanding of the just-war doctrine. In fact there seems to be a misunderstanding of the very nature of moral reasoning. The just-war doctrine starts from the moral principle that the order of justice and law cannot be left without adequate means for its own defense, including the use of force. The doctrine further holds that the use of force is subject to certain conditions and its justice depends on certain circumtances. The investigation of the fulfillment of these conditions leads the conscientious man to a consideration of certain political and military factors in a given situation. There is the issue of aggression, the issue of the measure of force to be employed in resisting it, the issue of probable success, the issue of the balance of good and evil that will be the outcome. The fact that his judgment must take account of military and political factors does not make the judgment purely political. It is a judgment reached within a moral universe, and the final reason for it is of the moral order.

There is some subtlety to this argument. But that is not, I think, the reason why the political community refuses to assimilate or accept it. The reasons are of the practical order. The immediate reason is the enormous difficulty of administering a statute that would provide for selective conscientious objection. The deeper reason is the perennial problem of the erroneous conscience. It may be easily illustrated.

Suppose a young man comes forward and says: "I refuse to serve in this war on grounds of the Nuremberg principle." Conversation discloses that he has not the foggiest idea what the Nuremberg principle really is. Or suppose he understands the principle and says: "I refuse to serve because in this war the United States is committing war crimes." The fact may be, as it is in South Vietnam, that this allegation is false. Or suppose he says, "I refuse to serve because the United States is the aggressor in this war." This reason again may be demonstrably false. What then is the tribunal to do?

Here perhaps we come to the heart of the difficulty and I have only two things to say. First, unless the right to selective objection is granted to possibly erroneous consciences it will not be granted at all. The State will have to abide by the principle of the Seeger case, which does not require that the objection be the truth but that it be truly held. One must follow the logic of an argument wherever it leads. On the other hand, the political community cannot be blamed for harboring the fear that if the right to selective objection is acknowledged in these sweeping terms, it might possibly lead to anarchy, to the breakdown of society, and to the paralysis of public policy.

Second, the reality of this fear imposes a further burden on the consciences of those who would appeal to freedom of conscience. Selective objection is not a trivial matter. As Ralph Potter has said: "The nation is ultimately a moral community. To challenge its well-established policies as illegal, immoral, and unjust is to pose a threat, the seriousness of which seems at times to escape the critics themselves, whether by the callowness of youth or the callousness of usage." It must be recognized that society will defend itself against this threat, if it be carelessly wielded.

The solution can only be the cultivation of political discretion throughout the populace, not least in the student and academic community. A manifold work of moral and political intelligence is called for. No political society can be founded on the principle that absolute rights are to be accorded to the individual conscience, and to all individual consciences, even when they are in error. This is rank individualism and to hold it would reveal a misunderstanding of the very nature of the political community. On the other hand, the political community is bound to respect conscience. But the fulfillment of this obligation supposes that the consciences of the citizens are themselves formed and informed.

Therefore, the final question may be whether there is abroad in the land a sufficient measure of moral and political discretion, in such wise that the Congress could, under safeguard of the national security, acknowledge the right of discretionary armed service. To cultivate this power of discretion is a task for all of us.

Selective Conscientious Objection: Warrants and Reservations

PAUL RAMSEY

1. Discretionary Armed Service

"Is military service in this country's armed forces an option exercisable solely at the discretion of the individual?" A quick answer to that question would be to say: "That depends on his discretion."

This is to say that whether an individual is apt rightfully to exercise the choice extended him by a system of optional service would depend on how his conscience—his discretion—has been formed and informed. Moreover, whether any government in securing the political common good could ever grant selective armed service at the conscientious discretion of individuals depends on whether the citizens of a nation are more like Socrates, who while suffering imprisonment and death for conscience's sake still effectually acknowledged "the conscience of the laws," than they are like Sophists putting in individualistic claims that their own subjective opinion is the measure of truth. Not everyone who is 18 or 60 years old has arrived at the age of political discretion.

This, of course, is only to state the problem of conscience in relation to military service. Yet it is a statement of the problem that needs a great deal of repetition and clarification today.

This calls our attention to a fundamental fact concerning man in his political existence. The individual is included within the common good of the nation-state (which is to date the most inclusive, actual political community that we have), but he is *not* included in the national common good *to the whole extent of his personhood*. The person transcends the political community, but again *not to the whole extent of his being*. The person does not exist simply to serve the state, but neither does the state (meaning political society, not merely the "government") exist simply to serve an aggregation of individuals. Some human rights touch the person and at the same time the common good so directly that they are absolutely inalienable. Others in the hierarchy of rights are inalienable only substantially: these pertain to the person given certain conditions of fact, but under other circumstances they can properly be restricted. They can be limited so that other rights and social values may better be served. There is, indeed, a distinction between the *possession* of certain human rights, and the claim that one of these rights may now justly be *exercised* in a given way.[1]

This means, for example, that while under some conceivable circumstances the state may secure the common good by directing a mathematician to teach mathematics, the state cannot tell him the mathematical truth he should teach. Similarly, a citizen may be required to serve in the armed forces and to be willing to lay down his life for his country. But this does not mean that his conscience is entirely included within the determinations of public policy. The question is how we are to understand the legitimate claims of personal conscience in conflict or in symbiosis with the legitimate claims of the national common good to which every individual also "belongs" in the very marrow of his humanity.

It is now well established in U.S. draft laws that allowance should be made for special status for men who "by reason of religious training and belief" are "conscientiously opposed to participation in war in any form." We shall later take up the recent judicial decisions that may have interpreted "religious" to mean "conscientious." The point here is that, to date, the tangible and readily understood test for either or both is that a man shall be opposed to participation in war in any form, and the further point that this provision of alternate service for the pacifist objector is not a *constitutional* right but a "right" granted by the "grace" of Congress in the positive legislation it enacts.

An individual's spiritual counselors may advise him that by the grace of Jesus Christ he should follow his own upright conscience or even his erring conscience on pain of making himself "good for nothing" (mortal sin). Still the pacifist objector is relieved of the obligation to bear arms not because of a constitutional principle, but because it has accorded with the policy of Congress thus to relieve him. Doubtless ours is a better society, the common good is better achieved, because of this. Doubtless Congress also, and not individuals or churches only, should recognize that in the forum of conscience there is duty to a moral power higher than the state. But the Congress is not *legally or constitutionally* bound to do this. In this there is a relic of the fact that while the person is transcendent he does not transcend the national common good to the whole extent of his being.

This means that persons whose responsibility it is to direct the community toward the political good, and the public processes by which the political society acts together, in one way rather than another, have their consciences too. The "right" of pacifist conscientious objection can be granted for the fostering of the consciences of free men only because in national emergencies there are a sufficient number of individuals whose political discretion has been instructed in the need to repel, and the justice of repelling, injury to the common good. No political society can be founded on a principle according *absolute* rights to possibly errant individual consciences. It is the aggregate-individualism of such a view, and not true conscientiousness, that makes such an account of political obligation a radically non-political and an ultimately inhumane viewpoint.

Absolute pacifists who are politically realistic have commonly recognized this. Some have as members of Congress felt themselves bound to *vote* for military appropriations, or at least not inhibit existing political purposes, even while by their lives and witness they tried to persuade "the conscience of the laws" that another direction might be taken by a political community resolved together to go the way they themselves must tread. While remaining faithful to the dictates of their own consciences, they have not been impelled to a confusion of categories, or made legalistic-pacifist use of the just-war criteria as if that doctrine governing the political use of armed force was designed to make peace by disqualifying one by one all wars. They have not been too ready to sign public manifestos that contribute to the "credibility gap" while hastily condemning the same from the side of the present Administration.

2. *Selective Conscientious Objection*

This brings us to "particular war objection" or "selective conscientious objection," which might be the meaning of the proposal that service in the armed forces should be an option exercisable solely at the "discretion" of the individual. The present writer argued as long ago as 1961 that there should be a category of "just-war objection" in the mind of the church and instituted by Congress in the draft laws it enacts. This was long before the current agitation over this matter of selective or particular-war conscientious objection. I may perhaps point this out without undue personal *hubris*, since I only followed the moral argument where it led. I wrote then: the church must "make the decision to support its members who refuse to fight because they believe a particular war to be unjust with the same vigor with which it has in recent years supported the pacifist witness within its ranks and within the nation. This would mean that the church will consciously attempt to obtain in military draft laws some status for those who refuse to fight unjustly as well as for those who have conscientious objection to all war. . . . If the decision is reached that the church's doctrine of just or limited war [is addressed only to magistrates or to topmost political leaders and military commanders, and] is *not* addressed to private citizens and soldiers, then, if also penance is good for anything, consideration should be given to reviving the requirement of forty days' penance following participation in any war[!]" [2]

Yet the reservations and conditions which must surround just objection to particular wars, and which indeed could make this a possible enactment of Congress, are the same as in the case of pacifist objection. This, too, depends on the "discretion" abroad in the land—on the forming and informing influences upon political consciences in our society. Ralph Potter, who has written the best essay I have seen on the subject of "Conscientious Objection to Particular Wars,"[3] believes that the granting of status to selective conscientious objectors would "demand a considerable upgrading of the level of political discourse in America." Such an enactment, he believes, would contribute to that goal. A selective objector would have to look to his reasons, and so would the members of his draft or review board. Appeals to *jus contra bellum* and *jus in bello* would require formulation, and empirical knowledge in applying these tests, and not slogans that do not admit the real possibility of *jus ad bellum*. A premium would be placed on the *discriminating* religious conscience and on a higher order of ethico-political reasoning than is fostered by a system that focuses attention, and with less refinement of men's judgment, upon the comparatively simple decision made by an intuitive conscience between participation in war and participation in no war.

I rather think it works the other way round. A considerable upgrading of the level of political discourse in America is among the conditions of the possibility of granting selective conscientious objection. At least, these two things can and may and must go together. The signs of the times are not propitious for either, nor are religious leaders contributing all they could either to the upgrading of public discourse concerning the morality of participation in war in general or to advancing the cause of conscientious discretion concerning particular wars. In the contest of extremist assertions that "this is Lyndon Johnson's war" or "McNamara's war" or that our leaders are committing "murder" and "genocide" or that this is a "race" war of white versus colored peoples, or that this nation's leaders are obsessed with a compulsion to play "world policeman" or are conducting a "holy war" against the legitimate aspirations of an underdeveloped people or are activated by a blind anti-communism—in such a context the proposition that "military service in this country's armed forces is an option exercisable solely at the discretion of the individual" has one sort of meaning.[4] That meaning should be refused by anyone who has any conception of the meaning of an individual's political obligation.

Yet in another context precisely this proposition could be defended as a proper enabling ordinance for the discriminating consciences of free men in politics. The question is whether we are nurturing such an ethos. No nation can grant draft exemption to conscientious objectors to particular wars if it is widely believed among the people that the tests of justice in war are mainly ways of securing peace by discrediting one by one all wars. The tests are rather directives addressed to every generation of young men, no less than to their political leaders, concerning how within morally tolerable limits they can and should protect and secure the relatively juster cause by resort, if need be, to a political use of armed force.

In order to sustain the individual consciences of generations of young men in the determination of the justice or the injustice of their participation in particular wars, there is need for spokesmen of the churches always to remember all the sons of the church wherever they may be—those in the armed services (as did the Vatican Council[5] and as did not the 1966 Geneva Conference of the World Council of Churches Conference on Church and Society) no less than those sons of the church who in conscience protest particular wars. There is need for church leaders when acting severally or collectively as citizens commending some particular policy and exerting strictly political pressure to use their "Reverends" as the regulations of Princeton University require me to use my "Professor," for purposes of identification only. Moreover, there is no profit in the unexplicated verdict of a congress of Christians declaring, as did the 1966 Geneva Conference, that recent U.S. actions in Vietnam "cannot be justified,"[6] when the need is for the clarification of decision-oriented and action-oriented standards for telling whether any particular war or act of war is justified or not, and for the creation of an ethos in which men are apt to be able to exercise the requisite moral and political wisdom.

In "workshops" on conscientious objection, sometimes sponsored by ministers and local church councils, has there been as much open and realistic debate over how responsibly to tell political justice in war and peace as there has been simple instruction to young men concerning their rights and privileges under the draft laws? As much concern over how to form *one's own* mature conscience as about how to act on an assumed particular opinion? If not, people's responses to this or any other war are left close to the visceral and emotional level, and our responsibility for constantly upgrading political discourse in this country has simply been abandoned.

No political community can be based solely on accrediting the claim that (in the sense that Nietzsche meant it) "at least everyone claimeth to be an authority on 'good' and 'evil.' "[7] The rejection of such individualism was the import of the provision in the just-war theory that to be just, an extension of politics into a resort to armed force must be legitimately or officially declared. That test was never meant to be used in legalistic-pacifist fashion to condemn a war merely because it is not *technically* "declared." It refers rather to the authority of the established political processes by which the political community directs its policy and exerts its united force one way rather than another. Nor was the provision meant *simply* to exclude "private wars" (or *private* peace-making expeditions to Hanoi on the part of U.S. citizens).

Instead, this provision expresses the basic requirement that for there to be a political community, capable of being an actor in the international community, there must be some way of identifying a nation's decisions or commitment, and some measure of internal authority accorded to this "voice" even by those of its citizens who dissent from it. "If the political community is not to be torn to pieces as each man follows his own viewpoint, authority is needed. This authority must dispose the energies of the whole citizenry toward the common good. . . ."[8]

Does this mean that there is no room for effectual conscientious objection to particular wars? Or that only the "upright" conscience should be allowed such rights, or only the consciences judged by legitimate social processes to be activated by a proper political "discretion"? It does not! Still there is a burden upon the consciences of selective objectors that can be identified.

There is, of course, no "third man" to insure that an individual has discerned the true justice and the really responsible political policy in opposition to the public conscience. There is no way to appeal to "objective obligation" beyond the good faith efforts of conscientious men seeking to discern in their sense of "subjective obligation" their real objective duties. Unless, therefore, selective or particular-war objection is granted to possibly errant consciences, it will not be accorded at all; and in no way will a discriminating transcendence of the person over the state be capable of coming into evidence while the state makes war.

If ever talk about "just-war conscientious objection," and about the limits drawn by moral law and the gospel, is to be reduced to action, there must be a manifold work of political intelligence directed toward making this an acknowledged part of citizen responsibility. There can be no question about the *moral* right. In the foregoing, I have spoken mainly about the conditions of the possibility of *exercising* this right, and the prerequisites to granting it *legal* status.

Still there would need to be acknowledged an important ingredient within the subjective consciences exercising objection to particular wars. This is a minimum acknowledgment of the authority of the laws. If political community is not to be torn to pieces between upright and errant consciences, or for that matter between various assertions of upright conscience disagreeing as to the justice of the cause, there must be in each some significant measure of acknowledgement that political authority must dispose the energies of the whole toward the common good as this has been determined by the legitimate decision-making processes of the community. This is simply the bracing requirement that a man should concede the judgments of justice that have been made on behalf of the nation *unless and until,* by looking to his reasons, he is searchingly sure in his own mind that the nation's course of action is unjust. This requires not *certainty* (since there is no "third man" or "impartial observer" to adjudicate between his personal conscience and the conscience of the laws), but it does require a degree of certitude attained in an inward wrestle for valid moral insight, and accepting a burden of proof favoring the authority of the commitment of the nation to which an individual belongs unless and until he has succeeded in winning his way with integrity to a subjectively sound decision by means of all the sources of enlightenment available to him in forming his own conscience.

This is a slight thing, and the agent's own; but it is no mean requirement. Especially not in a day in which it has become fashionable, as a first move, to disbelieve the moral credibility of one's own government; and when with no sense of political incongruity one young man in an anti-Vietnam protest could declare over television for all his fellow countrymen to hear that, of course he'd fight in Vietnam if he *knew* the war there was just, but since he didn't know he had to protest its immorality!

3. *The Burke Marshall Report*

A minority on the National Advisory Commission on Selective Service[9] wanted to recommend to the President that exemption be granted to conscientious objectors to particular wars. A reading of their arguments reveals that the acceptability of selective conscientious objection depends on the answers to two questions. Its acceptability depends first of all upon whether there exists in the ethos of this country a moral consensus or doctrine on the uses of military force that could be set alongside the time-honored doctrine that all uses of military force are inherently immoral in determining both to be statutory grounds for conscientious objection. Unless this is the case, it would seem that the proposal for particular-war objection is at bottom a plea for individualistic consciences, all sincerely moral no doubt, each to be able not simply to make his own determination of justice within some minimal agreement about everyone's political responsibilities, but rather free to *determine how he is going to determine* what is just or unjust for him to do, with *whatever degree* of recognition he may *choose* to give to the claims of his nation upon him. The latter view of the person and community and of freedom of conscience never composed the moral substance of political community. This draws our attention to the large issues that may lurk behind proposals of selective objection, and which must be brought to light and resolved before this could become national policy.

The possibility and acceptability of selective conscientious objection depends secondly upon whether we can articulate and reduce to actionable principles the "competence" of panels, mentors, and young men to determine whether judgments are "truly held" in the case of objection to a particular war no less than in the case of absolute pacifism. We must face the fact that no nation (except for extrinsic reasons) can accept an objector's statement that his political beliefs are "truly held" conscientious convictions. We must face the fact that the requirement of opposition to "participation in war in any form" provides some check, some clarification, of the conscientiousness of the objection which is at trial. We must face the fact that a viable substitute for this test that can be "taken hold of" must be found if we are to make provision for objection to particular wars. We must acknowledge, in other words, that no political society can allow exemption for purely political objection to its uses of military force, and we must find a way to distinguish between this and refusals to participate on moral grounds if we are ever to legislate exemption for selective conscientious objection. Without the manifold intellectual work that is needed to wrestle successfully with this distinction, the proposal of selective objection will remain an ideological protest—or else one that is based on the optimistic faith of philosophical anarchism that out of the self-determining freedom of individual consciences political community can be composed and its energies effectively disposed one way rather than another in the course of its history.

We who are proponents of particular-war conscientious objection need to take seriously the views of this distinguished and presumably morally sensitive group of our fellow citizens on the National Advisory Commission and find the way to answer them, if there is such a way. The Commission said: (1) "It is one thing to deal in law with a person who believes he is responding to a moral imperative outside of himself when he opposes all killing. It is another to accord a special status to a person who believes there is a moral imperative which tells him to kill under some circumstances and not kill under others." Moreover, it observed, the "classical Christian doctrine" on the subject of just and unjust wars, which would be interpreted in different ways by different denominations, is "therefore not a matter upon which the Commission could pass judgment."

Here a partial reply might be that this is a doctrine concerning justice on which more than Christians could and do agree, and also that neither the Commission nor competent panels in the future are required to judge this on its merits (any more than they are required to credit the pacifist's claim) in order to be able to recognize that consciences formed in these terms may be granted exemption. The crux of the obscurity that would need to be cleared up was in the Commission's second point. (2) ". . . So-called selective pacifism is essentially a political question of support or nonsupport of a war and cannot be judged in terms of special moral imperatives." Coupled with this was the judgment that conscientious objection which only goes so far as "political opposition to a particular war should be expressed through recognized democratic processes and should claim no special right of exemption from democratic decisions." To this the Commission added that (3) "the distinction is dim" between selective pacifism and selective disobedience to all laws, or conscientious opposition to the payment of a particular tax [e.g., the presently imposed 10% surtax, a chief reason if not the sole reason for which is the cost of the war in Vietnam]. Finally, (4) selective conscientious objection would pose a special problem for men already in the Armed Forces. "Forcing upon the individual the necessity of making that distinction [between the justness and unjustness of any war—or, in the minority's words, "the measure and mode in which military force is to be employed"]—

which would be the practical effect of taking away the government's obligation to make it for him—could put a burden hitherto unknown on the man in uniform and even on the brink of combat, with results that could be disastrous to him, to his unit, and to the entire military tradition. No such problem arises for the conscientious objector, even in uniform, who bases his moral stand on killing in all forms, simply because he is never trained for nor assigned to combat duty."[10]

A reply, and I think a sufficient reply, should be inserted here to the Commission's final point. The Commission is mistaken, at least from the point of view of the just-war doctrine on the uses of military force, in supposing that laws and practices based on notions of *jus in bello* (justice in war) would "take away" the government's obligation to make these decisions for the man in uniform, or would mean that the government would relinquish this primary obligation, or that the soldier on the "brink of combat" would have put upon him the "burden hitherto unknown" of making the *primary* decision concerning the justice of the "measure or mode" of the war's conduct. The presumption would rather be that lawful commands are just unless and until the soldier conscientiously believes he knows they are *un*just. This mistake about the presumption of legitimacy is one that is commonly made today not only in regard to *jus in bello* but also by persons who are too eager to transform *jus ad bellum* (the "just cause" for war) into a doctrine of *jus contra bellum*.

The Commission might have been more open to this understanding of the presumption, particularly since some, at least, of the decisions in an actual war situation have a clarity that can take them out of the shadowy realm of mixed political and moral decisions. It has recently been argued in regard to "opposition to particular weapons" that:

> Here perhaps the question of proof of sincerity and the probable effect on conduct of granting or denying exemption is not so very different from the case of the person opposed to war in any form. The morality of particular weapons is a question that can be rescued from the flux of uncertain facts and relative values, continuity of belief and expression may be demonstrable, and the determination of

the objector not to have a hand in the employment of these weapons may be as firm as the determination of the absolute pacifist.[11]

This paragraph speaks, of course, about decisions to go or not to go to war; and it must be said that "opposition to particular *weapons*" would hardly be the discriminations between just and unjust conduct in war countenanced by the just-war doctrine on the uses of military force. But Mansfield's point is well taken: because the continuity of belief and expression may be demonstrable here, this would be a basis of particular conscientious objection which, if granted, would not be subject to the chief reason the Commission supported exemption for absolute conscientious objection but not for selective objection. For the Commission found itself unable to distinguish in the latter case between conscientious moral objection and purely political opposition to a particular war.

We should press for the development in our military codes of the possibility of *defenses* that can be entered against a charge of disobedience to a "lawful command" proving that the command was not lawful because it called for an *unjust* action to be done. Even on the brink of combat or in the middle of combat it should be possible for a man who grants the presumption of legitimacy resident in every particular command to have, against the charge of disobedience, the possibility of a defense based on the grounds that he was commanded needlessly or wantonly to kill prisoners of war, or to perform acts of cruelty, to do something inherently immoral, or to make war in ways that are contrary to international conventions governing warfare to which his nation was a party. So understood, this should not be a burden disastrous to the soldier, to his unit, or to the entire military tradition, but a quite necessary element in the marginal morality of warfare. Having said this, the general proposal that selective conscientious objection be adopted still has to face the main reasons the Commission refused to recommend it.

4. What Happened on the Way to Selective Conscientious Objection?

Two things happened before we got started. These two preconditions are apt to void the current pleas coming from many quarters calling upon the nation to recognize, indeed encourage, more discriminating conscientious judgment concerning the justice of particular wars by instituting particular-war objection. Unless these trends or happenings are reversed, it is exceedingly doubtful whether Congress will grant or should grant exemption, with alternate service, to consciences more selective than the pacifist. Yet both *seem* irreversible.

The first is the steady erosion, for at least the last three or four decades, of shared basic convictions concerning normative structures in social ethics having for religious people final theological warrant. There has been a flight from the use of rational principles of analysis, and a lack of political philosophy or norms governing our deliberation upon moral questions. This means that there can be no fundamental moral consensus among or within the religious communities of our nation. At least a retreat from the articulation of the lineaments of a political philosophy is what happened in Protestantism.

What has happened in the absence of norms and intervening principles governing action is rather like a hectic game of hurley in Ireland which was once interrupted when the ball went into a tree. All efforts to dislodge it by shaking the tree and throwing stones at the branches having failed, one captain is said to have exclaimed to the other: "Ah, the hell with it, let's get on with the game!" The name of the game is casuistry with principles, decision-making that is believed to be more responsible because situations are so unique that there are no relevant, *specific* norms. Have not such views taken increasing hold among us, leading not to increasing discrimination and refinement in moral judgment but in the very opposite direction on every moral matter, including the morality of war?

The second thing that happened before we got started on the

way to selective conscientious objection was in the legal order. This too is extraordinarily apt to frustrate that conclusion, and in the practical order it may force the religious communities to *choose* between two "revisions" of our draft laws. We may have to decide which of two "liberalizations" we wish to support, selective conscientious objection to particular wars *or* the interpretation lately placed upon the *meaning* of conscientious religious objection by the U.S. Supreme Court.

In the case *Torcaso v. Watkins,* the Court had before it for decision the matter of a man who, elected Notary Public, refused to take the oath required by the state of Maryland that he believed in a Supreme Being. Instead of resolving this matter equitably on the narrow grounds of appeal to the Ethical Culture Society to which Mr. Torcaso belonged, a group long ago recognized by the courts as a "religion" because of its cult and practices, the Court chose rather to launch out upon an ocean of theological speculation, and it might have assigned Mr. Torcaso a godless religion *without* the trappings heretofore recognized (at law) as also necessary to there being a religion. The Court went so far in a *dictum* as to speak of "Secular Humanism" as also among the religious sects that do not believe in a Supreme Being.[12] *Dicta* of the Supreme Court that are in accord with the trends of the age have a way of becoming law.

The *Torcaso* case with its *dictum* about the meaning of religion almost immediately entered into the decision of our courts in conscientious objector cases. By a cluster of decisions the Court "constructively" imposed an assertedly constitutional meaning upon legislation enacted by Congress in regard to religious objection to military service. In this way alone could the Court, on the *Torcaso* construction of the meaning of "religion," avoid declaring the more limited and the more probable common sense meaning of legislation enacted by Congress to be unconstitutional.

The 1940 Selective Training and Service Act had granted exemption to those who by reason of their religious training and belief are opposed to participation in war in any form. Then there arose divergence in the decisions of the circuit courts of appeal. Some districts limited exemption to cases showing religious training and belief in an ordinary language sense of these expressions. One circuit, however, went beyond a cult-and-practices definition of "religion" to require a showing of belief in a Supreme Being to warrant the religious exemption. Because of this lack of uniformity, the Congress in 1948 added to Section 6 (j) of the 1940 Act a statutory definition of religious training and belief, requiring "belief in a relation to a Supreme Being involving duties superior to those arising from any human relation," and specifically excluded "essentially political, sociological, or philosophical views, or a merely personal code."

After that enactment, decisions on appeal in conscientious objector cases proved no more uniform than before. This finally brought the matter before the Supreme Court for resolution during its 1964-65 term. The thing to be noted concerning the Court's resolution of these dilemmas is the fact that, with *Torcaso's dictum* as its premise, the Court drove even deeper into the territory of theological interpretation, and even unfolded a speculative theory of conscience. It did not find a way, if indeed such a way was possible, to bend the uniform interpretation of the 1948 statute back either to the more tangible meaning of "religious training and belief," to the meaning "religion" usually has at law in other connections, or to require that some evidence of religious training, practices, or influences be shown upon beliefs held in good faith, and *nothing more*.

The hinge case was *United States v. Seeger*. The applicant had been reared in a devout Roman Catholic home and was a close student of Quaker beliefs, from which he claimed to derive much of his own thought. He frequently attended Quaker meetings. That would seem enough evidence of religious training and belief, in the law's ordinary view of these matters. The applicant did not rest his claim to exemption upon these facts, as perhaps he might have done before the 1940 Act was amended in 1948. Still this would not have prevented the Court from basing a decision in his favor on these facts had it chosen to do so. The Court might simply have struck down the 1948 requirement of "belief in a Supreme Being involving duties superior to those arising from any human relation" as *unconstitutional*. This would have returned the law of the land in the matter of exemption for conscientious objection to the 1940 Selective Training and Service Act, plus placing the lower courts on notice that the Supreme Court meant no additional (Supreme Being) test to be required under it.

Instead the Court strained to find the 1948 statute *constitutional*, and it was therefore driven to search in the inner recesses of "conscience" for the equivalent of (lower case) "supreme being" in most or many men. It searched for that paramountcy in natural conscience which the Congress, being composed of reasonable men, must not have meant to exclude by its reference to "a relation to a Supreme Being." Just as the Court's *dictum* in *Torcaso* created for the applicant "Secular Humanism" as a religion which it might have assigned him, so in *Seeger* the Court created for the applicant the equivalent of a relation to a Supreme Being which he disavowed, instead of resorting to the religious training and belief which (certainly in the law's manner of speaking) Seeger claimed, without himself basing the justification of his conscientious beliefs upon these things. The Court did not venture upon what might be called a strenuous effort to construe the findings of fact concerning the origin and descriptively religious nature of Daniel A. Seeger's beliefs in order to bring him under the statute. Instead it made what has been called a "strenuous statutory interpretation" of the 1948 legislation and of "conscience" in order to bring the statute over him. It said in effect that no matter what were Seeger's apprehensions of his own case, he did actually believe in (to use the "lower case" for the idea) the "supreme being" that Congress had in mind. As Professor John H. Mansfield of the Harvard Law School has written, "It is certainly permissible to wonder whether the authority of Congress is really any more respected by the sort of strenuous statutory interpretation that the Court indulged in to avoid a constitutional question than it would be by an outright holding of unconstitutionality."[13] This leaves us with an interpretation of the meaning of "religion" required to be read into Section 6 (j) of the 1940 Military Training and Service Act that would hardly be the meaning of religion where this has been noticed or legislation enacted in most other aspects of our law. And it leaves us with an interpretation of "a relation to a Supreme Being" in the 1948 statute as a certain supremacy or a transcendent element within the structure of a man's conscientious beliefs upon which the last word has certainly not been spoken. Fast upon the heels of this legal history and into *this* understanding of the meaning of conscientious objection, the proponents of selective objection are endeavoring and must endeavor to insert exemption from particular wars as an *additional* qualification.

It should be acknowledged that the Court was dealing with a mare's nest of religious assertions when it joined two other cases with *Seeger* for decision. In *Jakobson,* the claimant affirmed his faith in a "Supreme Being," "Ultimate Cause," or "Supreme Reality" which is "ultimately responsible for the existence of man." Arno S. Jakobson's appeal had been upheld by the second circuit court of appeals, even though he had stated that his relation to "Godness" was a "horizontal" one "through Mankind and the World," and not a "vertical" and "direct" one.[14] In *Peter,* the applicant for exemption rested his objection philosophically upon his "consciousness of some power manifest in nature" which is "the supreme expression of human nature" or "man thinking his highest, feeling his deepest, and living his best." These beliefs were affirmed to have been derived from reading and meditation upon "American culture, with its values derived from the western religious and philosophical tradition."[15] The ninth circuit court of appeals judged that Forest B. Peter's "respecting and loving . . . livingness in other objects and human beings" did not meet the statutory requirements; this was only a "personal moral code." His exemption was denied.

In the *Seeger* case the issue was presented squarely, since Seeger did not claim that his objection was based on a belief in a Supreme Being in *any* sense. His claim that he simply adhered to "a *religious* faith in a purely *ethical* creed," and that "pacifism . . . is for me a *transcendent* concern and it is in this respect that I consider myself *religious,*"[16] also gave the Court its lead in vastly expanding the meaning of the statute.

The lower courts had all pointed out the difficulty of draft boards distinguishing between "Godness," "goodness," "livingness" at the heart of things, or "a high state of order and even disorder within the physical universe governed by laws which are presently above my ability or that of any man to completely control or completely understand"—which one claimant alleged he believed in.[17] The courts had strongly suggested that if by "Supreme Being" Congress meant to limit the exemption, the statute was unconstitutional. They had drawn upon the ever broadening meanings in contemporary religious thought, and called attention to the fact that many modern men feel the internal demands of conscience as compellingly as the externally derived commandments of God have traditionally been felt. And in granting Seeger's exemption, the circuit court of appeals relied heavily upon a definition given by Judge Augustus Hand in a decision interpreting "religious training and belief" *before Congress added the "Supreme Being" specification* excluding a merely political, philosophical, sociological, or personal moral code: "a belief finding expression in a conscience which categorically requires the believer to disregard elementary self-interest and to accept martyrdom in preference to transgressing its tenets."[18]

It is important to notice that the Supreme Court endorsed in one respect and did not endorse in another respect the decision of Judge Irving R. Kaufman of the second circuit court of appeals in reversing Seeger's conviction and granting him exemption. It did *not* hold that "a line such as drawn by the 'Supreme Being' requirement between different forms of religious expression cannot be permitted to stand consistently with the due process clause of the Fifth Amendment." It did *not* hold that "a requirement of belief in a Supreme Being, no matter how broadly defined, cannot embrace all those faiths which can validly claim to be called religions" [here Kaufman cited *Torcaso*]. Instead, this was exactly what the Court proposed: a broadly defined (lower case) supreme being or transcendent principle in consciences to be called religious in properly grounding the exemption.

The Court, however, did endorse Kaufman's decision in another, crucial respect. The *Kauten* test, wrote Judge Kaufman, recognizes that in today's "skeptical generation . . . the stern and moral voice of conscience occupies that hallowed place in the hearts and minds of men which was traditionally reserved for the commandments of God." "When Daniel Andrew Seeger insists that he is obeying the dictates of his conscience or the imperatives of an absolute morality, it would seem impossible to say with assurance that he is not bowing to 'external commands' in virtually the same sense as is the objector who defers to the will of a supernatural power."[19] With this the Supreme Court agreed; but it construed this to be the meaning of the "Supreme Being" test.

Daniel Seeger's *"religious* faith in a purely ethical creed," his *"transcendent* concern" in pacifism,[20] seemed clearly to be a way out of a morass of subtleties, a way to grant Seeger exemption by an extraordinary interpretation of the 1948 statute. So the Court did *not* find that statute to be unconstitutional or rest Seeger's exemption upon his Catholic upbringing or upon the demonstrable influence of Quaker teachings upon him, or the fact that he frequently attended Quaker meetings, or upon the fact that he had a rather limited notion of a Supreme Being (as did, indeed, the government's brief against him) when he said neither "yes" nor "no" to that question. It did *not* revert to the 1940 requirement of "religious training or belief," or require Congress to revert to it. The upshot was rather to make such a reversion to an earlier test impossible, by virtue of the Court's anatomizing the meaning of the conscientious objection which Congress must have meant to require when it passed the 1948 statute. It is hard to see how there *could* be any reversal of this interpretation even if there *should* be.

Mr. Justice Clark, writing for the Court,[21] held that by amending the law in 1948 Congress intended only to clarify the meaning of "religious training and belief," and moreover that this was an expanding clarification and not a limiting one. Where the Congress required "belief in a relation to a Supreme Being," it meant to embrace all "religions," including godless religion. What then is the trial to be made of "religious belief"? The test to determine whether a belief is religious is to ask "whether a given belief that is sincere and meaningful occupies a place in the life of the possessor parallel to that filled by the orthodox belief in God of one who clearly qualifies for the exemption."[22] Thus there must be in the anatomy of a man's conscience some belief that forms its crux, comprises the organizing principle of his practical life, and has the paramountcy that "a relation to a Supreme Being" used to have or has for others. That, in fact, was what Congress meant to require.

It is not quite clear, we should note, that the Court has reduced *religious* exemption to the test of *conscientiousness*. Yet the Court's functional notion of religious belief comes close to that. "After this decision," Professor John H. Mansfield writes, "one is left to wonder whether there are any conscientious objectors who will not be found, whether they like it or not, to be religious objectors in the meaning of the statute . . ."; concerning the "non-religious conscientious objector," the question still unanswered is "whether under the Court's decision he still exists."[23]

There *may* be some merely political, sociological, philosophical, or personal objections that could not qualify for the exemption. Still the Court has reduced the religious belief conditioning the exemption to a speculative form of conscientiousness. On this basis it seems very clear that there are *some* conscientious beliefs concerning duties arising from merely human relations that in the anatomy of conscience involve duties superior to those arising from all *other* human relations which Congress did not mean to exclude in seeming to say so, and which could henceforth rightfully warrant granting the exemption. Moreover, it can scarcely be denied that there may be *some* political, philosophical, sociological, and personal moral outlooks that function in the lives of those who possess them as once did belief in a relation to a Supreme Being, and which also Congress did not mean to exclude when it went about saying so. It is the supremacy or commanding presence of an ingredient in conscience that has now to be assayed.

The ordinary citizen in his daily rounds—if he thinks about it

—may puzzle over why the meaning of "religious belief" is to be settled by "the place that the belief occupies in the life of the objector" and not by "the character of the truths believed." While religion cannot be satisfactorily defined *without* reference to the role belief plays in the life of a believer, he will suppose that religion cannot be defined by that *alone*, with no reference to what is believed.[24] In any case, generally speaking, the character and content of a belief, and not only how it is held, will have some effect upon whether the community will consider it wrong to require a person to act contrary to it.

Public acceptance of the *Seeger* decision, indeed the general commendation of it, has depended not on these intricacies or on the Court's actual ruling but on a consensus that when it comes to exemption for conscientious objection to "participation in war *in any form*" there are "really no convincing reasons why the religious objector should be exempt and not the non-religious objector."[25] The strange manner in which the Court reached this result is of no account; in fact, it is a widely held but false opinion that it reached it simply by saying so.

Nothing in the foregoing account has been meant to raise objection to these developments in juridical law-making. To the contrary, this extension of the meaning of conscientious objection may be an entirely laudable and necessary growth in our understanding and practices in a religiously pluralistic and secular age. Our purpose has rather been simply to present this first significant juridical "revision" in the meaning of conscientious objection that had already been accomplished before the peak, at least, of the movement toward adding a second significant revision, namely, conscientious objection to particular wars. It has been necessary for our account to be a rather full one in order to direct attention to the enormous practical problem and indeed the profound doctrinal issue whether any political community can extend the meaning of exemption from military service in both directions at the same time. Only *now* do we have before us the meaning of that conscientious objection which it is *now* proposed be no longer limited to objection to war "in any form."

The acceptability of the result of *Seeger* depended on our moral consensus that *in the matter of exemption from participation in war in any form* no important distinction should be drawn between religious, philosophical, or other personal grounds on which an individual might be driven to *that* conclusion. The fact that he had to enter objection to all wars already exerted its *heuristic* effect; that was clarifying as to whether this was an ultimate for him. He no more opposed one particular war than any other, and no more opposed his own nation's policy than any other. Given this anchorage, given this limit upon the exemption, no distinction should be made or needs to be made between religious and non-religious conscientious objection. With this we all concurred.

If anyone supposes, however, that the courts (or Congress), having just reached clarity on the meaning of religious objection to all wars—and holding that firm—are going to plunge immediately into the subtleties of distinguishing between "religious" and "political" objection, he is very naïve indeed. The test *itself* —opposition to war in any form—did more than any panel could (except for assaying a man's sincerity) to insure that his was *not* a merely political or strategic or personal opposition to one war rather than another, or against his own country's wars rather than those of some other. This test itself had a clarifying effect upon conscience, and upon what review boards and courts were to make trial of. The fact that this was the meaning of the exemption on one side enabled the courts to extend its meaning on the other. Because the *character* of the belief looked for was opposition to participation in war in any form it enabled the courts vastly to enlarge the meaning of the "religiousness" with which this belief has to be held in order to qualify for *that* exemption.

We have several choices before us: (1) This recent "revision" in the meaning of conscientious objection is more important than getting Congress to grant selective objection to particular wars; (2) Objection to particular wars which are believed to be unjust is more important than the extension of the exemption to non-religious objectors, and we should pull the laboring oar back upstream to a far more limited and precise meaning of "religious" to which selective objection could then be attached; or (3) We must, because *both* of these meanings of conscientious objection are right and just, now undertake the manifold intellectual labor of distinguishing between conscientious moral or ethico-political objection to a particular war and merely political opposition to it. It is only the man who gets exhilaration out of being a prophet without really trying who will imagine that there is a fourth alternative, i.e., who imagines that there is any point in simply protesting and petitioning or demanding that Congress grant status to particular-war objectors merely because, taken out of context, there are principled claims that can be made for this.

It is noteworthy that the National Advisory Commission on Selective Service in holding on to exemption only for objection to war in any form also held on to *Seeger*. This at least suggests that if anyone wants to work for particular-war objection with any hope of success he may have to work against *Seeger*. The Commission considered only the question whether there was need for the selective service statute to be amended in order "to assure as a matter of orderly form that the Supreme Court's interpretation of the law as set forth in the *Seeger* decision would be followed." It concluded that such an amendment would be unnecessary because "it is the obvious duty of the Selective Service System . . . to follow the construction of the law which has been placed on it by the highest Court in the land."[26] But the Commission was *not* set up to make recommendations to the Selective Service System! It was making recommendation to the President, who then would recommend to Congress. It might, therefore, have recommended legislation having the effect of narrowing the results of the *Seeger* decision; and I suggest it might have had to do so if at the same time it had endorsed particular-war objection.

The gravity of the problems surrounding the proposal of particular-war objection in the context of this recent extension of the meaning of "religious conscience" can be seen by simply recalling how utterly "categorical" and undifferentiated were many of the philosophical and personal ultimates claimed in the cases the Supreme Court has had before it. These categorical ultimates would now be applied to particular wars without the limiting, more tangible test of "religious training and belief" in any ordinary sense of these words and without the limiting and *heuristic* test that the objection must be to all wars.

Perhaps those objections were "categorical" because the statute now invites only grounds for opposition to war "in any form." It is said on behalf of selective conscientious objection that this would invite conscientious objections that are more thoughtful and discriminating, and might even help to raise the level of public debate over particular wars. Certainly no one should say that conscientious objection is any the less "religious" or "conscientious" because *reason* has entered into it. We should reject altogether the notion that an objection is the more conscientious or religious in nature because it is merely intuitive or has, as it were, entrapped the claimant who without giving reasons simply cannot do otherwise. Still the proponents of particular-war objection must see that the very argument advanced in favor of it is an argument against it. The fact that, presumably, particular-war objection would be more reasoned and discriminating is the characteristic of it that makes it, apparently, indistinguishable from any sensible political opposition to the nation's policy. How is a conscientious judgment that a particular war is stupid and therefore wrong to be distinguished from any other opposition to that war? Do we not need to articulate with some definiteness the criteria by which claimants themselves and then competent review boards could tell the difference between reasons of a philosophical, sociological, political, or personal nature for opposition to particular wars that qualify as exemptible *religious conscientiousness* and those that do not? Can "opposition" to the government's policy be simply made the grounds for alternative service? Should this be one ingredient in determining "who serves when not all serve" in the military forces? Would that be *fair?*

Let us suppose that, without the searching and clarifying burden upon claimants and panels which was the effect in some measure of the test of opposition to war in any form, it is still possible for a competent panel to distinguish the truly conscientious from the un-conscientious holders of these various beliefs. *Then* the question is how to distinguish between merely political opposition (which any political community must require to yield or to find expression only through established political processes) and the conscientious particular-war objection to which it is proposed that exemption be granted. If religious, philosophical, and personal creeds may all, in effect, qualify for religious exemption, how can the paramount claims *thence* arising be distinguished from purely *political* objection which will not be allowed, certainly not in time of war? It is not likely to prove any easier to distinguish one objection from another in the case of particular wars than to distinguish one conscience that is religious from another. But the point here is a *normative* one: if no line should be drawn between the variety of modern man's religiousness, why should any line be drawn between his various grounds for opposition to a particular war? Unless grounds for doing so can be found, selective conscientious objection would in the end mean exemption upon request, with only a determination of the claimant's good faith, sincerity, and deep-feeling in which what *he says* about his opposition has the casting voice. This would seem to be an unconstitutional favoring of those who feel deeply about their politics in determining who serves when not all serve. These are the issues *beneath* the unpersuasiveness of this proposal to the ordinary citizen or statesman. The latter will reflect as follows (and so far we have not deprived them of this argument): It would be the applicant who in World War II was a devout member of the German-American Bund, or today has formed his conscience quite sincerely according to the tenets of communism, or has found his spiritual home among the Viet Cong of this age or (lest the foregoing be dismissed as another expression of an inflexible anti-communism or of an anti-revolutionary "mystique") who believes with all his heart in the justice of the cause of future national enemy-X, who could most clearly qualify for exemption from one of these particular wars because in his conscience there is an ingredient functionally equivalent to a relation to a Supreme Being involving duties superior to those arising from all (other) human relations.[27] To determine the meaning of a valid conscientious objection to particular wars is certainly not going to be easier than distinguishing between "a relation to a Supreme Being" and "godness" or "livingness" or the "inscrutable order and disorder" that rules in a young man's mind. Nor, certainly, is it any part of the just-war doctrine (which, after all, is a theory of statecraft and of political authority and community) to warrant conscientious objection to unjust wars on a petitioner's claim that he is supremely devoted to "man thinking his highest, feeling his deepest, and living his best." How is particular-war exemption to be determined? To this question we have devoted too little attention.

The crux is that it does not yet appear, on the Court's anatomy of conscience, how one would distinguish between political objection and political loyalties, on the one hand, and the exemptible conscientious objection on the other, especially when the former are passionately held in disagreement with the nation's policy. The question is whether selective conscientious objection can be made compatible with the very nature of political community, and a nation's ability to act one way rather than another while counting that all citizens acknowledge the authority of this action until and unless they clearly must say it is unjust. Coupled with the proposal that a nation recognize as well objection to particular wars, it does not yet appear that, as consciences are formed in the modern period, this revision would not have ominous consequences upon our remaining sense of political community and the claims this places upon everyone.

5. The Way Ahead

I do not believe that the conclusion from this must be to abandon the case for selective objection. To the contrary, the case for this is an intrinsic moral one while the obstacles are in the empirical order, however deeply imbedded these are in our culture and law. They may be so deep within the hearts of non-religious, non-political modern men as to be insurmountable in our time. Still a serious search for a viable implementation of selective conscientious objection is required by our conviction that men live in more than this one earthly city, that life in the kingdom of politics does not encompass men to the whole extent of their beings, and that the character and institutions of these kingdoms should be open to transformation and elevation by that other City to which we, with all men implicitly, belong. The *transcendence of the person* requires us to ask whether this must be manifested only by the insights and vision we strive to put into public debates over national policy. To say this *is* the only bearing of morality upon politics and war is *not* an amoral view of politics. Quite the contrary. Still we should press the question whether in regard to the state's activity involving the killing of man by man, a way cannot be found by which the transcendence of the personal in its claims upon persons can come to expression in yet another way, in exemption granted to conscientious objection to particular wars.

There are only a limited number of options—each difficult to *think through* and difficult to execute—if we really mean to be going to particular-war objection. In listing these alternatives, I assume that John Courtney Murray is quite correct in the recommendation he made in the interest of "good public argument": "The issue of selective conscientious objection must be distinguished from the issue of the justice of the South Vietnam war."[28] We cannot think straight about this matter unless these two issues are separated. But the fact that the political issue of the tragic conflict in Vietnam is, like most political issues, also a moral matter does not settle—it only opens—the question whether our moral judgments should enter into political decision through the procedures of public debate in a democratic society, obliging us then to support the direction given our nation's action while continuing to dissent from it, or whether the transcendence of the person and fundamental moral claims in the matter of war requires that particular-war objection be granted.

The premise that a political act is a moral act certainly does not perform for us the manifold intellectual labor required to distinguish in which matters the one or the other of these conclusions is proper. To approach the question of particular-war objection from the point of view of generalized rights of civil disobedience is already to have abandoned political reason. Finally, the morality of the political act does not automatically enable us to know the lineaments of a system of selective conscientious exemption that would be ethico-politically *right*, much less one that would be practicable.

The limited number of difficult options follow, I believe, from the evidence I have here analyzed or alluded to. They follow also from the warrants and reservations in the just-war doctrine on the uses of military force, which doctrine arose from serious thought about the nature and responsibilities of statecraft in light of the transcendent claims of the person upon the structures of political action. (So did also, of course, the processes of a democratic politics.)

1. It might be the case that, in order to institute a system of selective service that requires no man to fight a war or a mode of war he conscientiously believes to be unjust, we would have to choose at this juncture between proceeding on the way to selective conscientious objection and first attempting to restore to the comprehensions of men the meaning of religious claims, of genuinely transcendent claims, upon conscience.

However, this may not be a necessary or an acceptable disjunction. Fr. Murray does not believe that it is. He has stated that on the National Advisory Commission he advocated "that the grounds for the status of conscientious objector be not only *religiously* or *non-religiously* motivated opposition to participation in war in all forms, but also *similarly* motivated opposition to participation in particular wars."

2. In that case, our task is only the enormous one of re-educating an age in the meaning of political justice and of justice in war. Our nation would have to "make its way to some discriminating doctrine . . . on the uses of force." "Our national tradition of confused moral thought on the uses of force" would have to be brought to an end, and reversed. We would have to become a people who no longer deny that a nation has *jus ad bellum*, or strive to render this inoperative or no basis of policy;

and who, when the *jus ad bellum* we refuse to acknowledge comes into play, tend then to deny that there is *jus in bello* governing our conduct in war. Granting that those strange, latter-day understandings of religion which we have reviewed have at least the virtue of according to the conscience of every man as man its proper importance, and assuming the recovery of a national capacity for political reason, it would still be incumbent upon us to *show how* selective conscientious objection could be made to work without being destructive of political community (and this means of the nation and its power to act with one will and way in the nation-state system).

The truth is that every time we endorse or propose selective conscientious objection to our fellow countrymen, we are mainly making a proposal to ourselves, and delivering a judgment upon ourselves. This self-incriminating judgment can be summed up in the obvious fact that we who are the vocal voices in church and in academic community have done very little to articulate and transmit an adequate political philosophy in the present day. It may be exhilarating to get behind this reform. But it is another thing again to create the conditions of its possible enactment—or, for that matter, even to imagine how we are going to do this. To raise the level of public debate in any nation of the modern world so that there could be a *proper* adoption of selective objection seems insurmountably difficult. We ought not to think we have made any advance if we succeed simply because modern weapons eliminate the need for many men in order for force to be used, and eliminate in some measure also the need for integral, purposive political community, because opposition to national policy can be shrewdly accommodated by exemption from particular wars. Nor should we rejoice if this proposal commends itself to our contemporaries simply because it is one more step in the erosion of imperative political obligation by an omnivorous individualism and by apolitical optimism about the trustworthiness of men's moral sensibilities.

But can it be expected that in making our way as a nation to some more discriminating doctrine on the uses of force we can really reach the minimum requirement of clarity in recognizing

Selective Conscientious Objection / 61

the difference between moral objection to a particular war and political objection to a particular war? *This is the sticking point,* and one which in my judgment Fr. Murray too quickly assumes would be solved by a greater degree of common, articulated, moral and political discourse. There seem to be two obstacles in the way of assuming that political self-re-education would have as one of its fruits that we would learn to draw an acceptable line between conscientious moral and conscientious political objection to particular wars. One difficulty is simply the fact that we are morally a pluralistic political community no less than we are religiously a pluralistic people, and are apt to remain so. Can we come to agreement on what is to count as conscientious moral objection any more than on what counts as a religious belief? The other, and a deeper, obstacle may lie in the fact that moral reasons and political reasons (which are admittedly inseparable) may intrinsically not be distinguishable enough for this to be a foundation of the proposed system.

This brings us to two remaining ways in which particular-war objection might be made possible and determined to be desirable.

3. With certain findings of fact, selective objection might be accorded without attempting to distinguish between moral and political objection, whether because the line cannot be drawn practically or because the distinction is believed to be impossible in principle. Exempt status could be granted as a politically wise and humane accommodation, not as a response to a *moral claim* (transcendent or otherwise), let alone a human or constitutional *right* which Congress must grant. All that would be assayed would be a young man's "sincerity," his "conscientiousness," how deeply he feels his objection to be, whether moral or political, and whatever the nature of his moral or political beliefs, their substance or worth. This seems to be the main thrust of what Vatican Council II had to say on this subject, if its statement is transposed from universal to particular objection. Among agreements which are designed to make military activity and its consequences less inhumane, the Council stated, it also "seems right that laws make humane provisions for the case of

those who for reasons of conscience refuse to bear arms, provided however they accept some other form of service to the human community."[29] On condition that this does not frustrate the political purposes of a nation in its legitimate determination to use military force, governments should seek, among other things, to relieve the burdens and frightfulness of war by holding in check the enforcement of military service upon persons conscientiously opposed to service in a particular war. It will be a better political community if this can be done. This, with the judgment that selective objection in this sense can likely be extended in our society today, but not as an ethico-political *claim*, is the view to which Quentin Quade subscribes. This would be a political judgment, itself a moral judgment, on the part of a society, to the effect that to extend exemption to conscientious objectors on moral/political grounds to service in a particular war would conserve an individual and a common good that is more important than the degree of unfairness to those who are not so deeply opposed or who support the present direction of American foreign policy. On some suppositions of fact, however, this conclusion could be rebutted, since it is not based on an inherent moral claim, as against a distinguishable "merely" political objection. The judgment would be reversed if to grant the exemption would frustrate the disposition of the energies and will of the nation one way rather than another. Moreover, if the *fairness*-features of the situation seemed uppermost, then the war could be judged less totally burdensome if strong objectors to a particular war were entered into a lottery system along with the college-bound and with high school "drop-outs" alike in determining who must serve when not all need serve.

4. The final possibility seems to the present writer, given the present understanding of religious conscience in our law and given the present understanding of political justice and of the tests of the justice of a nation's war-policy, to be the only way in which we might begin to introduce selective conscientious objection as a matter of principle, or as the recognition of a *moral claim*. I put this suggestion forward only as one long *question*. It is a move which I judge calls for thorough investigation and manifold thought.

The proposal is that in thinking about the justice to be invoked or the conscientious objection to participation in a particular war to be explained before a competent panel by claimants to exemption from military service, we would need to move in two different directions at the same time in setting such a claimant's and panel's terms of reference.

First, we should cease to look into the anatomy of conscience itself to find grounds for the objection that are functionally equivalent to duties superior to those arising from any human relation for a traditional religious believer in a relation to a Supreme Being. In that direction we are not going to discover a workable distinction between conscientious moral objection and conscientious political opposition to particular wars, even if this were either a theoretically possible or a morally and politically defensible distinction. Therefore, one of the conditions of the possibility of selective objection based in any measure on the transcendence of the person or on moral principle or the inherent claims of conscience would be that we cease to look for this in political positions that are "truly held."

We should look rather to where the claims of humanity have, in the matter of war, been largely registered and given some shape or form not wholly subject to the passions and strongly held opinions of the moment, namely, to *jus gentium*, to international law, to agreements and treaties and conventions expressing men's agreements as to justice and governing the conduct of men and nations in war. This would be to build upon Jacques Maritain's suggestion that "knowledge of the primordial aspects of natural law" are known directly by no reason, no conscience, other than God's, and that these elements of a transcendent justice are "first expressed in social patterns rather than in personal judgments"—not simply in any sort of social patterns, but in the *jus gentium*, or the common law of human civilization.[30] Perhaps a system of particular-war objection could be erected upon the double foundation of conscientious inclinations moving a person to claim the exemption and of clarifying objective features in the agreements of men concerning justice in war. The proposal is, therefore, that the class of exemptible conscientious objections to participation in particular wars shall be those based on opposition to the war because of the claimant's conscientious belief that the war is in violation of international conventions and the "laws of war" and in violation of those of these agreements to which his nation was and is a party. Other sorts of objection to particular wars, which are also of course moral appeals and claim moral warrant (as do the opposing and the prevailing opinion), shall nevertheless be regarded as falling wholly within the legitimate due processes of democratic society, from the burdens and outcome of which no participant can claim exemption.

Secondly, those who hold, vaguely or in more precise terms, to the just-war doctrine on the uses of military force should distinguish between what we may call the teleological or consequentialist tests in this doctrine and the deontological tests. We should distinguish between what is stupid and therefore morally wrong and what is inherently wrong (even if not stupid). It is one thing to determine whether and when a war is rightful, another thing to determine in *prohibitiva* what is rightful or wrongful in war. It is one thing to determine that the overall "cause" of war is just, another to determine whether the war is conducted unjustly. And between the two tests of just conduct of war, it is one thing to determine whether the mode of warfare is excessive in terms of what is at stake (or is likely to lead to proportionately greater evil than the evil prevented) and it is another thing to determine or conscientiously to believe that acts of war are being "aimed indiscriminately" and are in direct violation of the moral immunity of noncombatants from direct, intended attack.

In all these cases, in these pairs, the proposal is that the *second* be recognized as a possible basis of a creditable claim to conscientious objection to participation in a particular war, because in these respects the claimant would state his belief that something is unjust no matter what are the good policy-consequences alleged by others or by the government. A challenge to or rejection of the alleged policy-consequences would not be allowed as basis of a claim to exemption because, while equally a moral claim, such judgments would not be distinguishable from merely political opposition to a particular war or from disagreement with the general course of the nation's foreign policy.

Taken together, these two stipulations would constitute a minimal and a somewhat clear, non-sectarian agreement concerning how citizens would go about distinguishing between claims to conscientious objection that may be accorded exemption, on the one hand, and, on the other, their opposition to particular wars or support of them (also properly expressed in terms of verdicts of "just" and "unjust" war) which simply indicate that there are points of view in significant political debate. The one overruled in the course of determining the nation's policy would then have rights of continuing dissent but no intrinsic claim to conscientious objector *status*.

It cannot be too often repeated that, if we have no more objective terms of reference for the meaning of the proposed conscientious objection than the Supreme Court's anatomization of conscience, then all talk of applying this to particular wars is beating the breeze. The proposal then amounts to a claim favoring one religion over another, or one political opposition over another, or stronger dissent over weaker dissent, which will not likely be granted and perhaps should not be granted; or else this would be a claim to normless, individualistic dissent that could not begin to be considered compatible with a citizen's responsibility. Such a proposal will not be adopted by a political community whose people still have a will to be a *people* and have any remaining sense of *res publica*—except as an accommodation hedging for some men the burden of directly serving the cause they oppose, which may prove unfair to men less certain that the current policy is wrong. Hence the proposal that acceptable claims to exemption on grounds of conscience be linked with specifiable features in international law and in agreements governing warfare in the international system to which one's own nation was and is a party. These grounds in *jus gentium* are often the same; in any case they fall within the same range of ethico-political considerations as the tests of *inherent wrongfulness* (the deontological tests) in the just-war doctrine on the uses of military force.

The teleological tests—which would be excluded as bases of

claims to status as a conscientious objector—are the test of justice in the overall "cause," the test whether the war was undertaken in the "last" reasonable "resort," and the test of proportionately greater good or lesser evil in the effects. To say that objection on these grounds would not be an admissible claim is *not* to say that opposition to the war for these reasons would be any the less moral. The proposal only recognizes that the course of the nation's policy was set by precisely these same considerations, on which men may disagree who are exercising the same conscience, and that in these respects conscientious moral objection cannot be distinguished from serious political opposition to that particular policy. The place for the interplay of conscience on *these* points is and must remain in the public forum, in continuing dissent until "the conscience of the laws" is persuaded or in conscientious objection that bears the burden of *refusing* to serve.

Here may be introduced an interpretation of "just cause" which, I would say, was its essential meaning in ages past and which, in any case, must be its accepted meaning in today's world if there is any hope of discriminating between conscientious political viewpoints that are the very substance of political discussion (and also the basis that may be equally claimed for any prevailing political policy) and conscientious moral claims that might be allowed special status as grounds for exemption from particular wars. To understand the just-war doctrine we must link together the several teleological tests that a war must be for "just cause," that it must be officially "declared" by proper authority, that war must be in the last reasonable resort, and that not even every just cause is worth the fires of war. These tests are properly linked together because *legitimate declaration* of war was always thought to entail competent judgment concerning the justice of the cause, the cost/benefits and judgment as to whether to refrain longer from resort to arms could be only out of a desperate and unreasonable hope for a peaceful solution.

What must this be taken to mean? To answer this question, a choice has to be made between two "models" concerning a judgment declaring a particular war to be just in these respects, warranting its initiation. One model is expressed by "the *tribunal* of war," the other is expressed by "an *arbitrament* of arms."

The idea that just war is a tribunal entails a belief that killing in the war is an "execution" of a court's "sentence." This view seems to require that the justice or injustice of the cause be sunclear to all observers; that the capital punishment of the "guilty" can rightfully be exacted; that the initiation of the use of force by one side is clearly in accord with an objective distinction between the "guilty" and the "innocent"; that a warrior is only a hangman acting within a quasi-juridical order.

The idea that just war could ever appeal to such a commonly accepted understanding of guilt or innocence may have had some semblance of credibility within "Christendom" with its common understanding of rights and dues. On the other hand, it may well be that the "model" of a "tribunal" of war executing an agreed upon justice and punishing offenders is a romantic notion having no correspondence to any actual state of human affairs in the past or in the present.

In any case, this is not the human condition politically in the modern world. If now one holds in mind the model of war as a "tribunal," and "declaration" as executing sentence upon the "unjust," he goes so far astray as not to be able, on this basis, to be a proponent of selective conscientious objection to wars that are unjust. This model will force one rather to become a pacifist in regard to all wars, and to give up the case for conscientious objection to particular wars;[31] or else it will force one in the direction of justifying all the decisions of proper political authority as the highest decisions concerning political justice that we can certainly know.

I can only assert, therefore, that the requirement that the cause of war be just in all these respects, coupled with the requirement that the war be declared by the authorities or by the established processes of decision-making presumed to be competent to make these determinations, always actually meant resort to an "arbitrament" of arms, not resort to anything properly to be called a "tribunal" rendering its verdicts by the light of an objective certainty as to the universal justice of the cause. In any case, the model of an "arbitrament" of arms is the one that more correctly exhibits mankind's struggles for justice in the nation-state system with its politically embodied justices on which men do not always agree. There would be world political community with an enforcing authority if we did so agree, and no more need to be loyal to the justice we know, or tragically, to determine the justice of the cause of war by the light of the apprehensions of justice that we have, and which are always less than the "universal view" presupposed by the tribunal-model.

This does not mean that these tests laid down by the just-war doctrine on the uses of force are of no more avail. Nor does it mean that they are addressed only to the topmost magistrates or political leaders of the nations. In modern democratic society they are addressed to every man who must say whether the war is justified or unjustified in these terms. This does mean, however, that decision as to whether the cause is just, whether the end will be a more just and peaceful order, whether what is at stake is worth the costs paid and exacted, and whether there were better ways out that were *possible*, all these are decisions falling within established political due-processes by which a nation has the political *authority* (which is more than the *power*) to dispose the energies of the whole citizenry toward the realization of its agreement as to the national and the international common good. If we do not stand as a nation for the justice we know, we are not as a people likely to come into that land where a wider, perhaps a universal, view of justice can become known. As individual citizens we are not apt to come into that land either, unless we allow the nation the *moral authority* to do this, even while, it may be, persevering in conscientious dissent on all these points from some particular policy.

I suggest that this entails that as a matter of moral and political *principle*[32] men who feel their conscientious moral and political objection to the prevailing judgment as to the justice of the over-all "cause," etc., to run so deep that they cannot and will not participate in a particular war should not claim to be exempted from the consequences of such refusal. Theirs is only another reading of the particular political encounter their nation went to meet, and by an application of the same moral/political tests governing whether war is justified or not.

We are permitted another conclusion when it is not a question of estimating the rightfulness of a war, involving such vast and at the same time uncertain and mixed moral and political calculations of the political good to come. In the matter of estimating rightfulness and wrongfulness in war there may be grounds for distinguishing more clearly between conscientious objection to a particular war based on conscientious claims as moral claims, on the one hand, and, on the other, "truly held" political opposition.

The analogy is with the situation in military justice when a man in the Armed Forces charged with disobedience to a lawful order is allowed to enter as a defense the fact that he was ordered to do something inherently immoral or contravening the "laws of war" to which, in treaties and conventions, his nation was a party. If his commanding officer said, "We're going down this valley to take all the territory this side of yon river," and ordered him to go, he is not allowed as a defense to try to prove that this was quite unwise as a tactic, or did not conform to the contours of the strategic encounters going on or to the contours of what was politically at stake in the world. He is not allowed as a defense to try to prove that he conscientiously *believed* the command, in this sense, to be wrong morally and politically. He is not allowed as a defense to state that he believed that he was commanded to use *excessive* force, and therefore that the order was not a lawful one. But he is allowed as a defense against a charge of disobedience to a "lawful order" to show that he was ordered to kill prisoners of war, etc., and that therefore the command was *not a lawful* one. For men on the brink of combat or in the midst of combat there is a clear enough difference between the rightfulness of a particular engagement and what would be wrongful *in* that particular engagement. Further to clarify or enlarge the class of such legitimate defenses linked to international conventions and agreements to which his nation was a party would be an improvement in military justice. (For example, a defense against a command to use many of the forms of gas or micro-biological warfare.) There are principled reasons for these defenses; they would not simply be an easement of the burdens of obedience for men strongly opposed to some command or tactic. Moreover, such an ingredient in the procedures and decisions of courts martial would allow, in some measure, at least, for the growth through case-law of what we do actually regard as rightful or wrongful in war in response to the claim that the order was for the defendant an *inherently* immoral one.

This is only an analogy; crucial differences between defenses against a charge of disobedience in war and recognizing or assessing claims to particular-war objection will have to be brought out. But the foregoing may be a helpful analogy. The differences are that in claims to exemption from the liability of combatant service on grounds of selective conscientious objection the claimant would not be attempting to demonstrate that the war is *in fact* in violation of international law or inherently wrongful in its conduct, nor would he bear the burden of proving that the "laws of war" to which he makes appeal do have in international law the construction he places upon them. Nor would a competent review panel have a duty to make a determination concerning such alleged findings of fact and of law or right. Instead, the claimant would have to show that, beyond the conscientious moral/political nature of his objection, these are *his* terms of reference, that *his* conscience has been formed in these terms, and that he cannot participate in a particular war because it is *his* conscientious belief that the war violates canons of conduct clearly governing nations at war. The panel would have the duty of determining that these are his reasons and that the claimant's conscience has in fact been formed to this sort of objection and not as an excuse for claiming exemption that is actually based on general opposition to the course of the nation's foreign policy or to the judgment that resort to military force was required by this policy in this instance. The claimant would not simply be asserting, nor would a review panel probe his conscience to find out *only* how deeply he feels his conviction, that the nation should not go down a particular valley in the political encounters taking place in the world.

His case would not be *wholly* unlike that of the universal pacifist who dissents, as it were, "from the history of nations; his position does not single out his own country for adverse judgment."[33] or one war and not others. True, the selective objector singles out a particular war and not all wars, and he singles out his own country in this war for special rebuke and perhaps not others equally. Still he dissents not from the particular resort to war as such, but from this particular sort of war as a part of the history of warfare and of the history of nations. While he bears the burden of rebuking this particular war and not others or more than others, and of rebuking his nation's war in this particular case more than others, he could gain no standing to enter conscientious objection with any claim to exemption on grounds that single out the entire justice of his own nation's cause in a particular war or the recent course of his nation's foreign policy which later seemed to require a resort to military force. It is the latter and not the former claim that would seem to be indistinguishable from strongly held political opposition—which belongs to the history of political debate, to the forum of political debate, to the history of democratic determination of national policy by established procedures, and to the history of continuing dissent (from which no man should dissent).

Under the proposed system of selective objection I see no reason why conscientious objection to certain modes of warfare (such as nuclear) might not be allowable grounds (although I myself do not believe a particular weapon-system is the mode of warfare censured on just-war principles). This would certainly become a ground if there were international agreement proscribing the use of nuclears to which one's nation was a party. There would be another arguable ground, under conditions of a supposable particular war, if there is "customary international law" proscribing *first* use of nuclear weapons. But these and other cases I have given are only illustrations. The point is to link exemptible cases with the formation of conscience by reference to ethico-political agreements in the international system to which the nations are parties. In the case of claimants and review panels under the proposed scheme (much more readily than in the analogy I used with defenses in military courts) it is possible to anticipate that, upon claimant's reference to the "laws of humanity" and to something he believes *inherently* wrongful in war on which there is no clear international convention, there would be developed a body of case-law and precedents exhibiting our agreement as a people concerning inhumanity and injustice in war sufficient, at least, for us to be willing to grant exemption from military service to any man who conscientiously believes that a particular war violates men in these particular respects. Again, there would be no burden of showing or of reviewing whether findings of fact or of international law or of a true and actionable universal justice are sufficient to sustain the claimant's judgment, but only a showing that his conscientious objection had in fact these terms of reference.

One thing more should, in conclusion, be observed. It has sometimes been proposed that one "chamber" of the United Nations should be directly elected by the people of the nations, while as entities and actors in the international system nations would continue to be "represented" in the other "chamber." This would be a step toward achieving an international legislative authority, radically altering the present structure of the United Nations which is carefully erected upon the nation-state system. The same thing can generally be said of the World Court, which serves to interpret the meaning and force of treaties among the nation-states. Even when a nation agrees to compulsory adjudication before the Court, this can be rescinded, even as a decision to act through the United Nations is a national decision. The proposal that one "chamber" of the United Nations represent people and not the nations is an attempt to envision how the nation-state system is going to be able to fetch forth from itself something more than the nation-state system, namely a genuinely world public authority and more of a legislature for mankind.

There is a comparable structural problem in the world *juridical* order. How is the nation-state system going to fetch forth from itself, by the action of nations, a juridical order and international law that is founded in more than agreements between nations and their willingness case by case to abide by these conventions? The proposed scheme of selective objection might be a small step toward making the agreements between states concerning what is rightful and wrongful in war *the law of the land,* in the sense of the people's reference to them and not simply the government's. There would be no international tribunal rendering judgment upon the claims of consciences who in the cause of humanity make reference to international agreements and law; such courts would still hand down judgment upon states and treaties, etc. There would, in fact, be forthcoming from review boards acting within the body politic *no* findings of fact or law or justice upon the claims of humanity at work in the conscience of claimants. In fact, the contrary would be the case. In particular-war objection as with objection to participation in war in any form, it would still hold true that "if the government refrains from compelling a person to participate in war over his conscientious objection, it does not thereby accept the individual's judgment on the moral question."[34] The reason it does not do this is that *government* even in its decisions to resort to military force is a moral act (strange as this may seem to a typically modern mind).

By enacting the proposed system of selective conscientious objection, however, we would at least have taken the step of saying that a man who forms his conscience in terms of *jus gentium,* and not only in terms of his conscience's own inner demands or in terms of political disagreement with his nation's policy, may have a case in the body politic for exemption from participation in a particular war which, he judges in these terms, is being disposed wrongfully by the country's political leaders in the exercise of their proper authority to decide to go down one valley rather than another in today's world. This would mean to introduce into the body politic some recognition of the transcendent claims of the person and of humanity as these have taken and are taking specifiable form in the international juridical order. This would be the state's acknowledgment of some transcendence over its particular decisions on the part of this juridical order, resident within its own body politic, even when it does not agree with or think it possible to act in accord with these claims. This would exert some influence on the state's action in shoring up and keeping in repair, up-dating and improving, those conventions and agreements in which it expresses its sense, as an actor in the nation-state system, of the agreements as to justice which are to the world's common good. I should think that a *conscientious* "conscientious objector" would not want his objection to count for less than this, or for exemption to be allowed him as a political easement or because only he knows, or says that he knows, that he represents a higher justice.

NOTES

[1] Jacques Maritain: *Man and the State* (University of Chicago Press, 1951), pp. 101, 117, 135.
[2] *War and the Christian Conscience* (Durham, N.C.: Duke University Press, 1961), pp. 128–129, 132–133. It is the purpose of the present essay now to test this proposal by bringing to bear upon it the full force of a hopefully adequate political philosophy, to analyze the conditions of a possible enactment of particular-war objection, and to think through certain questions concerning the reservations necessary if, upon just-war warrants, selective conscientious objection is choiceworthy and feasible.
[3] In Donald Giannella, ed., *Religion and the Public Order*, Vol. 4, (Cornell University Press, 1968).
[4] This was the package of particulars condemned as misguided and war-prolonging forms of dissent by the Freedom House political advertisement in *The New York Times*, November 30, 1966, and signed by persons as disparate as former President Eisenhower, Senator Jacob Javits, Dean Acheson, James B. Conant—and the present writer.
[5] "Those who are pledged to the service of their country as members of its armed services should regard themselves as agents of security and freedom on behalf of their people. As long as they fulfill this role properly, they are making a genuine contribution to the establishment of peace." *Pastoral Constitution on the Church in the Modern World (Gaudium et Spes)*, par. 79.

⁶ For a fuller treatment of this too-particular condemnation, see my *Who Speaks for the Church? A Critique of the 1966 Geneva Conference on Church and Society* (New York and Nashville: The Abingdon Press, 1967.)
⁷ *Thus Spake Zarathustra*, II, xxvii.
⁸ *Pastoral Constitution on the Church in the Modern World*, par. 74.
⁹ *In Pursuit of Equity: Who Serves When Not All Serve?* Report of the National Advisory Commission on Selective Service, Burke Marshall, Chairman (U.S. Government Printing Office, Washington, D.C., 1967). See pp. 9 and 48–51 for both the minority and the majority positions.
¹⁰ I omit the Commission's report of the view of a smaller minority, and its answer to them. These members would have cut through the obstacles in the way of granting exemption to selective objectors by not requiring "that they show that their objection to combatant service is on properly moral ground," and would have coupled a probably generous use of this excusal with the elimination of the present alternative of some form of civilian service. Instead, objectors to particular wars would be "required to serve in a noncombatant *military* capacity, under conditions of hardship and even hazard, and perhaps for a longer period (for example 3 years)." This meat-axe approach to the problem, a "more narrow option" especially occasioned by opposition to the Vietnam war, is indeed an alternative, perhaps the only alternative to the present requirement of opposition to participation in war in any form, unless and until we can show how purely political objection is to be distinguished from moral or ethico-political objection in a system of selective service that allows conscientious objection to particular wars.
¹¹ John H. Mansfield (Harvard Law School): "Conscientious Objection—1964 Term," in *Religion and the Public Order* (Donald Giannella, ed., Chicago: University of Chicago Press, 1965), pp. 3–81 and pp. 80–81.
¹² 367 U.S. 488 (1961), at 495, n. 11. Cited in evidence were watered-down versions of some of the more questionable aspects of the theologies of Paul Tillich and Bishop J. A. T. Robinson. For the box this places the Court in, in ever distinguishing the "secular" purpose and primary effect of *any* legislation from its possibly secondary "religious" consequences, and its difficulty now in stopping short of saying that any instruction in any values in the public schools amounts to an "establishment" of "religion," see Paul G. Kauper, "Schempp and Sherbert," in *Religion and the Public Order* (Donald Giannella,

ed., University of Chicago Press, 1963), pp. 3–40 at pp. 22–23; and Paul Ramsey, "How Shall We Sing the Lord's Song in a Pluralistic Land?" in *Journal of Public Law*, Vol. 13, No. 2 (1965), pp. 353–400 at pp. 385–386.
13 *Op. cit.*, p. 6.
14 *United States v. Jakobson*, 325 F.2d 409 (2d Cir. 1963).
15 *Peter v. United States*, 324 F.2d 173 (9th Cir. 1963.)
16 *Record*, p. 99, United States v. Seeger, 380 U.S. 163 (1965), italics added.
17 *MacMurray v. United States*, 33 F.2d 928 (9th Cir. 1964).
18 *United States v. Kauten*, 133 F.2d 703 (2d Cir. 1943), at 707.
19 *United States v. Seeger*, 326 F.2d 846 (2d Cir, 1964). Excerpts printed in *The New York Times*, January 21, 1964.
20 It is high time our Judges and Justices cease citing, as they have done since *Torcaso*, Paul Tillich in support of their interpretation of the meaning of "religion." Obviously, such a thing as "pacifism" must be, for Tillich, of *less than* "ultimate concern"; and the fact that Seeger said "pacifism, *among other things* . . ." would mean that his was not the "transcendent concern" Tillich has written about. Judges and Justices, however, can scarcely learn better when a good many theologians have, after a moment's hesitation, declared these decisions to be in line with some of the best trends in modern theological analysis.
21 *United States v. Seeger*, 380 U.S. 163 (1965). See also: 326 F.2d 846 (2d Cir. 1964), cert. granted, 377 U.S. 922 (1964).
22 *Ibid.* at p. 166.
23 Mansfield, *op. cit.*, pp. 7, 81.
24 *Ibid.*, pp. 9, 33–34.
25 *Ibid.*, p. 76.
26 *In Pursuit of Equity*, p. 48. See also p. 9
27 The fact that such a man would not make a good soldier is *not* to the point of whether exemption for cause of conscience should be granted. Neither is it to the point to argue that, because of modern military technology, a nation might be able to fight its wars without requiring those conscientiously opposed to particular wars to serve. The question precisely is whether *under these conditions*, when fewer men are needed, opposition to a particular war *should* be an element in determining who will be required to serve. Is selective objection a *fair* national policy, and could it be made consistent with the integrity and disposition of a nation's policy?

[28] "War and Conscience." Subsequent quotations are from this address.
[29] *Pastoral Consititution on the Church in the Modern World*, par. 79. See also my article "The Vatican Council on Modern War," *Theological Studies*, Vol. 27, No. 2 (June, 1966), pp. 195–197.
[30] *Man and the State*, p. 92.
[31] This is the legalistic-pacifist use of the just-war doctrine, one example of which is to be found in Gordon Zahn's article "The Test of the Just War," *worldview*, Vol. 8, No. 12 (December, 1965), pp. 10–13. Protestant pacifists also allow the just-war doctrine strength enough to condemn any particular war brought under review, just before its own demise. The question such use of the just-war doctrine as anything other than an ethico-political theory of statecraft poses most urgently is: can a pacifist tell a just war?
[32] I.e., excluding for the moment the possibility that selective conscientious objection could be granted as an accommodation to limit the burdens of war by not requiring particular-war objectors to serve (or to be entered into a lottery system).
[33] Donald A. Giannella: Religious Liberty, Nonestablishment and Doctrinal Development, Part I, "The Religious Liberty Guarantee," *Harvard Law Review*, Vol. 80, No. 7 (May, 1967), p. 1415.
[34] John H. Mansfield, *op. cit.*, p. 39.

War and the Jewish Tradition

EVERETT E. GENDLER

AT the outset, two source-problems of some seriousness confront any Jewish approach to the issue of "just war" doctrine, individual conscience, and selective conscientious objection.

The first of these Professor Julius Kravetz has called an "embarrassment of poverty."[1] For reasons easily enough understood, there is no great corpus of biblical and rabbinic legislation dealing directly with these issues. Augustine and Aquinas may have fancied that their findings about just and unjust wars would have application to the body politic of Christendom, represented by the Christian kings. The rabbinic fathers had no such hopes that Roman Emperors would seek their religious findings, nor could Maimonides and other Jewish medieval scholars expect their halachic deliverances to be heeded by regnant powers. Naturally, then, there was no felt urgency to formulate anything so directive of the use of power as a fully elaborated "just war" doctrine, and the elements we do have are somewhat incomplete and unsystematic. As for the biblical material, it too is somewhat limited in extent, and its *locus classicus* in Deuteronomy places it, documentarily at least, well after the period of the Conquest of the Land. Nevertheless, as I will indicate, there are quite valuable elements in both the biblical and rabbinic material, however limited in quantity and comprehensiveness this material may be.

The second problem is the application of such source-material as we have to present circumstances. The social, political, religious, and human context of the material differs considerably both from our present self-understanding and our present situations, and these differences must be kept clearly in mind. Even within the same historical and social setting, the application of rules to cases is often difficult, as the workings of any legal system indicate. When there are additional differences the difficulties are compounded.

These two source-problems do not, of course, dictate that the grave issues confronting us should be avoided, nor do they render the source-material inapplicable. They do, however, urge upon us a constant appreciation of the difficulty and subtlety of the task, an appreciation which, combined with the felt sense of the present urgency of the issue, may yield certain findings which are both fair to the sources and relevant to our own times.

One last introductory caution. The following material, while hopefully an accurate presentation of some major teachings of the Jewish tradition in these areas, does not pretend to be comprehensive. A comprehensive treatment would necessarily extend far beyond the limits of an essay, developing many points that are only alluded to here. (References to fuller treatments of some of the relevant issues will be found in the footnotes.)

1. Biblical Material

Most discussions of the biblical material focus on the specific regulations of *Deuteronomy* 20, and these will be considered. However, without some preliminary indication of the variety of communal contexts within which armies were mobilized in biblical times, there is great danger that invalid analogies will be drawn with our own times. To reduce this danger, a brief summary of some parts of Roland de Vaux's fine survey of Israelite Military Institutions will be helpful.[2]

Recruitment of fighting men. Details of the nomadic period are scanty, but it seems reasonable to assume that "there is no distinction between the army and the people." By the period of the Judges, however, there is more information, some of it of particular relevance for us. Most significant are the following findings:

a. During this period individual tribes and families decided within their own intimate groupings whether or not to respond to the general call to arms. "During the period of the Judges, the response to these appeals depended on each group, which made its own decision. The Song of Deborah twice insists on this freedom to fight or not to fight *(Jg.* 5:2 and 9), and expresses nothing stronger than reproach or regret about the tribes which chose to stand aside *(Jg.* 5:15-17)."

b. "The units of the army were based on those of society. The unit was the clan *(mishpahah)*. . . ."

c. The voluntarism extended to individuals within the clan and tribal groupings. "Gideon's action against the Midianites is even more typical; of the 32,000 men who answered his call, he sent home all who had no heart to fight, and only 10,000 remained; of these, he chose 300. . . ."

d. "From time to time, two enemy forces would agree to settle the issue by single combat."

e. ". . . it must not be forgotten, even now, that the warriors of Israel were upheld by their firm belief that Yahweh fought with them and that he could grant them victory whatever the odds against them (I *Sam.* 14:6; 17:47)."

This period of small group autonomy and individual voluntarism was succeeded by a period of professional armies with mercenaries and chariotry, "the work of the first kings of Israel," and still later (and at times simultaneously) by conscript labor forces and conscript armies as well.

These latter developments were ambivalently regarded within the biblical literature. On the one hand there is a stream of thought distinctly favorable to the monarchy (I *Sam.* 9 and 11, praise of the Davidic dynasty, etc.). On the other hand, there is a strong current severely critical of the monarchy and its implications for the life of the people.

"Then all the elders of Israel gathered together and came to Samuel at Ramah, and they said to him,

'Consider, you have become old and your sons do not follow in your footsteps. Now set up for us a king to judge us like all the nations.'

But the thing was evil in the sight of Samuel, when they said, 'Give us a king to judge us.'

Nevertheless Samuel prayed earnestly unto the LORD; and the LORD said to Samuel,

'Listen to the voice of the people according to all that they say to you; for they have not rejected you, but they have rejected me from being king over them. Like all the deeds which they have done to me from the day I brought them up from Egypt even to this day, inasmuch as they have forsaken me and served other gods, so they are also doing to you. Now therefore listen to their utterance, except that you shall certainly warn them, and show them the procedure of the king who shall reign over them.'

Then Samuel told all the words of the LORD to the people who were asking of him a king; and he said,

'This will be the procedure of the king who shall reign over you: he will take your sons and appoint them for himself for his chariots and for his horsemen; and they shall run before his chariots; and he will appoint for himself commanders of thousands and commanders of hundreds, and some to do his plowing and to reap his harvests and make his implements of war and the equipment of his chariots. He will take your daughters for perfumers, for cooks, and for bakers. He will take the best of your fields and your vineyards and your olive orchards, and give them to his servants. He will take the tenth of your grain crops and of your vineyards and give it to his eunuchs and to his servants. He will take your male and female slaves, and the best of your cattle and your asses, and make use of them for his work. He will take a tenth of your flocks; and you yourselves will become his slaves. Then you will cry out on that day because of your king whom you will have chosen for yourselves; but the LORD will not answer you on that day.' "—*I Sam.* 8:4–18.

The legislation restricting the king in *Deuteronomy* 17:14–20, and passages from *Hosea* (7:3–7, 8:4, 13:9–11) reveal the continuation of suspicion and hostility toward the king as divine surrogate and usurper. In this latter respect, the attitude toward the census of the people for military purposes is especially significant.

"Now the LORD was again angered against Israel, and he incited David against them, saying,

'Go number Israel and Judah!'

So the king said to Joab and the commanders of the army which was with him,

'Go about now throughout all the tribes of Israel, from Dan even to Beersheba, and take a census of the people that I may know the number of the people.'

Joab said to the king,

'May the LORD your God add to the people a hundred times as many as they are, while the eyes of my lord the king look on! But why does my lord the king take delight in this thing?'

But the word of the king prevailed over Joab and the commanders of the army. Therefore Joab and the commanders of the army went out from the king's presence to take the census of the people of Israel. They crossed the Jordan and started from Aroer, and from the city that is in the midst of the torrent valley, toward Gad and on to Jazer. Then they came to Gilead and to the land of the Hittites, to Kadesh; and they came to Dan, and from Dan they went around to Sidon, and came to the fortress of Tyre and all the cities of the Hivvites, and of the Canaanites; and they went forth to the Negeb of Judah at Beersheba. When they had gone about through the whole land they came to Jerusalem at the end of nine months and twenty days; and Joab gave the number of the census of the people to the king, and Israel consisted of eight hundred thousand able-bodied men who drew sword, and the men of Judah were five hundred thousand.

But David's conscience smote him after he had numbered the people. Then David said to the LORD,

'I have sinned exceedingly in what I have done. But now, O LORD, take away, I pray thee, the iniquity of thy servant, for I have done very foolishly.' "—*II Sam.* 24:1–10.

In the words of de Vaux: "Thus the tradition of a people under arms persisted, but the mass response to a call from a leader inspired by God had given place to mobilization organized by the royal administration. The first indication of this development can be seen as early as David's reign: his census had a military purpose and was equivalent to drawing up a register for conscription, but this step was condemned as an abandonment of the rules of a holy war, and a profanation (cf. verses 3 and 10)."

Varieties of Biblical wars. Scholarly classifications of biblical wars tend to coincide. Thus Kaufmann distinguishes three main types: Wars of Conquest, Wars of Liberation, and Wars of Empire, with one intermediate type, Wars of Tribute.[3] De Vaux's division into wars of conquest, defensive wars, and wars of expansion, is essentially the same. The basic biblical legislative differentiation is, however, confined to the distinction between wars with "towns that lie very far from you" and wars with "towns that belong to nations hereabout."

> "When you invest a city, you must offer it terms of peace. If it agrees to make peace with you, and surrenders to you, then all the people to be found in it shall become forced laborers for you, and serve you. But if it will not make peace with you, but wages war with you, you are to besiege it, and when the LORD your God delivers it up to you, you must put every male in it to the sword; but the women and children and live stock and everything that is in the city, that is, all its spoil, you may take as your booty, and yourselves use the spoil of your enemies which the LORD your God gives you. So shall you treat all the cities that are very far away from you, that do not belong to the cities of the nations here. However, in the cities of the peoples here, which the LORD your God is giving you as a heritage, you must not spare a living soul; but you must be sure to exterminate them, Hittites, Amorites, Canaanites, Perizzites, Hivvites, and Jebusites, as the LORD your God commanded you, so that they may not teach you to imitate all the abominable practices that they have carried on for their gods, and so sin against the LORD your God."—*Dt.* 20:10–18.

The primary characteristic of wars of conquest, the *herem*, "the anathema carried out on the vanquished enemy and his goods," was understood to be by the express command of God, applied only to the "seven nations" inhabiting the promised land (cf. *Dt.* 7:2), and characterized these wars only and no others. "The characteristic quality of the wars of conquest is that they are exclusively Canaanite. . . . Ammon, Moab, Edom, and Aram, whose lands were never promised to Israel, are excluded from these wars."[4] From the Biblical text itself it is clear that the *herem*, the total destruction of persons and goods, is limited in application to a single category of conflict: the wars of conquest of the promised land. Any additional instances, such as the total destruction of the Amalekites, were exceptions and understood to be only at the direct instigation of God, not by inferential human discretion.

There is one other characteristic, common to all the varieties of biblical wars, which requires some clarification: the holy or sacred character of the wars. De Vaux uses the term "holy war," a term which appears to suggest what we might designate an ideological conflict, but de Vaux is emphatic in rejecting such an identification. To attempt to spread one's faith by force of arms was utterly foreign to Israel, and until the time of the Maccabees the concept of a war of religion had not appeared. "Israel did not fight for its faith, but for its existence." War was indeed "a sacred action, with its own particular ideology and rites," but so were many other actions and activities, and the religious character of biblical war was quite distinct from those distortions which we designate medieval religious or modern ideological "crusades." De Vaux summarizes the meaning of this in the following words: "This is the principal fact: it was Yahweh who fought for Israel, not Israel which fought for its God. The holy war, in Israel, was not a war of religion."

The sacred character of biblical war was reflected in such acts as sacrifices prior to marching to battle *(I Sam.* 7:9; 13:9, 12), the consultation with Yahweh by means of the Urim and Tumim *(I Sam.* 23:9 f.; 30:7 f.), requirements of ritual cleanliness for combatants *(Jos.* 3:4) and for the camp *(Dt.* 23:10–15), and the frequent presence of the Ark *(Num.* 10:35–36).

Most important for our considerations, however, are the implications for the combatants of the sacred character of biblical war. "Faith was an indispensable condition: they had to have faith and to be without fear *(Jos.* 8:1; 10:8, 25). Those who were afraid did not have the necessary religious dispositions and were to be sent away *(Jg.* 7:3; cf. *Dt.* 20:8, where the dismissal of such men is explained by a psychological reason, which was not the original reason for the custom)."

With the establishment of the monarchy ". . . this strictly sacred character of war disappeared with the advent of the monarchy and the establishment of a professional army. It is no longer Yahweh who marches ahead of his people to fight the Wars of Yahweh, but the king who leads his people out and fights its wars (*I Sam.* 8:20). The combatants are no longer warriors who volunteer to fight, but professionals in the pay of the king, or conscripts recruited by his officials."

De Vaux traces this "profanation" of war as it became the state's concern; adduces prophetic retentions of the original idea which serve as the bases for criticism of the later secular wars of the Jewish state; and analyzes the reappearance of certain elements of the holy war in the Maccabees (which do not, however, make theirs a holy war in the older sense, but rather a "war of religion": "The Maccabees and their men are not inspired by God; God did not order the war and he does not intervene directly in it"). He makes very clear, in short, the non-transferable nature of the "holy war" and so enables us to guard against that fearful tendency to identify our own impulses and ideologies with the sacred as such.

Specific Biblical regulations. The major remaining, though sketchy, biblical regulations concerning the waging of war find their classic formulation in *Deuteronomy* 20.

> "When you go out to battle against your enemies, and see horses, and chariots, forces greater than your own, you must not be afraid of them; for the LORD your God who brought you up from the land of Egypt is on your side. When you are on the eve of a battle, a priest must come up and speak to the people. He shall say to them, 'Listen, O Israel; today you are on the eve of a battle against your enemies; do not be faint-hearted, nor afraid, nor alarmed, nor stand in dread of them; for the LORD your God is going with you, to fight for you against your enemies and give you the victory.' Then the officers shall say to the people, 'Whoever has built a new house, but has not dedicated it, may leave and return home lest he die in the battle, and another dedicate it. Whoever has planted a vineyard, but has not had the use of it, may leave and return home, lest he die in the battle, and another get the use of it. Whoever has betrothed a

wife, but has not married her, may leave and return home, lest he die in the battle and another marry her.' The officers shall say further to the people, 'Whoever is afraid and faint-hearted must leave and return home, so that his fellows may not become faint-hearted like him.' As soon as the officers have finished addressing the people, the army commanders shall place themselves at the head of the people."—20:1-9

(Verses 10-18 cited above)

"When you have to besiege a city a long time in your war on it in order to capture it, you must not destroy its trees by taking an ax to them, because you can eat their fruit; you must not cut them down; for are trees in the field men to be besieged by you? It is only trees which you know are not fruit trees that you may destroy and cut down for the construction of siegeworks against the city that is waging war with you, until it is razed."—20:19-20

Of these provisions, those respecting the morale functions of the priest and the officers can be well understood in the light of de Vaux's discussion of the role of faith in the rallying of men to combat. One also notes the necessity of individual consent, as it were (verse 8), a provision highly significant for our own considerations.

In the case of siege warfare outside the promised land, peace terms must first be offered, and if the population accepts, it may be subjected to forced labor but to nothing else (verses 10-11, cited above). If it refuses, the possibilities are specified in verses 12-15, including the execution of the males and the appropriation of the remaining persons and property.

The *herem* provisions of verses 16-18 have already been discussed above, leaving two final elements for comment: rules of exemptions (verses 5-7) and limitations on destruction (verses 19-20). In both cases, the penetrating comments of Johannes Pedersen are especially illuminating.[5]

With respect to personal exemptions or deferments, Pedersen suggests that the following profound human consideration is at work: ". . . the army should only admit to its ranks men who can be entirely merged in the whole and act as part of it. In the military laws of *Deuteronomy* we find the following passage (verses 5–7). In these three laws we find the same considerate spirit which prevails in many of the laws of *Deuteronomy* and which is generally characterised by the honourable name 'humane.' A close inspection will show, however, that the laws are not considering casual instances, but something greater and more profound. In all three cases a man has started a new, important undertaking without having finished it yet. In such a case something has been created, which is greater than the man himself, a new totality has come into existence. To make a breach in this prematurely, that is to say, before it has attained maturity or has been finished, involves a serious risk of sin. This risk must be avoided for the sake of the cause itself, and the man who came to the army after committing such a breach might mean a danger much more than a help in the psychic whole constituted by the army." (pp. 9–10.)

As for the law requiring that the enemy's trees be spared to some extent: "Here there is a demand for the moderation characteristic of the old time. Life is to be respected, it must not be entirely destroyed, . . . Reduction is allowed, but not extermination." (23, 24.)

Or in the beautiful summary of this spirit by Isaiah:

> ". . . the Lord Who created the heavens
> (He is God!),
> Who formed the earth and made it
> (He established it),
> He did not create it a wasteland,
> He formed it to be inhabited!" (45:18.)

2. Rabbinic material

As I have noted, one does not find ready-at-hand a fully developed rabbinic formulation of a "just war" doctrine, and the problem of application is further increased by the fact that much of the legislation presupposes the existence of a divinely established state in the Holy Land. Further, since such a state was regarded as divinely ordained, it is especially perilous to extrapolate from permissions granted it to any other situation.

Neither does one find a systematic elaboration of the individual moral considerations considered appropriate for determining individual participation or non-participation in any given conflict. Yet there is, scattered throughout the classical rabbinic writings, some significant amount of teaching relating to these questions, material which, with due caution, is quite relevant. Much of it is biblically based, though it often goes beyond the biblical texts, sometimes expanding, sometimes modifying, sometimes applying them. I will attempt to show that some selections from these teachings are pertinent to the specific issues confronting us.

The traditional rabbinic classification of wars distinguishes three types: *milhemet hovah* (obligatory), *milhemet mitzvah* (mandatory), and *milhemet reshut* (discretionary) *(Talmud Sotah, 44b)*. For almost all practical purposes, however, the first two categories are one, leaving in effect the distinction between mandatory and discretionary wars *(mitzvah* and *reshut)*.

Which specific wars fall into these categories? Although there are some points at issue, it is widely agreed among rabbinic authorities that mandatory wars obtained in only two or possibly three instances: (a) Joshua's war of conquest against the seven Canaanite nations (directly commanded by God); (b) the campaign against Amalek (directly commanded by God); (c) a war of clear and immediate defense against an attack already launched (included by Maimonides but not classical-rabbinic).[6]

Instances of discretionary wars *(reshut)* include the following: (a) expanding the boundaries (perhaps to strengthen one's strategic position); (b) increasing one's power or prestige.[7] In the opinion of all, such wars anticipatory of future power-political problems are at best discretionary *(reshut)*, even in the case of the divinely ordained state, and thus subject to the checks and limitations to be indicated below.

Especially significant with respect to classification is one particular case, that of "preventive" or "pre-emptive" attack. In the classic statement of the issue in the *Talmud*, Raba, discussing a difference of opinion between the Rabbis and R. Judah, says the following:

> "The wars waged by Joshua to conquer Canaan were mandatory *(mitzvah)* in the opinion of all; the wars waged by the House of David for territorial expansion were discretionary *(reshut)* in the opinion of all; where they differ is with regard to wars against heathens so that these should not march against them. One calls them mandatory *(mitzvah)* and the other discretionary *(reshut)* . . ." *(Sotah* 44b.)

Or, in the wording of the *Talmud Jerushalmi:*

> "Rabbi Judah designated discretionary *(reshut)* a war in which we attacked them, and obligatory *(hovah)* a war in which they attacked us."

In short, the majority opinion of Talmudic thinking is that a war "pre-emptive of future danger . . . is at best a *milhemet reshut."*[8]

In evaluating these classifications it is well to keep in mind that they are largely theoretical findings after the fact, and further that subsequent authoritative opinions tend to reduce severely the range of "discretion" in the case of *milhemet reshut.* Thus Maimonides forbids the waging of war against any nation before peace offers are made to it, and insists that even in the case of a supposed *milhemet mitzvah* (mandatory war), "if the inhabitants make peace, accept the seven Noahide commandments, and submit to certain conditions of taxation and service, one may not kill a single person."[9]

There is also evident among Jewish authorities a strong tendency to emphasize limitations on the so-called "discretionary" wars. Thus Rabbi David S. Shapiro, in a learned and well-documented essay, states the following:

> "The category of *milhemet reshut* includes wars against the avowed enemies of Israel, nations that flagrantly violate the Seven Commandments and recognize no international obligations. This kind of war may be declared only after the sanhedrin of seventy-one, the highest tribunal in Israel, the king of Israel, and the high-priest through the Urim and Tumim have given their approval. Its purpose may not be conquest, plunder, or destruction. It may be waged only for the protection of Israel and for the sanctification of the name of God, that is the imposition of the Seven Commandments. . . .

No war may be waged against a nation that has not attacked Israel, or that lives up to the fundamental of the Universal Religion. Even Edom, Ammon, and Moab, who had throughout their history displayed hostility to Israel, were not to be attacked, not to speak of those nations who were not bellicose. It would seem that the *milhemet reshut* was limited by the ideal boundaries of the Holy Land." [10]

And the eminent Israeli halachist, Rabbi Shelomo Yosef Zavin, suggests that "in fact a war of attack, though designated a *milhemet reshut* (discretionary war), is forbidden to the nations of the world." [11]

With this caution in mind, it will now be of value to consider briefly the traditional significance of these distinctions among wars. In the three cases of *milhemet mitzvah*, it is the rabbinic view that such wars may be initiated by the king without his consulting the Court of Seventy-One, that the claim of conscription applies to all, even those specifically exempted by the provisions in *Deuteronomy* 20:8 and 24:5, and that all may be coerced to participate. It is interesting (and ironic) that Maimonides takes those critical threats in *I Samuel*, cited above, and reads them as sanctions for such acts by the ruling power!

On the other hand, in instances of discretionary wars *(reshut)* it is rabbinic opinion that the king may not involve the people without the sanction of the Court of Seventy-One and the sanction of the Urim and Tumim (oracles) consulted by the high priest, and that the various exemptions do indeed apply. Thus while reducing in some respects the application of biblical exemptions, the rabbinic authorities in other respects extend them. Relying on *Deuteronomy* 24:5,

> "When a man is newly married, he is not to go out with the army, nor be counted with it for any duty; he is to be free at home for one year, to enjoy himself with his wife whom he has married,"

the rabbis apply it as follows:

> "The following do not move from their place (to join the army and then claim exemption): He who built a new house and dedicated it, planted a vineyard and used its fruit, married his betrothed, or took home his brother's childless widow. . . . These do not even

supply water and food or repair the roads (for the army)." *(Mishnah Sotah* 8:4.)

The exemption in such cases is thus total.

We further note in passing that the provision of *rakh levav* ("tender of heart") in all opinions applies to all cases of discretionary war, a fact of some import since no war today can be regarded as either *hovah* or *mitzvah*.[12]

Other elements of rabbinic teachings are relevant to our current considerations, for example, attempts to limit destruction of resources during war. Among the provisions from the classical rabbinic tradition attempting to limit the destructive consequences of war, the following are clearly relevant to our own age:

1. "It is forbidden to cut down fruit-bearing trees outside a (besieged) city, nor may a water channel be deflected from them so that they wither, as it is said: 'Thou shalt not destroy the trees thereof' *(Deut.* 20:19). Whoever cuts down a fruit-bearing tree is flogged. This penalty is imposed not only for cutting it down during a siege; whenever a fruit-yielding tree is cut down with destructive intent, flogging is incurred. It may be cut down, however, if it causes damage to other trees or to a field belonging to another man or if its value for other purposes is greater (than that of the fruit it produces). The law forbids only wanton destruction." (Maimonides *Code*, "Laws of Kings and Wars," Ch. 6, Law 8.)

2. "Not only one who cuts down (fruit-producing) trees, but also one who smashes household goods, tears clothes, demolishes a building, stops up a spring, or destroys articles of food with destructive intent, transgresses the command 'Thou shalt not destroy.' He is not flogged, but is administered a disciplinary beating imposed by the Rabbis." *(Ibid.,* Law 10.)

3. "It was after these things and this loyalty, that Sennacherib, king of Assyria, came and invaded Judah, and besieged the fortified cities and expected to take them. When Hezekiah saw that Sennacherib had come determined to attack Jerusalem, he decided in council with his princes and his leading men to stop the water of the fountains that were outside the city, and they helped him. Indeed a great crowd of people collected and stopped up all the fountains

92 / *A Conflict of Loyalties*

and the torrent that coursed through the midst of the land, saying,
'Why should the kings of Assyria come and find abundant water?' "
—*II Chron.* 32:1–4.

"It was Hezekiah who stopped the upper springs of Gihon and directed the waters straight down on the west side of the city of David."—*II Chron.* 32:30.

"Our Rabbis taught: Six things King Hezekiah did; in three they (the Sages) agreed with him, and in three they did not agree with him . . . and he closed up the waters of Upper Gihon, and they did not agree with him. . . ."—*Pesahim* 56a

Other teachings are directly applicable to traditional attempts to limit injury of persons during war. The rabbinic tendency to modify the biblical meaning of certain texts toward what we might designate "humane ends" was noted above with Maimonides' insistence that even the "seven nations" were first to be offered peace rather than herem, and that such acceptance meant that "not one person was then to be slain." The attempt to prevent unnecessary injuries and deaths during conflict, especially among noncombatants, is expressed in a number of rabbinic rulings:

1. "When siege is laid to a city for the purpose of capture, it may not be surrounded on all four sides but only on three in order to give an opportunity for escape to those who would flee to save their lives, as it is said: And they warred against Midian, as the Lord commanded Moses (*Num.* 31:7). It has been learned by tradition that that was the instruction given to Moses." (Maimonides, *op. cit.*, Ch. 6, Law 7.)

2. "(During their festivals) One should not sell them (gentiles) bears, lions, or anything which may injure the many." *(Mishnah Avodah Zarah* 1:7.)

"The reason is because they may injure the many." *(Talmud Avodah Zarah* 16 a,b.)

Maimonides spells out more fully the implications of this dictum:

3. "It is forbidden to sell to idolators any weapons of war. Neither

may one sharpen their weapons nor make available to them knives, chains, barbed chains, bears, lions, or anything which might cause widespread injury. One may sell to them shields or shutters which are purely defensive." (Maimonides *Code*, "Laws of Murder and Defense," Ch. 12, Law 12.)

One notices, incidentally, that the nature of the weapons themselves, and *not* the purported intentions of their users, determines the prohibitions!

In further treating this provision, Maimonides extends the principle to include indirect supplying of such material, and makes clear that the prohibition applies to Jewish brigands as well:

> 4. "That which is prohibited for sale to idolators is also prohibited for sale to Jews who are suspected of then selling such material to idolators. Likewise, it is forbidden to sell such weapons to Jewish brigands *(listim.)*" (Maimonides *Code*, "Law of Idolatry," Ch. 9, Law 8.)

Zavin, relying on Maimonides, states the following principle as well:

> 5. "In all cases of *milhemet reshut* (discretionary war), it is forbidden to kill women and children." (Zavin, *op. cit.*, p. 44.)

There is no developed rabbinic doctrine on the scale or dimensions of any given conflict, although some of the previously indicated limitations suggest that in practice any war had to be rigorously bounded. Two further remarks on this specific question should be cited, however:

> 1. "R. Eleazar said: Every war which is waged with more than sixty thousand men is waged in disorder *(milhemet irbuviah,* a chaotic war)." *(Song of Songs Rabbah,* IV, 4.)

> 2. "Samuel said: A government which kills up to one out of six (by going to war) is not punished. . . ." *(Talmud Shevuoth* 35b.)

implying, of course, that beyond this such a government is liable to punishment. From Rashi's comment, this would seem to apply to those conscripted by the king, and would refer to the casualty rate among the soldiers themselves. From the current text reading, however, it would appear to apply to the nations attacked. In either case, however, it clearly excludes a war of "attrition" or a war of mutual extirpation.

Rabbi Immanuel Jakobovits, addressing himself to the issue in modern terms, states emphatically:

> "A major source in the *Torah* for the law of self-defense is the provision exonerating from guilt a potential victim of robbery with possible violence if in self-defense he struck down and, if necessary, even killed the attacker *before he committed any crime (Ex.* 22:1). Hence, in the words of the rabbis, 'if a man comes to slay you, forestall by slaying him!' *(Rashi; Sanhedrin* 72a). Now this law confers the right of self-defense only if the victim will thereby *forestall* the anticipated attack and save his own life at the expense of the aggressor's. But the defender would certainly not be entitled to frustrate the attack if this could be done only at the cost of both lives; for instance, by blowing up the house in which he and the robber encounter each other. Presumably the victim would then have to submit to the robbery and even to death by violence at the hands of the attacker rather than take 'preventive' action which would be sure to cause two deaths.
>
> In view of this vital limitation of the law of self-defense, it would appear that a defensive war likely to endanger the survival of the attacking and the defending nations alike, if not indeed of the entire human race, can never be justified. *On the assumption, then, that the choice posed by a threatened nuclear attack would be either complete mutual destruction or surrender*, only the second alternative may be morally vindicated." [13]

Besides such regulations dealing with the body politic and its policies, there are a number of rabbinic teachings which deal with considerations of conscience for the individual facing a situation of war. Most significant is the fact that in these life-and-death confrontations, restraint, limitations, and scruples are explicitly affirmed as appropriate. This is so in both individual and collective confrontations.

1. "It has been taught by Rabbi Jonathan ben Saul: If one was pursuing his fellow to slay him, and the pursued could have saved himself by maiming a limb of the pursuer, but instead killed his pur-

suer, the pursued is subject to execution on that account." *(Talmud Sanhedrin* 74a.)

2. Especially revealing are the classical rabbinic comments on the anticipation of war between Jacob and Esau, deriving from the following verse in *Genesis* (32:8):

" 'Then Jacob was greatly afraid and was distressed.' R. Judah b. R. Ilai said: Are not fear and distress identical? The meaning, however, is that 'he was afraid' lest he should be slain, 'and was distressed' lest he should slay. For Jacob thought: If he prevails against me, will he not slay me; while if I am stronger than he, will I not slay him? That is the meaning of 'he was afraid'—lest he should be slain; 'and was distressed'—lest he should slay." *(Genesis Rabbah* 76:2.)

Another rabbinic comment ascribes to Jacob the following sentiment: "If he overpowers me, that is bad, and if I overpower him, that is bad!" [14]

3. There are two classical statements, referring to the same verse in *Genesis*, which affirm explicitly that murder *(shefichut damim)* is a category applicable to armed conflict:

" 'And Jacob was greatly afraid and was distressed.' One might think that Jacob was literally afraid of Esau, fearing that he might not be able to defeat him; but this is not the case. Why, then, was Jacob afraid of Esau? Because Jacob took seriously the prohibition against murder *(shefichut damim)*. And so Jacob reasoned as follows: If I succeed and kill him, behold, I have transgressed the commandmend 'thou shalt not murder.' And if he kills me, woe is my lot! Hence it is written: 'And Jacob was greatly afraid and was distressed.' " [15]

Even more remarkable is the comment of Rabbi Shabetai Bass, compiler of *Sifte Hahamim,* the classic subcommentary on the commentary of Rashi. Bass takes explicit note of the Talmudic permission to defend oneself, yet suggests that murder is still an issue, even in a situation of armed combat!

". . . Yet one might argue that Jacob surely should have had no qualms about killing Esau, for it states explicity, 'If one come to slay thee, forestall it by slaying him.' *(Talmud Sanhedrin* 72a; *Berachot*

96 / *A Conflict of Loyalties*

> 58a and 62b.) Nonetheless, Jacob did indeed have qualms, fearing that in the fray he might kill some of Esau's men, who were not intent on killing Jacob (for only Esau had this intention) but merely fighting against Jacob's men. And even though Esau's men were pursuing Jacob's men, and every person has the right to save the life of the pursued at the cost of the life of the pursuer, nonetheless that provision applies which states: 'if the pursued could have been saved by maiming a limb of the pursuer, but instead the rescuer killed the pursuer, the rescuer is liable to capital punishment on that account.' Hence Jacob rightly feared lest, in the confusion of battle, he kill some of Esau's men outright when he might instead have restrained them by merely inflicting injury upon their limbs." [16]

Thus Bass, whose subcommentary is a summary of "the best work of his fifteen predecessors who had commented on Rashi," [17] relays the opinion that even in an actual combat situation, the principle does obtain that the least possible and least injurious force should be applied, even to combatants!

4. Rabbinic comments on Abram's participation in the War of the Kings *(Genesis* 14) sustain the validity of this concern.

> "After these things the word of the Lord came unto Abram in a vision, saying: 'Fear not, Abram. . . .' *(Genesis* 15:1). This relates to the verses from *Proverbs:* 'Fortunate is the man who fears perpetually; But he who hardens his conscience shall fall into evil' *(Prov.* 28:14); and 'A wise man is fearful and turns away from evil, but a fool is overbearing and careless' (14:16). Who is the wise and fortunate man alluded to? Abraham. And of whom was he afraid? Of Shem, for he killed in battle Chedarlaomer, King of Elam, and his three sons, descendants of Shem. . . . Thus Abram was afraid, saying: 'I have killed the sons of a righteous man, and now he will curse me and I shall die. . . .'" (Midrash Tanhuma on Lech L'cha, 19, ed. Buber.)

Even more telling is the further speculation in Midrash Tanhuma:

> "Still another reason for Abraham's fear after killing the kings in battle was his sudden realization: 'Perhaps I violated the Divine commandment that the Holy One, Blessed be He, commanded all men, "Thou shalt not shed human blood" *(Gen.* 9:6). Yet how many people I killed in battle!' "(—*Ibid.*)

For this reason too the Midrash imagines Abram needing divine reassurance.

Among other explanations of the grounds for Abram's fear, R. Levi suggests the following:

> "Abraham was filled with misgiving, thinking to himself, Maybe there was a righteous or God-fearing man among those troops which I slew. . . ." (Midrash Rabbah on *Genesis*, 44:4.)

There are, of course, other explanations advanced which take Abram's fear in the most self-concerned sense; he feared for his life when the avengers of the dead would set out for him. Yet the interjection of scruples about killing in the midst of conflict is highly significant for our considerations, and that Abram needed direct divine reassurance indicates that the bloodshed consequent upon warfare was not to be lightly regarded.

5. The provision in *Deuteronomy* 20:8, which provides exemption from combat for one who is "fearful and/or tender-hearted," has received comment from the rabbinic tradition also:

> "R. Akiba says: 'Fearful and tender-hearted' is to be understood literally, viz., He is unable to stand in the battle-ranks and see a drawn sword. R. Jose the Galilean says: 'Fearful and faint-hearted' alludes to one who is afraid because of the transgressions he had committed. . . ." *(Sotah* 44a.)

Lest Rabbi Akiba's interpretation be understood in purely "medical or psychological" terms, the *Tosefta* cites Akiba's position in these words:

> "Why are both terms, 'fearful' and 'tender-hearted,' specified? To indicate that even the most physically fit and courageous, if he be a *rachman* (compassionate, gentle), should be exempted. . . ."

There are, further, teachings which concern obedience to established authority.

1. The respect which Judaism accords the law is well-known, and this respect extends to the civil laws of the secular state. Frequently cited is the rabbinic dictum: *dina d'malchuta dina*, "the law of the government is the law."

Not so often cited, however, are the precise conditions in

which this dictum is asserted. The four Talmudic instances concern: the validation of a deed of sale, the method for acquisition of real property, tax collectors exceeding their authority, and extortioners, official oppressors, or tax-farmers behaving illegally.

All four cases involve monetary matters or matters of civil procedures, not matters of life and death. Furthermore, in the two cases where officials exceed their rightful authority, the dictum does *not* determine the issue, but rather tax-refusal/resistance/evasion is countenanced! (Cf. *Talmud Gittin* 10b–11a, *Baba Batra* 54b, *Baba Kama* 113a, *Nedarim* 27b–28a.)

2. In the *Talmud* a discussion is recorded between Resh Lakish and R. Johanan concerning the respect which should be shown a king. At issue is a legend that Moses struck Pharaoh in contempt and anger just before stalking out. While one of the rabbis is of the opinion that no matter what the ruler's nature, respect must be accorded him because of his office, the other maintains that a ruler's wickedness should call forth contemptuous behavior in his presence! Thus, it is not at all certain that the man in office is to be accorded the respect due the office if he, in that office, violates the dignity of the office itself.

3. There is on record a specific case in which constituted authority commands an act contrary to the most basic moral teaching of Judaism. In such a case, the *Talmud* and later rabbinic tradition are at one in counseling refusal no matter what the personal consequence.

> "In every other law of the *Torah*, if a man is commanded, 'Transgress and suffer not death,' he may transgress and not suffer death, excepting idolatry, incest, and shedding blood. . . . Murder may not be practiced to save one's life. . . . Even as one who came before Raba and said to him, 'The governor of my town has ordered me, "Go, and kill so and so; if not, I will slay thee."' Raba answered him, 'Let him rather slay you than that you should commit murder; who knows that your blood is redder? Perhaps his blood is redder.'" (*Talmud Sanhedrin* 74a.)

4. Many instances could be cited of disobedience to established authority, whether Jewish or non-Jewish, where such au-

thority violated the basic moral and religious convictions of Judaism. Abraham, Moses, Elijah, Jeremiah, Shimon bar Yochai, Jochanan ben Zakkai, etc., are the heroes of numerous tales and legends lauding their refusals to obey illicit authority and unjust laws.

It should be mentioned, finally, that a well-established principle of Talmudic law is: "There is no agent for a sinful act." This is held to mean that a responsible adult cannot evade the legal consequences of the act committed by pleading that he was "merely following orders."

More precisely, in the opinion of the *Talmud* he is guilty of following the wrong orders: "If there is a conflict between the words of the Master (God) and the words of the student (man), whose are to be obeyed?" *(Talmud Baba Metzia* 10b; *Kiddushin* 42b, 43a.)

3. Coda

The foregoing selections should already have suggested some direct implications, both negative and positive, for our own situation. It is clear that the biblical period prior to the establishment of the monarchy was characterized by intimate family and tribal groupings, considerable local autonomy, and a high degree of voluntarism with respect to recuitment of fighting men. Professional armies and conscription of individuals by the central monarchy seemed to some of the prophets a serious violation of divine intent. The first biblical record of monarchical conscription receives unqualified condemnation.

It should be evident from these facts that any attempt to validate a centralized and bureaucratized system of mass conscription on the basis of early biblical practice and later prophetic evaluation is a serious misreading of the meaning of that tradition.[18] Inferences from an intimate community to a mass society are extremely dubious, to say the least.

It is further evident from the biblical material that there were distinctions among categories of wars; that "ideological wars" have no biblical basis; that individual willingness to participate in war was an indispensable condition; that a premature breach in a man's involvement in life was explicitly prohibited; and finally, except for the limited specific cases of the wars of conquest (from which no analogies to modern times can be drawn in any respect), a war which destroys the bases of human existence, i.e., a war of scorched earth or extermination, is strictly prohibited.

One further detail should be made explicit. There were two occasions on which exemptions were granted: *before* conscription *(Dt.* 24:5) and *after* entering the ranks *(Dt.* 20:5–8). This option did not apply once a force went off to battle, but it did apply during what we might call the training period, when the implications of war became evident to the person. It is, in fact, precisely to such a situation that the provision of *Rach-levav* (tender of heart) applies.

The rabbinic material, though not a complete statement of a "permissible war" doctrine, evidently supplies significant criteria for determining whether or not one should participate in a given conflict. It is further evident that individual scruples were regarded as appropriate to war situations, that obedience to established authority is *not* sufficient justification for participation, and that individual responsibility for actions could not be evaded by appeal to superior human authority.

It seems evident from the foregoing that Judaism cannot be characterized, in the strict sense of the term, as a "pacifist" tradition. It seems equally evident that Judaism does not regard every war as permissible, nor does it regard every means of prosecuting war as permissible. It is further evident that while Judaism is highly respectful of duly constituted authority, this does not absolve the individual from the duty of making responsible moral decisions. Neither these moral decisions nor their bases are delegated to human authority in any unchallengeable way.

If the above be an accurate rendering of an essential part of the Jewish tradition, it would appear that "selective" conscientious objection on moral grounds is a fundamental teaching of Judaism and a fundamental demand of its adherents.

NOTES

[1] Julius Kravetz: "Some Cautionary Remarks," in *CCAR Journal*, Vol. XV, No. 1, January, 1968, pp. 78–79 (Central Conference of American Rabbis).

[2] Roland de Vaux: *Ancient Israel: Its Life and Institutions* (New York: McGraw-Hill Book Company, 1961). Especially pp. 213–267.

[3] Yehezkel Kaufmann: "Traditions Concerning Early Israelite History in Canaan," pp. 304–309, in *Scripta Hierosolymitana*, Volume VIII. Jerusalem, 1961.

[4] *Ibid.*, p. 304.

[5] Johannes Pedersen: *Israel: Its Life and Culture*, Vol. III–IV (Oxford University Press, London, 1959).

[6] Cf. Maimonides *Code*, "Laws Concerning Kings and Wars," Ch. 5, Law 1.

[7] *Ibid.*

[8] Cf. the sensitive article by Prof. Irving Greenberg of Yeshiva University on "Judaism and the Dilemmas of War," in *Judaism and World Peace: Focus Viet Nam* (Synagogue Council of America, New York, N.Y.).

[9] Maimonides, *op. cit.*, Ch. 6, Law 1.

[10] David S. Shapiro: "The Jewish Attitude Towards War and Peace," in Leo Jung, ed., *Israel of Tomorrow* (N.Y., 1946), p. 237.

[11] Rabbi Shelomo Yosef Zavin: *L'or Hahalacha* (Tel Aviv, 5717), p. 17.

[12] Such a statement may appear doubtful today given the strong feelings concerning the value, perhaps even the sanctity, of the reestablished State of Israel. Without entering into the question of any of the specific wars involving the modern State of Israel, it is surely clear that in the strict sense of the terms they cannot be regarded as anything more than *reshut*. As recently as 1946, before the establishment of the State of Israel, Rabbi Shapiro could plainly state: "Since the destruction of its state, Israel can no longer wage wars, for its war-declaring agencies are no longer in operation. All attempts at armed reconquest of the Holy Land are expressly forbidden. God has imposed an oath upon Israel to that effect. The Land of Israel will be restored to its people in God's own good time." *(op. cit., ibid.)* It must also be remembered that so inspired a teacher as Jeremiah raised serious questions about particular wars involving the ancient Jewish State, that very State established by

Divine edict according to the Biblical tradition. To insist that all wars today are at most *reshut* is simply to insist that every single one must be subject to serious moral evaluation, and that no claims of sanctity can serve to exempt any conflict whatsoever from this moral judgement.

13 In *Tradition:* A Journal of Orthodox Jewish Thought, Vol. 4. No. 2, Spring, 1962, p. 202. Cf. also the paper by Morris Laub: "Maimonides on War and Peace (with Special Application to Vietnam)." Available from the American Jewish Congress, 15 East 84 Street, New York, N.Y. 10028.

14 Lekach Tov, cited in *Torah Shlemah* (ed. M. Kasher), Vol. 6, page 1266, footnote 49.

15 Schechter Genizah Manuscript of an early edition of Midrash Tanhuma, cited in *Torah Shlemah, ibid.*

16 Sifte Hahamim on *Gen.* 32:8.

17 Louis Ginzberg in *The Jewish Encyclopedia* (New York, 1904), Vol. 2, p. 584.

18 Cf. the outrage expressed by Rabbi Aaron Samuel Tamaret as early as 1905 at the violation of individual existence by modern collective nationalist demands (in *Judaism,* Vol. 12, No. 1, Winter, 1963, esp. pp. 42–46).

Dissent: The Tradition and Its Implications

MULFORD Q. SIBLEY

WHAT we call today selective conscientious objection is a reflection of the spirit of dissent in general; and dissent has had a not inconsiderable place in the experience of the American people. The United States has exemplified in its life both resounding objections to prevalent trends in the culture and equally strong attempts to suppress those objections. This ebb and flow between the pole of rebellion and that of conformity will illustrate both the problems and the promise of dissent.

I will examine the notion of dissent as it has been reflected in the religious culture; in general politics; in the impetus to utopian withdrawal; in the tradition of non-violence and civil disobedience; and in the vicissitudes of the peace movement. The last section will explore the implications of dissent and of selective conscientious objection as a species of dissent.

1. *The Tradition of Religious Dissent*

The United States was settled just after the first two generations of the Protestant Reformation had passed. Its early history reflects, therefore, both the religious protest of Protestantism and the criticism of orthodox Protestantism and Catholicism by sectarian movements. There were dissenters within movements of dissent; and later on dissenters to the dissenters to movements of dissent. The result has been a nation which, in terms of religious affiliations, has been a puzzle to most of the world; for the United States—despite the tendency in recent years to merge religious denominations—still remains one of the most divided nations in terms of formal religious commitments.

The colony at Plymouth was, of course, established by British dissenters from the Established Church who had found even Holland too constricting an environment for the adequate expression of their particular notions about the relations between man and God. After the foundation of a relatively orthodox establishment in Massachusetts, dissenters within it—like the great early exponent of religious freedom, Roger Williams—seceded, thus affecting profoundly the religious environment of the colonies.[1]

Perhaps the most radical of the dissenters in early days were the Baptists and the Quakers. The former might be either "Calvinist" or "non-Calvinist" in outlook and stressed radical decentralization in church government. As for the early Quakers, they were bold religious innovators who dissented not only from the ancient church of Christendom but also from the major stream of the seventeenth-century British Protestant tradition. Whereas Catholicism had maintained that the Church is the defining authority of religious faith and orthodox Protestantism had identified the *Bible* as the ultimate basis, Quakers discovered that same authority in the voice or the spirit within each individual man and woman. There was, to be sure, an important corporate side to early Quakerism in this country—the voice within was to be checked against the witness of the Meeting—but in the end Quakerism held that the individual must make his own decision as to how he should exemplify his faith in everyday life.[2]

Thus Quakerism, like so many of the heterodox Protestant sects, contributed to that individualism which was to constitute so important a note in both the religious and the social heritage of American culture. Groups like the Quakers and tendencies like that of "antinomianism"[3] helped contribute to a relatively early breakdown of the original "theocracy" of Massachusetts. And this religious dissent affected all aspects of life.

Sectarianism became an important note in American religious consciousness and worked against what Ernst Troeltsch has called the "church type" of organization—the large, monopolistic aggregation reflected in so much of the religious life of Europe.[4] Sects within sects made American religious experience a fissiparous one, to a degree rarely understood outside this country.

This tendency to dissent and to separate can be illustrated by reference to well-known facts of religious history. Already in the eighteenth century, the "Great Awakening" shook religious complacency and orthodoxy; and the impact of the Wesleys on American life counteracted any tendencies which might have existed to impose uniformity. Out of the "congregationalist" stream emerged unitarianism, which became so important a challenge to the orthodoxies of the nineteenth century, even though unitarianism itself, in certain respects, tended to harden into a new kind of orthodoxy.

When this hardening of the religious arteries became evident to certain nineteenth-century souls, they dissented and sought once more a kind of original revelation which would by-pass the organizational inertia of both unitarianism and congregationalism. Thus Emerson and the Transcendentalists, strongly influenced by European idealism and romanticism, as well as by Hinduism, tried in the concept of the "over-soul" to emancipate themselves from the thralldom of religious respectability. About the same time, "perfectionist" cults under men like John Humphrey Noyes issued novel proclamations of religious nonconformity. Both Perfectionism and Transcendentalism led to unusual dimensions of social and political dissent as well as to religious eccentricity.

In pre-Civil War days, too, the rise of the Latter Day Saints (Mormons) illustrated both the dimensions of dissent and the strong cultural efforts to suppress it. Hounded out of the East and Middle West by social and legal pressures, the Mormons eventually found refuge in the West, thus in a sense re-enacting the saga of those dissenters who had established several of the original American colonies.

The split in Methodist and Presbyterian organizations over the issue of slavery illustrated yet another aspect of religious dissent before the Civil War. Among other things, these divisions demonstrated that dissent might take a "conservative" as well as a "radical" form.

Meanwhile, the immigration of large numbers of Roman Catholics was to add quite a different minority element. While Catholics had been present in relatively small numbers from the very beginnings of American life, their impact on American culture became great only after the Irish troubles of the nineteenth century and the immigration of Irish Catholics. A preponderantly Protestant religious culture began to be diluted by what, to the orthodox Protestant tradition, was a strange set of beliefs and customs. Until recent years, indeed, Catholics have possessed a "minority" psychology, which was rooted in their early experiences.[5] Subjected to all kinds of social pressure, they courageously maintained their faith but in the process developed many of the characteristics often associated with dissenting minorities in general—extreme defensiveness, a sense of alienation from the main cultural stream—plus a determination to pass on their own beliefs through a separate educational system at a time when the developing public schools were dominated by "Protestant" ideologies and teaching.[6]

Since the Civil War, the tension between church and sect types has continued. Typically, when religious organizations veer far in the direction of rigid church types, dissenters secede in order to regain what they think of as the original religious experience which, in their view, has been lost in the emphasis on size, property, and religious respectability. The secession of the Nazarenes from the Methodist Church in 1912 is a good example of this kind of dissent; and while some may argue that the Church of the Nazarene since then has taken on many of the characteristics of the large body from which it originally seceded, the original dissent was indeed an exemplification of a common pattern in American culture. And many other examples might be mentioned, whether of "conservative" or of "radical" dissenters. An example of the former was the organization in 1941 of the American Council of Christian Churches in protest against what its founders thought of as the too-liberal tendencies of the Federal Council of Churches.

Similar issues have arisen in connection with the Jewish religious tradition. The development of "Reform" and "Conservative" congregations in protest against the "Orthodox" tendencies was originally an exemplification of the spirit of dissent, aided and abetted, of course, by the ancient tradition of congregational autonomy in the Jewish community. But Reform and Conservative congregations often develop their own kinds of religious rigidity, leading some Jews to dissent from them as well—either in the direction of some kind of "ethical culture" or of disaffiliation from any formally religious group. To some extent, indeed, the prophetic tradition in Judaism is closely related to the role of the dissenter, even when that dissenter calls himself an atheist or an agnostic.[7]

I have mentioned thus far only formally organized religious groups, but "anti-religious" dissent has also had a real impact on American culture. Many Europeans have observed that one of the most striking features of American life has been its strong religious note, but atheists, agnostics, and the "anti-religious" in general have also played important roles. The village atheist who challenged all formal religious belief is more than a myth. In almost every town he constituted a radical critic of those who regarded themselves as God-centered. In the early days, writers like Tom Paine, who perhaps can best be described as a deist, were critical of all organized religious groups. Paine paid a terrible price for his dissent: he was virtually ostracized and was berated unmercifully by the orthodox.[8] In the latter part of the nineteenth century, Robert Ingersoll played a role not dissimilar to that of Tom Paine. As an "agnostic" affected by Darwinian biology, he challenged most of the religious commitments of the orthodox and became the *bête noire* of the preachers. Men like Ingersoll challenged the exponents of traditional religion to think about the relation of science to religion and helped to produce the stream of religious liberalism and modernism of the twentieth century. They were supported, at a more scholarly level, by men like Andrew White, who, in his book on the "warfare" between religion and science, performed a similar service.[9]

The atheistic-agnostic dissenting tradition has been carried on in the twentieth century by several minority currents. Many of those who have sought to clarify the theory of separation of church and state have come from the atheist-agnostic stream of dissent.[10] At the level of popular dramatization, such great dissenters as the late Clarence Darrow have done much to carry on the challenge to religious orthodoxy. In the Scopes trial of the twenties, the confrontation between Darrow and William Jennings Bryan exhibited the sharp conflict between the small minority of agnostic dissenters and the much larger body of those who continued to repeat the formulae of orthodoxy. About the same time and on the level of high journalism, acrid commentators like H. L. Mencken performed a similar function.

American religious culture, whether Catholic, Protestant, or Jewish, has been very much affected by the idea of "progress." Hence the stream of dissent on this issue assumes an unusual importance. Throughout American history, there have always been those who challenged the notion that human history would go on indefinitely or was progressive. Most orthodox views, to be sure, paid lip service to the view that history might come to an end some day. But only dissenters like the Millerites in the nineteenth century professed to see the end of history within a very few years. In the twentieth century, perhaps the best reflection of apocalyptic dissent has been the sect known as Jehovah's Witnesses.[11] The Witnesses have despaired of human progress and have consistently anticipated a decisive, imminent, and violent end to historical experience. Dissenters *par excellence,* they have come on the whole from the economically and socially deprived and in many respects seem to resemble first-century Christians. Regarded as eccentrics even by many eccentrics, they are an excellent example of how extreme dissenting sects can affect the general course of human history; like St. Paul in the Roman Empire, they have utilized the courts to the fullest extent and in the process have deeply affected American law.

But while sectarianism has been a hallmark of religion in the United States, we might well ask whether most religious groups, sectarian or not, have escaped the overriding and unifying effects of what some have termed the "religion of nationalism."[12] We ought also to note the effect of the modern ecumenical movement on possibilities of dissent in the future.

On the first score, it can be argued—as, indeed, it has been by a well-known scholar of religion in the United States[13]—that despite the sectarianism so ubiquitous in American experience, the real "religion" of the American people has been "Americanism" or

"American nationalism." To a considerable extent this has undoubtedly been true. But although it has affected groups ideologically, it has not substantially prevented organizational dissent; and it makes all the more significant the existence of those movements—like Jehovah's Witnesses—which dissent ideologically from the "religion of nationalism."

With the development of the ecumenical movement, on both a national and a world scale, the problem of dissent in American religious life is put in a different perspective. Consolidation and confederation of churches, with inherent tendencies to greater bureaucratization, may provoke forms of dissent which can hardly be envisioned. American religious organization in our day is torn. On the one hand, it has been affected by the spirit of American "efficiency" and the desire to avoid duplication and overlapping, as well as by the laudable desire to be "one" in the faith. On the other hand, the element of dissent which has constituted so important a factor in the religious consciousness will undoubtedly conflict, to some extent, with this tendency to consolidation.

While religious dissent has played a highly significant role in the past history of American culture it is, like other facets of dissent, confronted by new difficulties. The imperatives of technology tend to impose their uniform patterns on all expressions of human life, whether labeled religious, political, or social. We may well wonder whether the religious eccentric will be able to flourish in an age of ubiquitous technological imperatives. Can he, as in the past, appeal periodically from the rigidities of church-type religion to what he regards as the original springs of religious insight? Will he find it psychologically possible to revolt? Or will he succumb, stifle his tendencies to dissent, and confine his mutterings to the purely private sphere?

2. Dissent in General Politics

Politics, interpreted broadly, can refer to a very substantial segment of human experience. I will later discuss direct action, nonviolent resistance, civil disobedience, the utopian surge, and the peace movement as expressions of dissent. Insofar as they seek deliberately to order society or to affect public policy, all of these represent, in one sense, political activity. First, however, I will discuss politics as it is identified with its more formal reflection in dissenting political parties; with dissenting ideologies; and with *ad hoc* groups outside those to be considered later.

Parties. In a day when the "two-party system" seems to have become a kind of sacred cow for the preponderant currents of American culture, it is easy to forget the checkered party history of the United States and the role of minor parties and movements. The two-party system itself has not always occupied the position it holds today. In the beginning, the Founding Fathers were suspicious of all political parties as incompatible with republican government (a position shared by such exponents of democracy as Rousseau). Later, when parties of some kind had begun to be accepted as part of the social order, there was no assurance that they would be two in number. As a matter of fact, during the latter part of Madison's administration and throughout most of Monroe's (roughly, 1816 to 1824), this country was virtually a one-party nation. And throughout many States of the South, one-party systems have been the rule in modern times.

And "third" and "minor" parties have characterized the scene on many occasions, often playing significant roles in their dissent. Before the Civil War, such parties as the Anti-Masons and the Know-Nothings proclaimed doctrines which were outrageous to the orthodox but which forced men to think out their positions on secret societies and on new immigrants. By the fifties, the major issue of the day had become slavery; yet both major parties—the Whigs and Democrats—either evaded the issue or gave such ambiguous answers that they became increasingly unacceptable to many. Minor parties like the Liberty Party and the Free-Soil Party really grappled with the questions which men were raising, thus contributing to the debate. While the major, orthodox parties gave unclear answers, the minor parties, in dissent, often stated relatively clean-cut alternatives. At its birth and for a few years thereafter, even the Republican Party was a minor party and in this stage of its career was less evasive than after it had become a major grouping.

In the American two-party system the parties might differ from each other on issues initially, but they very rapidly come to espouse essentially the same principles—where any principles can be discerned. They become "church-type" as over against "sect-type" organizations. In the beginning, the Republican Party took a relatively clear stand on slavery and several other issues, thus differentiating itself from the Democrats. But after the Civil War, both major parties became essentially spokesmen for a burgeoning capitalism. While there might be relatively minor differences— Democrats stood for "free trade" and Republicans for "protection"—even those tended to fade. Differences within the two major parties tended to be greater than clear-cut differences between them. In fact, by the middle of the twentieth century, it was not wholly inaccurate to speak of the Demo-Republican Establishment, within which two segments of slightly different emphases existed. Many praised this Establishment precisely because there were hardly any "ideological" differences between its two wings.[14]

Under circumstances of this kind, the role of third parties in dissent was essentially one of supplying the contesting ideologies which the Establishment lacked. Repudiating the evasions and the obscurantism of the two major parties, the minor groups felt called upon to take eccentric and unorthodox positions. In the post-Civil War period, for example, the Greenback Party advocated an expansion of the currency and in effect anticipated the respectable applied Keynesianism of the 1950's. The rise of socialist parties— the Socialist Labor Party, for instance, and the American Socialist Party—enabled some segments of the electorate to challenge the premises of industrial and finance capitalism; for such a challenge was impossible within the framework of the major groups. Sometimes the minor dissenting parties made proposals which were much later taken over—without credit, of course—by the major parties: thus the "immediate demands" of the Socialist Party in 1912 included such items as Social Security, which, after a generation, were embodied in New Deal legislation under the auspices of the Democratic Party. This is not always true, of course; the Vegetarian Party, which from time to time has nominated candidates for the presidency, has had no direct influence on the major party establishment.

It should be emphasized, too, that many minor parties are very short-lived. Thus the party which sponsored the candidacy of Robert La Follette in 1924 dissolved not long after his defeat. The Jobless Party of 1932, a product of the Great Depression, disappeared immediately. While the Progressive Party of 1948 originally gave promise of surviving the election, its life, in the end, proved to be very brief. But even where parties were tiny or short-lived, they often brought to the surface issues which might otherwise have remained hidden.

It has often been observed that American radical parties exhibit many of the same characteristics as religious sectarianism; they tend to split up into small groups, each of which may emphasize what is to some a comparatively minor point of doctrine. The variety of radical dissenting groups since the twenties can be indicated if we call the roster of their often very similar names: Communist Labor Party; Communist Party; Workers Party; Proletarian Party; Workers Socialist Party; Socialist Workers Party. Each splinter embodies some point in the on-going dialectic; and dissenters within dissent, in the long run, could conceivably be extremely significant even politically.

The ambivalence of American culture about minor dissenting parties, however, is as important as the existence of the parties themselves. On the one hand, Americans profess an abstract commitment to the notion that all political parties should be heard. On the other hand—and particularly in the twentieth century—they seem to fear genuine competition with the Establishment parties. Thus they have enacted laws in many states which make it extremely difficult for minor groups to appear on the ballot. They virtually outlaw certain types of parties. When dissent wishes to form a party, it meets both legal and economic difficulties.

But this very effort to crush organized dissent makes it all the more imperative that the Establishment parties be challenged. In politics, as in economic life, there is a strong tendency to monopoly. Aside from any specific contributions they may make, the very existence of minor parties helps check this tendency, which, if pushed very far, kills both the letter and spirit of republican institutions.

Dissenting Ideologies. Aside from dissenting parties, each of which may reflect a particular ideology, American politics has produced ideologies often unconnected with parties but nevertheless of great significance for political debate.

One might instance anarchist dissenters in this connection. According to their principles, anarchists, being against all authority, can hardly organize parties which attempt to carry on electoral and ordinary "political" work. Yet anarchism, by challenging all authoritarianism at its roots, has rendered a notable service to political society. Native American anarchism was reflected in the nineteenth century by such figures as Josiah Warren. There was a strong anarchist strain in early Abolitionism. "Individualist" anarchist contentions were exemplified, late in the nineteenth century and early in the twentieth, by such writers as Benjamin Tucker, who repudiated State structures root and branch, on the ground that they always tend to destroy the integrity of the individual.[15] Communist anarchism—reflected in such figures as Alexander Berkman and Emma Goldman—was closely connected with the outlook of Peter Kropotkin, the great European anarchist who rejected both the authoritarianism of the Marxists and what he regarded as the dictatorship of modern capitalism. Emma Goldman advocated birth control (long before Margaret Sanger), questioned most of the orthodox shibboleths of her day, was imprisoned on many occasions, and challenged not only American capitalism but also the authority patterns of the Soviet Union. She dissented from liberalism, conservatism, the Communist Party, and capitalist authoritarianism. She died in exile from the United States, thus illustrating the limits imposed on dissent by American culture.[16]

Aside from anarchism, there have been many other ideological currents which have not necessarily found embodiment in formal political parties but which have represented dissenting outlooks. One thinks of feminism, for instance, which, to be sure, was partly reflected in a minor party for a time, but which has always been to a great extent beyond party. The ideology of the Single Tax is another example; although a factor in formal politics for a brief period, it has mainly been influential in an indirect sense. The ideology of the Townsend Movement in the thirties, which to most appeared to be a "crank" outlook, affected, despite the orthodox viewpoint, American attitudes toward aging and the problem of retirement.

Ad Hoc Organizations. American politics has been characterized by the activities of many *ad hoc* groups, which often take positions in strong dissent from prevalent currents. In many respects, these groups have greater potentialities for affecting the political process than do the political parties. Thus the American Civil Liberties Union, founded by an anarchist during World War I, seeks to apply the generalities of the Constitution to particular cases; and in defending the freedoms of frequently very unpopular groups—Communists, Fascists, and nudists, for example—often finds itself in sharp dissent from the general society.

Anti-Vivisection societies lobby for legislation against the predominant opinions of prestigious scientists. Societies for the prevention of cruelty to animals often fight lonely battles for legislation or adequate administration. Civil rights organizations struggle against majority inertia or outright hostility. Committees to defend the rights of conscientious objectors are themselves dissenters defending the position of a tiny minority of dissenters.

Often *ad hoc* dissenting groups fight against hopeless odds, as do minor political parties. Many never gain their objectives but, like the dissenting parties, continue their agitation. Even though they never "win," they provide focal points for discussion which is vital in politics. Just as early suffragettes, in dissent, willingly went to jail for their convictions, so scores of *ad hoc* groups may flourish for a time, often for eccentric causes, and vanish. But even if their membership is miniscule and they are never successful, they serve to shake up the political process—always a good—and to preserve the personal integrities of those who commit themselves to a cause.

If politics is the effort of man to order his collective affairs deliberately—instead of depending on Fortune, instinct, or folkways—then dissent, whether in the form of minor parties, eccentric ideologies, or *ad hoc* organizations, plays a very vital role. For without dissent, men's imaginations are restricted, their adaptability declines, and they tend to slide into indifference and to become the prey of accidental forces and designing private groups. Only with the presentation of dissenting views can that continuous re-shaping of the social order, which is politics, be carried out. Without the expression of dissent, even radical dissent, inertia tends to set in and, for want of a rational ordering, human affairs are shaped by pre-political factors or by sheer brute force. Happenstance and force still play an enormous role in collective affairs but dissent can reduce that role. Without dissent, an active political consensus cannot be developed—instead, there is formed a specious consensus which is doomed to disruption when those forces which have remained under the surface of life break through. Dissent gives voice to those forces before they become embittered and irrational.

3. *The Utopian Impetus and Dissent*

Some students of American culture stress its alleged monolithic pattern, but others rightly point out that the elements of eccentricity in American history heavily qualify such interpretation. The so-called utopian movements illustrate nicely the sharp challenge to predominant ways of thinking and acting.

Between the War of 1812 and the Civil War, thousands of Americans were dissatisfied with the development of commercialism and industrialism, the apparent loss of community, and the seeming general decline of idealism. Some sought answers in general political reform through the party system. Others—like Thoreau and similar literary figures—challenged Americans by writing about the issues which they conceived to be uppermost. Yet others, animated by both religious and "secularist" ideals, strove for better social orders by withdrawing from the general society in the hope that they could, in isolation, provide standards which others might emulate. The utopians believed that through the establishment of intentional communities they could find answers to the questions so many Americans were asking about their rapidly expanding society.

Thus Robert Owen and his son were responsible for New Harmony, Indiana; and colonies under the inspiration of Etienne Cabet were founded in Texas, Illinois, and Iowa. Brook Farm, the experimental utopia so intimately associated with the Transcendentalist movement, became one of the best-known of the colonies. All the colonies expressed unease about private property and all sought to check the impersonalism which they saw arising under conditions of the increasingly complex division of labor. They met with varying degrees of success, some of them surviving into the post-Civil War period and even into the twentieth century, but all counteracted those tendencies to uniformity in American culture which acute foreign observers like Alexis de Tocqueville were describing.[17]

Most of the nineteenth-century utopian experiments, which developed under the impetus of early industrialism, were inspired by European theorists. Another type of utopia had been with the United States from pre-industrial days under religious inspiration. Mennonite and Amish communities, for example, had challenged basic assumptions of American culture from colonial days. Under the guidance of a theology which despaired of making the general society fully "Christian," they rejected the magistracy, spurned military service, and in general rejected complex ways of life in favor of a very simple, isolated agrarian existence. Similar to them were the Hutterite communities of the Middle West, which from time to time—particularly in World Wars I and II—were subjected to severe pressure from business and nationalist interests. Experiments of this kind have frequently been looked upon with suspicion, partly because they appeared so "queer"—questioning as they did so many assumptions of the "American Way of Life"—and partly because they provoked jealousy by reason of their sometimes astounding agricultural success.[18]

The Shakers, an eighteenth-century movement, exerted an important influence on dissent in the nineteenth century. Seeking community in celibacy, in close and cooperative organization, and in shared experiences of song and dance, the Shakers contributed not a little to the general culture through their manual skills; and their experiments encouraged yet other utopian ventures.[19]

I have mentioned the Mormons as a dissenting religious group, but Mormonism may also be looked upon as a utopian social movement of considerable importance. The very endeavor to encourage polygamy, in face of a rigid monogamous culture, was one of the boldest experiments of the nineteenth century—a venture which survives, in isolated colonies of Mormons, into our day.

One of the most remarkable examples of American-inspired utopian dissent was the Oneida community which flourished in upstate New York between 1848 and 1878. It differed so sharply from orthodox patterns and etched itself so memorably on the American consciousness that no history of dissent in America can fail to mention it. Founded by John Humphrey Noyes, Oneida was established in religious and social dissent alike. Noyes rejected his orthodox Calvinist background, was caught up in the early nineteenth-century revivalist movement, and eventually became a kind of Manichaean Christian. Oneida rejected monogamy and instead established Complex Marriage, in which every man was regarded as the husband of every woman and sex relations were carried on apart from any intent to reproduce the species. This meant that the Oneidans had a system of birth control—coitus reservatus or Male Continence—which many regarded as remarkably successful. Complex Marriage implied a close relationship between variety in sex experience— Oneidans were encouraged to have relations with many of the opposite sex and not to develop exclusive attachments—and the development of integrated personalities, thus anticipating certain psychoanalytical views of the twentieth century.[20] During the last ten years of the experiment, children were deliberately produced through "selective breeding," in which the community paired individuals with each other for reproductive purposes. The colony was communist economically, both consumers' and producers' goods being owned by the group, with distribution of consumers' goods according to need. Oneida was remarkably open to new scientific knowledge—including Darwinism—in a day when it was often being rejected by popular culture.

As a whole, utopian dissent challenged the growing capitalist economic developments of the general culture and sought to prevent what its leadership thought of as the inevitable disintegrating tendencies of a society increasingly devoted to private profit. The social innovations of the colonies were often startling examples of what uninhibited dissent could do, once it is freed from the seemingly inevitable rigidities of orthodox social organization. Where the colonies failed, it was usually not for economic reasons. Oneida, for example, was remarkably successful economically and disintegrated because of a clash between older and younger generations, conflict of personalities, and external pressures. The student of American dissent might well ask whether the many eccentric experiments of the nineteenth century could be initiated and flourish in the increasingly conformist culture of the mid-twentieth.

4. Protest, Non-Cooperation, and Civil Disobedience

A sensitive and intellectually alive individual will always be in some tension with any given historical social order; for the *status quo* at any particular time will always fall short of or distort the ideals which prophets exalt. On occasion, the tension will become acute and almost unbearable.

It is in situations of this kind that protest, non-cooperation, non-violent resistance, and civil disobedience may develop. When action takes the extreme form of civil disobedience—deliberate, overt violation of a law deemed to be unjust—the tension between moral norms and socio-political "reality" has obviously reached a crucial point.

The idea of concerted non-violent resistance (sometimes taking the form of civil disobedience) is an old one in American thought and practice. In colonial Pennsylvania, for example, many Quaker judges at one point resigned rather than carry out an order requiring administration of oaths.[21] Quakers, denied admission to Massachusetts, kept returning until one of their number was hanged—an important event in breaking down intolerance in the Bay State. Colonial legislatures carried out a kind of perpetual resistance campaign against the demands of colonial governors for more revenue; like the British Parliament, they would often refuse to appropriate money until particular grievances were redressed by the Executive. In Pennsylvania, legislators like David Lloyd conducted a long campaign to secure greater legislative prerogatives from the Proprietor, William Penn, himself a dissenter in religious and political matters; and the Quakers in the Legislature kept proprietary and royal governors in constant turmoil by resisting demands for money to be used for war.[22] Eventually, the pressure for war appropriations became so great (in a colony which had long before ceased to be Quaker) that Quaker members of the Legislature resigned rather than participate in uneasy compromises with their convictions.

In Pennsylvania, too, private citizens were not loath to resist non-violently what they deemed to be illegal or immoral demands. On one famous occasion, for example, the British government enacted a tax which was to be paid by all shipping proceeding down the Delaware River into the ocean. Quaker merchants argued that this was a violation of their legal rights. Several merchants thereupon sailed down the river, refusing to heed the warning to pay their taxes. The authorities, after warning them, took to a small boat and moved rapidly down the river to overtake the Quaker vessel, which they soon did. The merchants considerately threw out a rope to the tax men, assisted them to mount the sides of the ship, and then set the small boat adrift. The revenue agents thus had to remain on the ship while it continued its trip, untaxed, to the ocean. In the end, tactics of this kind won the day, the tax was recognized as illegal, and the non-violent resistance was thus successful in gaining its objectives.[23]

The whole history of resistance to what was regarded as unjust taxation is a fascinating chapter in the story of American dissent. Building on well-known British precedents of the seventeenth century, private citizens challenged allegedly illegitimate levies and boycotted the goods upon which they had been imposed. The Boston Tea Party was only one of the more dramatic episodes in this struggle.[24] It can be plausibly maintained, in fact, that had these essentially non-violent methods of resistance prevailed, the objectives of the American Revolution might have been attained more rapidly than by means of war, and without its enormous moral and social costs.

The firmness of the "antinomians" in New England helped break the stranglehold of the theocracy in politics as well as in religion. In Pennsylvania, the sturdy resistance of Quaker Meetings to alarms about Indian warfare—alarms sometimes deliberately concocted by the authorities to force the raising of armies —helped preserve one of the noblest dissenting experiments in history and kept Pennsylvania free from Indian warfare for more than two generations. The non-violent resistance to militarism helped confound the orthodox statements of the textbooks and public opinion about "defense"; and the axioms of that vast majority of mankind who regard themselves as "practical" were shaken.[25]

Although the founders of the American Republic were not pacifists, the proposition that large standing armies and military conscription were dangers to republicanism was central to early American politics. In this respect, even orthodox American leaders were dissenting from traditions that either had been or were to be important in Europe. In a sense, the French Revolution established the idea of national military conscription as a hallmark of modern nationalism;[26] and for many years the United States was in dissent. To be sure, the militias of the several States were supposed to be composed of all able-bodied males; but the principles were loosely enforced, there were legal limitations on the use of militias, and the notion of a nationally administered system was foreign to the American ethos. Daniel Webster, early in the nineteenth century, termed military conscription a species of slavery. Many interpreted the Constitution as permitting use of the State militias only for "defense" against invasion. Thus on one occasion a body of New York militia, when ordered to invade Canada during the War of 1812, resisted non-violently by throwing down its arms at the international border.

Dissent / 121

The first nationally administered and enforced system of military conscription was that of the Civil War. Resistance to it was widespread and sometimes took the form of anti-draft riots, as in New York City. Not a few Americans, apparently, sympathized with the riots and hoped they would succeed in frustrating the conscript system. Many did everything they could to avoid military service—by fleeing to the woods or into the West, for example, or by taking advantage of the law and hiring substitutes.

When Woodrow Wilson helped devise a new conscript system at the time of World War I, he sought to avoid some of the administrative errors present in the Civil War scheme and as a result World War I conscription did not provoke actual riots. But there was considerable dissent about its adoption, some vigorous non-violent resistance after it went into effect, and not a little propaganda against it during the war. Socialists particularly opposed its passage and continued to denounce it even after it became law. Some were sent to prison (under the Espionage Act) for circulating statements like the following:

> Conscription is upon us; the draft law is a fact!
> Into your homes the recruiting officers are coming. They will take your sons of military age and impress them into the army;
> Stand them up in long rows, break them into squads and platoons, teach them to deploy and wheel;
> Guns will be put into their hands; they will be taught not to think, only to obey without questioning.[27]

Even after the tradition of conscription had begun to have a place in American life, it was still regarded merely as a wartime measure and not as an institution conceivable for peacetime America. Thus there was enormous opposition in Congress to the adoption of a peace-time conscription measure just before American entry into World War II. Subsequent renewals, since the war, have usually been adopted by overwhelming margins, however, which has led many to conclude that the early American attitude to conscription has indeed been reversed. Resistance from 1945 to 1965 appears to have been confined to a relatively few conscientious objectors. Since 1965, however, with the onset of the Vietnamese war, both political and individual opposition to conscription seems to have been revived. Those who burn draft cards in our day are very much in the spirit of Civil War and World War I protesters and resisters.

Meanwhile, the tradition of direct-action dissent and propaganda has been reflected in many other areas of American life. From time to time, for example, those agitating for women's suffrage in the early part of the twentieth century would engage in acts of civil disobedience and thus have to suffer jail sentences. Demonstrations before the White House helped dramatize the plight of the women and served to place non-violent pressure on Woodrow Wilson, who, very reluctantly, became a convert to the cause.

Jehovah's Witnesses have refused to salute the flag, even against school board regulations and prevalent opinion, and have won legal recognition of their right to dissent from what they regard as a religious exercise.[28] Christian Scientists have on occasion refused to obey compulsory vaccination laws. The Amish have stood up against compulsory school laws, in the name of religious principles.[29] And there are still "Old Mormons" married to more than one wife who risk prosecution for conscientiously violating State "anti-polygamy" laws and the federal "white slave" statute.

But perhaps the best-known tradition of direct action has been that in the realm of race relations. From the latter part of the seventeenth century, opposition to the institution of slavery began to grow—very slowly at first but after a century at a more rapid pace. Some eighteenth-century men, like the Quaker John Woolman, thought that opposition to slavery could be strengthened by refusal to use goods made by slave labor; thus Woolman tried to dress in coarse home-spun materials and for this and other acts was thought of as an extreme eccentric by those who had little sympathy with or understanding of his moral motivations. Before the end of the eighteenth century, it had become a rule of the sect that no Quaker could have slaves.[30]

After the renewed grip of slavery, with the coming of the cotton-gin, opposition took many forms. Although it was at first rather disreputable in all sections of the country, agitation for emancipation eventually attracted many of the most notable spirits of the nineteenth century. They used many methods—propaganda, demonstrations, and the boycott of slave-made goods. When certain States enacted legislation separating the races on railroads, some Negroes conducted "sit-ins" to defy the segregation. When strict fugitive slave legislation was passed by Congress, organized opposition to it not infrequently took the form of civil disobedience. The so-called Underground Railroad, which was organized and directed by some of the most dedicated and intelligent dissenters in pre–Civil War days, was a gigantic exemplification of civil disobedience; thousands of Americans cooperated to frustrate the purposes of the Fugitive Slave laws by helping Negroes to escape from the South to Canada, where they would be free from Congressional statutes seeking to return them to servitude.[31] In developing this attitude of "selective" law defiance, the Underground Railroad conductors were building on the old American tradition of non-cooperation and non-violent resistance.

Unfortunately, the bitterness, estrangement, and irrationality engendered by the Civil War made the solution of the so-called race problem still more difficult. Had Americans continued to use only non-violent direct action, they might have accomplished far more than through war, and without the physical and spiritual devastation associated with violence. While the war resulted in formal legal emancipation, the main battle for freedom still lay in the future. And by the end of the nineteenth century new restrictive laws were being added by Southern States to keep the Negro population subordinate.

When direct action began to be resumed in somewhat systematic form during the 1940's, the way had been prepared by some improvement in economic status, the development of a theory of non-violent resistance by men like Bayard Rustin, the establishment of such organizations as the Congress of Racial Equality, and a series of legal victories in the courts spearheaded by the National Association for the Advancement of Colored People. The Montgomery bus strike came in the fifties and later, in the sixties, the widespread sit-ins, freedom rides, and civil disobedience.[32]

The non-violent resistance of the Civil Rights movement illustrated several points characteristic of direct action (as contrasted with legislative action) in general. First, by no means all of it constituted civil disobedience. Mass demonstrations, for example, were clearly within the law, as were such acts as peaceful picketing and many boycotts. Secondly, even where some acts violated local ordinances (some of the sit-ins, for example) their initiators often held that they did not violate a higher law (the Constitution, for example). In fact, in some instances local law was regarded as clearly a violation of congressional statutes or the Constitution and its violation was seen as a way of testing its legality. Curiously enough, the American constitutional system provides no method for testing the constitutionality of an alleged statute except by means of an individual deliberately violating the statute in the hope that he will be arrested and tried, when he can plead unconstitutionality of the violated "law." Much of the "civil disobedience" of the Civil Rights movement had this character; the dissenter was violating a claimed law in order to show that it was really no law. Finally, where genuine civil disobedience did occur (deliberate violation of a law admitted to be law by the violators), it was under conditions which exemplified a high sense of responsibility: the violators carefully deliberated before acting, they gave the benefit of any doubt to the law, and they were ready to accept the penalties.

In his *Letter from Birmingham Jail*, Martin Luther King illustrates the character of Civil Rights civil disobedience. He demonstrates great respect for law but argues, in effect, that often one shows greatest respect when deliberately violating the law while accepting the punishment attached. Laws which are unjust, he contends—echoing W. H. Seward's nineteenth-century doctrine of the "higher law"—undermine respect for law in general. Thus the civilly disobedient are appealing from a particular positive law to the *principle* of law, which, to be acceptable in the long run, must embody an element of justice, or at least not run counter to it.

Protest, non-violent resistance, and civil disobedience could be illustrated in many other aspects of the American tradition—in the labor movement, to take only one instance—but our examples will have illustrated the role of dissent in this context. The spirit of non-violent resistance has had roots deeply embedded in American life and its modern exemplifications simply renew that spirit.

5. *The Peace Movement and Dissent*

As the United States has been drawn more and more into the vortex of international politics, the issues of war in general and of peace tactics in particular have assumed increasing importance for American dissenters. Men like Thomas Jefferson envisioned a United States which would be a new departure in human history: it would avoid the urban congestion of Europe, experiment with systems of public education, and above all escape the perpetual quarrels which appeared to characterize so much of European history. Obviously, however, Jefferson's vision has been implemented in a most imperfect manner and among the casualties has been the hope that America might escape from what the late Charles A. Beard once called "giddy minds and foreign quarrels."[33] The problem of war, from the early part of the nineteenth century, became an increasingly significant one for dissenters of all types, particularly when governments pledged to peace became involved in wars which they expected the public to support almost automatically.

The peace movement was born with the foundation of the American Peace Society in 1828. Building upon the experience of local peace societies which had been established in Massachusetts and elsewhere, the national society soon found dissent and division within its own ranks, the division often turning on controversies between those who rejected war in general but supported most particular wars and those "absolutists" who insisted on rejecting all wars. On the whole, the "non-absolutists" won the day and the "absolutists" became dissenters within the peace movement. This has continued to be one of the central themes of the peace movement ever since.[34]

In such wars as the conflict with Mexico, however, opposition to the war was so widespread that it inevitably included both absolutists and non-absolutists. Among the latter was Abraham Lincoln, who in his speeches in the House of Representatives berated President Polk for his actions which had led the country into war. In attacking the war, Lincoln spoke for thousands of dissenters of all kinds, most of whom, undoubtedly, did not reject all war but only "unjust" conflicts like that with Mexico. Others, like James Russell Lowell in the *Bigelow Papers*, seemed to reject all war:

> Ez fer war, I call it murder,—
> There you hev it plain an' flat;
> I don't want to go no furder
> Than my Testyment fer that.

In fact, the dissent of all types was so strong and so outspoken that had national military conscription existed, we cannot doubt that selective conscientious objection would have been widespread. Many years later, General Grant—himself a military officer in the conflict—would in his *Memoirs* denounce the war as one of the most unjust ever waged by a powerful State against a small country.

In pre–Civil War days, of course, the whole peace movement was interwoven with what was at first a very small abolitionist cause. Leading figures among the abolitionists, like William Lloyd Garrison, were also advocates of an absolute pacifist position. Thus, in 1838, the declaration of the New England Non-Resistance Society, which Garrison supported, announced:

> Our country is the world, our countrymen are all mankind. . . . The interests, rights, liberties of American citizens are no more dear to us, than are those of the whole human race. Hence, we can allow no appeal to patriotism, to revenge any national insult or injury. . . . We register our testimony, not only against all wars, whether offensive or defensive, but all preparations for war; against every naval ship, every arsenal, every fortification; against the militia system and a standing army; against all military chieftains and soldiers; against all monuments commemorative of victory over a foreign foe, all trophies won in battle, all celebrations in honor of military or naval exploits. . . .[35]

Obviously, statements of this kind, particularly when combined with radical abolitionist arguments, constituted a kind of dissent within dissent, for the predominant stream within the peace movement was much broader. The so-called moderates were particularly perturbed by statements in the declaration which repudiated all government, thus adding anarchism to criticisms of preparation for war. Like conflicts between moderates and radicals in our own day, the struggle reflected real divisions about strategy as well as ultimate ends.

Later on, however, the dilemmas of the abolitionist-radical peace combination came to the fore. Suppose slavery could be abolished only by organized violence? What would be the pacifist-abolitionist position? Henry David Thoreau spent a night in jail for refusing to pay his poll-tax to a government which supported slavery and waged the Mexican War. And in his great essay on *Civil Disobedience* he asserted a general right and obligation of men to disobey commands of a government which were morally wrong. Yet Thoreau, despite his attack on the Mexican War, supported the violence of John Brown in 1859[36] on the plea that Brown was seeking through his rebellion to overthrow slavery; and later, the author of *Walden* upheld the Civil War on the same ground. Read in the light of his vindication of John Brown, *Civil Disobedience* can be seen as a statement defending the right and duty of what we should today call selective conscientious objection; Thoreau opposed the Mexican War on the ground that it was unjust but supported Brown and, later, the Civil War.

Thoreau, then, was never an absolutist on the peace issue and one can discern a pattern of consistency between his earlier and later positions. The same was true of Emerson. But avowed absolutists like Garrison had a more difficult time. In the end, they felt they had to renounce their complete rejection of war in order to support a particular war whose objective to them was just. In other words, they surrendered their absolutism only after a soul-searching struggle.

Some, to be sure, remained consistent absolutists. Among these was the eminent literary figure Elihu Burritt, a self-educated blacksmith who thought it mistaken to believe that the Civil War could truly emancipate the Negro. He continued to oppose all war, including the Civil War which according to so many was waged for "freedom." War, Burritt contended, always had a tendency to enslave; and while it might seemingly "free" the slave in a formal sense, it could not truly emancipate him. Because war is basically wrong morally, it cannot contribute in the long run to moral ends.[37] Traditionally pacifist groups like the Mennonites, Quakers, and Brethren, of course, agreed with Burritt and suffered on both sides of the line during the Civil War. Both opinion and law were against these dissenters. While there were, to be sure, some "fighting Quakers," the great bulk of the so-called peace churches remained true to their convictions.

During the Spanish-American War, absolutists and many moderates alike found themselves the objects of public criticism because of their opposition to the war. The Universal Peace Union, one of the most vigorous peace organizations of the time, was expelled from its national headquarters by a hostile opinion and lost much of its pre-war support.[38] Outspoken groups like the Anti-Imperialist League (which did not hold an absolutist position on war) exposed the horrors of the Philippine Insurrection— the "water cure" administered by American troops to prisoners, the orders of the American General Jacob H. Smith to kill all males over ten years of age, and the wiping out of whole villages, including women and children. Had national conscription existed, there would have been numerous "selective" conscientious objectors.

World War I constituted a crisis of a peculiar sort in the peace movement. As the first foreign war in which national conscription existed, the question of personal attitudes was posed dramatically for many. Because the war appeared to be waged for noble ends, under leadership which was supposed to be "liberal," it is not surprising that most of those who had been affiliated with peace movements before the war should have passively or actively supported the war. The leadership of conservative peace organizations like the Carnegie Endowment for International Peace gave its blessing on the ground that the war would lead to a firmer peace. A substantial minority of the peace movement, however, both absolutists and non-absolutists, were adamant in their opposition.

The attitude of the Socialist Party will illustrate the dilemmas which its members confronted. Before the war, the party had discussed the peace issue relatively little and when it did, it usually held that only complete achievement of socialism could lead to the elimination of war. Only after the outbreak of the war in Europe did it begin to think seriously about what its position should be if the United States were to become involved. In its 1917 convention, the majority of the party denounced the war and refused to give it political support. Some socialists, however, could not accept the majority resolution and many of these—among them some of the best-known figures—left the party altogether, thus becoming conscientious dissenters to dissent.

Many who supported the majority resolution were jailed for their opposition to the war, which was often expressed in leaflets such as the following:

Censoring God

The publishers of Bibles are away behind with their orders. The war has created an unprecedented demand for them, especially for the New Testament.

This is good news. We hope the purchasers of these books will read them.

They will probably have to do it on the sly, however. For, as you know, the Bible is treasonable nowadays. It says, "Thou shalt not kill." But our latter day commercial and political saints will have none of it. They are a whole lot wiser than God. . . . They have amended the commandment by striking out the word "not" so as to make it read, "Thou shalt kill." Before any more Bibles to go press, we suggest that that word be gouged out of the plate. Of course, it will leave a blank spot on the page. But that's all the better. It will call the attention of the present and future generations to the fact that our wise commercial and political saints overruled God and censored his word.[39]

Or the one entitled *Cheer Up:*

> *Cheer Up!* By Cary E. Norris
> Cheer Up, Boys!
> Wave your caps and shout for joy;
> For a kind, beneficial government has
> bought 200,000 coffins for you.
>
> . . .
>
> It is not customary to purchase the coffin
> until after death;
> Therefore, such thoughtfulness and consideration
> on the part of the government ought to be fully
> appreciated.
>
> . . .
>
> Just think of the sad condition of the poor French and
> German boys;
> Shot to death, torn into shreds, broken and mangled
> past all recognition, and no coffin.
>
> . . .
>
> Girl, say, "Good-bye" to your sweetheart with
> a smile on your lips.
> Part of him may come back;
> But if you never see him again try not to think of him
> with his arms and legs blown off;
> With great holes torn in his body;
> With his face crushed beyond all resemblance to a human;
> Just think of him peacefully sleeping in the coffin
> provided for him by the benevolent government and imagine that
> his last words were: "We are taking Democracy to Germany."
> Then, cheer up!
> And then cheer up some more.[40]

For his opposition to the war expressed in an Ohio speech, the great Socialist leader Eugene V. Debs served a term in Atlanta Penitentiary and became a kind of rallying point for all those who dissented from support of the war, whether absolutist or non-absolutist.

Dissenting conscientious objectors played an important role in opposition to World War I. Because the law was very narrow in the recognition it gave to objectors and failed to provide for a system of alternative civilian service, many served terms in prison, including military prisons like Fort Leavenworth. Some were subjected to indignities of all kinds, such as the torture of being suspended by the fingers with the toes barely touching the floor. Some died as a result of their harsh treatment. The problems were particularly difficult for those who had no formal "religious" attachments but grounded their objections on ethical and philosophical considerations. And of course there were those who opposed World War I but not necessarily all war.[41] While most intellectuals—as is true in most wars—supported World War I, a few dissented and the brilliance of their dissent has made it memorable. Perhaps the best example is Randolph Bourne, who based his opposition on the spirit of his teacher John Dewey's philosophy, even while Dewey himself became an apologist for the war.[42] Bourne died before the conclusion of the peace treaty, greatly disillusioned by the attitudes of his fellow intellectuals.

Between the two World Wars, the American peace movement was unfortunately often divided. But there were many high points of dissent. The "Oxford" pledge, in which one promised never to fight in a future war, was taken by many college students. In the twenties, journals like *The World Tomorrow* sought to maintain an element of idealism in a pleasure-seeking generation. Organizations like the Women's International League for Peace and Freedom and the Fellowship of Reconciliation held aloft the banner of non-violence. Strong personalities like the late A. J. Muste dissented from some of the basic premises of the culture.

In World War II, political dissent was not nearly as great as in World War I, despite the fact that the Socialist Party (now much smaller than during World War I) refused, in its convention of 1942, to "bless" the war. Conscientious objectors, however, provided a sharp element of dissent, whether in alternative civilian service camps or in jail, where some 6,000 objectors and Jehovah's Witnesses served terms. The devoted Witnesses, as a matter of fact, were widely imprisoned not only on the Allied side but also in Germany.

Since World War II, the American peace movement has had to confront the great wave of McCarthyism in the fifties and the so-called limited and Vietnamese wars. Beset by some of the same problems which affected the cause before the Civil War and between the two World Wars, "peace" dissenters have had to face an increasingly centralized State which, in terms of national government expenditures, can only be described as a "warfare State." In political terms, the movement was relatively unorganized until the time of the Vietnamese war beginning in 1965; after that year, it was seeking more and more to find some kind of an organizational basis for action. Individual conscientious objection has apparently grown but political unity in the peace movement is still to be achieved.

One unusual form of dissent should be noted in the period since 1965. Several persons, including the well-known Quaker leader Norman Morrison, expressed their moral outrage at the Vietnamese war by burning themselves to death, thus emulating several Buddhist dissenters in Vietnam.

The Vietnamese war raised anew the issue of selective conscientious objection, itself a very old question. Selective Service Acts since World War II have required one to be opposed to all war by reason of "religious training and belief" in order to be classified as a conscientious objector. Obviously such a formula does not recognize all genuine conscience; for there are those who reach their convictions without "religious training" and there are also men who conscientiously oppose some wars but reserve their judgments about the moral legitimacy of other conflicts. A society which excludes some forms of conscientious objection—forms which may embrace the majority of actual objectors—cannot legitimately be said truly to recognize conscience. But the dissenting objector, whether recognized by law or not, must continue to dissent or lose his soul.

The peace dissenter today, whether absolutist or selective, quite obviously builds on a very long American tradition.

6. The Implications of Dissent

What are the implications and what is the significance of dissent?

We may suggest two answers: first, the dissenter—including the selective conscientious objector, who is a particular type of dissenter—is an officer of society and carries out important social functions; and, second, he has a moral right and duty to dissent in order to preserve his own integrity.

The Dissenter as an Officer of Society. The dissenter acts as an officer of society in two respects: first, by challenging the orthodoxies, whether in words or in action, he breaks new ground upon which the majority may later build; and, second, even if the dissenting view never becomes predominant, its expression forces the orthodox to re-examine their premises, look at their consciences, and clarify their outlook. Without dissent, they will tend to become complacent and, as John Stuart Mill pointed out, their own position will become a mere form whose rational foundations, if any, will have been forgotten.

Let us illustrate these two propositions. Social change requires initiation and a challenge of the prevalent patterns. The dissenter offers this challenge. Change, to be sure, may not always be desirable; but assuming for the moment that a given change is in fact a desideratum, a dissenting group must be the agency for initiation. Insistence by early legislatures on redress of grievances before they would appropriate money helped establish precedents which checked tyrannical tendencies. Dissent and civil disobedience in connection with the Underground Railroad not only assisted many slaves to gain their freedom but was an important factor in developing a conscience against slavery. Similarly, direct action, including civil disobedience, contributed enormously to real, if all too slow, racial integration in Civil Rights. In some instances, as in the case of the early militant suffragettes and advocates of feminism, there can be little doubt that dissent aroused a sentiment which eventually received majority support. Dissenting socialist parties initiated proposals which provided the groundwork for major party enactments, even when the long-run objectives of the socialist parties were not attained. Selective conscientious objection in our day can keep alive our moral sensitivity and may eventually be an important factor in the elimination of war.

Even where dissenting movements were not successful, in the usual sense of the term, there can be little doubt that in some instances they sharpened orthodox consciousness and forced supporters of the established order to re-examine premises and clarify objectives; and if rationality and clarity be desiderata, this was a signal contribution. Thus Quaker dissent about war has never won the day and conceivably may never do so; but can there be much doubt that it has forced war-makers to deal with issues and answer questions with which they might not otherwise have grappled? Darwinian "agnostic" dissenters did not make most American agnostics, but by challenging orthodox belief systems they contributed enormously to more sophisticated views of religion. Utopian experiments did not transform the nation, but they did provide a stimulus for thought and speculation which has not been lost to this day. The American Communist Party did not convert most Americans, but without its agitation the debate about issues like poverty, war, and totalitarianism would have been less advanced than it is today. Jehovah's Witnesses did not make most men Witnesses nor did they invent the idea of religious liberty, but through their very existence and their obstreperousness they forced the organs of society to think more clearly about the meaning of freedom. Selective conscientious objectors may remain a minority for many years and through many wars, but they compel those in charge of the war machinery to weigh questions they might not otherwise consider.

The dissenter thus occupies a social office. It is a role having some of the characteristics associated with the functions of the ancient Hebrew prophet who was always challenging complacency, asking questions about the *status quo*, and either changing the *status quo* or compelling its guardians to re-examine and defend it.

The Dissenter and Personal Integrity. But aside from his strictly social office or role, the dissenter in expressing his convictions —whether by oral and written expression, demonstration, or going to jail—reminds us that man is more than a social being. While society is a necessary condition for the development of personality, personality is more than a social product. It has ends and visions of its own and cannot be reduced to a mere instrumentality of social ends. The person has an obligation to himself to speak and act in accordance with his deepest convictions, even if these lead to basic dissent and possibly death. One must be true to oneself, lest the person lose that wholeness which is itself a value.

An integrated or whole personality reflects the good, the true, and the beautiful. It is like a work of art, about which one does not ask, "What is it good for?" The eccentric—however extreme his eccentricity—dramatizes anew the fact that a man is more than a unit to preserve or reform society.

When the Greenback Party hopelessly, and even to the accompaniment of jeers, advocates its peculiar views, its members may never have a great impact on the community; but their dissent is, nevertheless, valuable. When Eugene V. Debs goes to prison for denouncing World War I, we need not defend him solely in terms of his social role; we can also suggest—as many did indeed suggest—that there is something of the good, the true, and the beautiful in his act. When the selective conscientious objector resists the draft and formulates his reasons for doing so, he is fulfilling a duty to himself and whatever his social service may be, he is justified in his objection.

The critic may argue, to be sure, that such views lead to "anarchy," that the very existence of both society and personality depends upon conformity to certain mutually held expectations about conduct. In response, we reply that while community does indeed entail some uniformity in behavior, the great danger is not from those who would limit uniformity but rather from those who would extend it into all areas of life. Complex, bureaucratic society is always tending to reduce persons to mere things and in the absence of dissent, the possibility of mere thinghood is a genuine one. The risks from dissent are minimal; those stemming from the thrust to make men mere instruments of the group or the power structure are enormous. Viewed in this light, Walt Whitman's advice "to the States" to "resist much, obey little" does not seem exaggerated.

The dissenter, then, holds an important social office. But he is also obliged to dissent to maintain his own integrity as a person; and personality, however humble in relation to social status, is a thing of beauty, an expression of truth, and a reflection of the good.

NOTES

[1] On Williams and other early dissenters about religious freedom, see Anson Phelps Stokes, *Church and State in the United States*, 3 vols. (N.Y.: Harper, 1950; rev. one volume edition, 1964).

[2] The tension between a corporate and an individual "witness" has played an important role in Quakerism from the beginning.

[3] Antinomian: against "law." Anne Hutchinson, one of the great rebels of New England, was regarded as an antinomian. In general, all those who tended to reject external authority in religious affairs were given this label by their critics.

[4] See Ernst Troeltsch, *The Social Teaching of the Christian Churches*, 2 vols. (N.Y.: Macmillan, 1931).

[5] On Catholic reactions to and understanding of American culture, see, for example, Gustave Weigel, *Faith and Understanding in America* (N.Y.: Macmillan, 1959) and Richard J. Regan, *American Pluralism and the Catholic Conscience* (N.Y.: Macmillan, 1963). Such well-known journals as *Commonweal*, from time to time, treat of such issues as the decline of a "defensive" psychology among twentieth-century Catholics.

[6] Although the great nineteenth-century movement for free public education appeared to advocate "non-sectarian" schools, a considerable proportion of all the elementary and secondary educational institutions, then and now, have been strongly influenced by Protestant and non-Catholic assumptions and teaching.

[7] On American Judaism and its divisions, see Nathan Glazer, *American Judaism* (Chicago: University of Chicago Press, 1957). See also Marshall Sklare, *Conservative Judaism: An American Religious Movement* (N.Y.: Free Press, 1955). Joseph Roth in his novel *Job* (N.Y.:

Viking, 1930) portrays an Orthodox Jewish immigrant gradually losing his faith in the context of the American environment.

[8] Paine's great offense was that he wrote *The Age of Reason*, a pioneer essay in the "higher criticism" of the Bible and a book which attacked so many orthodox shibboleths that its author became anathema to almost everyone. Only a handful of individuals attended Paine's funeral in 1809.

[9] Andrew White, *A History of the Warfare of Science with Theology in Christendom* 2 vols. (N.Y.: Appleton, 1896).

[10] Thus Vashti McCollum, who protested "released time" religious education in the Champaign, Illinois, public schools and who won her case in the Supreme Court, was a professed atheist. Her father had been president of the American Association for Advancement of Atheism. For an account of her struggle, often against great odds, see Vashti McCollum, *One Woman's Fight*, rev. ed. (Boston: Beacon Press, 1961).

[11] See Edgar R. Pike, *Jehovah's Witnesses: Who They Are, What They Teach, What They Do* (N.Y.: Philosophical Library, 1954). Consult also William J. Whalen, *Armageddon Around the Corner* (N.Y.: John Day, 1962).

[12] See Carlton J. H. Hayes, *Essays on Nationalism* (N.Y.: Macmillan, 1926) for an analysis of nationalism as a religion.

[13] Will Herberg, *Protestant, Catholic, and Jew* (N.Y.: Anchor, 1960).

[14] Some political scientists have argued, for example, that it is better to compromise differences within each party than to have "ideological" parties struggle in the legislative body. The dogma that there should be no differences between parties on foreign policy has also had considerable effect on American thinking. It sometimes appears that both academics and laymen seek to abolish all that which is characteristic of politics.

[15] See Benjamin Tucker, *Individual Liberty* (N.Y.: Vanguard, 1926).

[16] See her remarkable autobiography, *Living My Life* (N.Y.: A. A. Knopf, 1931).

[17] Alexis de Tocqueville, *Democracy in America*, 4 vols. (N.Y.: G. Dearborn and Co., 1838).

[18] Hutterite communities were subjected to the pressures of the Liberty Bond drives during World War I, in part, no doubt, for "patriotic" reasons but also because many in the community were suspicious of dissent in general.

[19] The Shakers had their center near Albany, New York; but some

moved to the Middle West and others as far north as Maine and as far south as Kentucky.

[20] The views, for example, which suggest that free sex expression and political freedom go hand in hand. Among those propounding this thesis were the late Dr. Wilhelm Reich (in such works as *The Mass Psychology of Fascism*). Reich himself was a notable twentieth-century dissenter in medicine and psychoanalysis.

[21] Although the order of 1703 required administration of oaths only to those who could conscientiously take them, Quaker judges deemed it an offense that they should be asked to administer oaths which they themselves could not take.

[22] Thus in 1701 Penn himself as Governor had to lay before the assembly a request of the King asking for a contribution of £350 toward erecting forts on the frontiers of New York. All knew that Penn opposed the grant on religious grounds; yet the Governor felt a moral obligation to put the King's request before the Legislature. The Assembly refused to appropriate the money but said that they would be willing to help "as far as their religious persuasions would permit." See Samuel M. Janney, *The Life of William Penn* (Philadelphia: Hogan, Perkins and Co., 1852), pp. 429–430.

[23] See Janney, *op. cit.*, pp. 492–493.

[24] In general, see Arthur M. Schlesinger, *The Colonial Merchants and the American Revolution* (N.Y.: Columbia University Press, 1918).

[25] One non-Quaker biographer has commented on the Pennsylvania experiment, perhaps too fulsomely: "For the only time in the history of the world, a whole country had accepted the Sermon on the Mount for its working policy, and found it neither impossible of performance nor unpractical in operation." Mabel R. Brailsford, *The Making of William Penn* (London: Longmans, Green, 1930), p. 351.

[26] Conscription was adopted by France in the name of equality of sacrifice and "democracy." But militaristic nationalism and the notion of democracy are basically incompatible with each other. Historically, the former has won out over the latter.

[27] Irwin St. John Tucker, *The Price We Pay* (1917), a pamphlet of the Socialist Party.

[28] On the flag-salute controversy in general, see David Manwaring, *Render Unto Caesar* (Chicago: University of Chicago Press, 1962).

[29] On October 24, 1967, the UPI reported that the Supreme Court refused to intervene in a conflict between Amish parents and laws of the state of Kansas requiring them to send their children to school after the eighth grade.

[30] George Fox was always antagonistic to slavery but some of his followers in the United States became complacent. Although the first American statement against slavery came from a Friends Meeting in 1688, some Quakers owned slaves and it was not until well into the eighteenth century that a complete "testimony" against it developed. See V. F. Calverton, *The Making of America* (N.Y.: John Day, 1939), pp. 175–177.

[31] Like anti-war dissent in modern America, the dissent expressed in the Underground Railroad was frowned upon by much orthodox opinion which appeared to hold that civil disobedience was always wrong.

[32] On direct action in the Civil Rights movement as related to the theory and practice of non-violence, see Mulford Q. Sibley, "Direct Action and the Struggle for Integration," *Hastings Law Journal*, V. 16, Feb., 1965, pp. 351–400.

[33] In 1940, Beard published his booklet *Giddy Minds and Foreign Quarrels*, in which he denied that it was America's duty to become involved in military actions abroad. His was the voice of many early Americans; but by 1940, it was beginning to be a dissenting voice.

[34] A generation ago, Devere Allen developed the theme of the conflict between "absolutists" and "non-absolutists" in the American peace movement. See his *The Fight for Peace* (N.Y.: Macmillan, 1930).

[35] The declaration had a profound effect on Leo Tolstoy. It is reprinted in Allen, *op. cit.*, Appendix V.

[36] In his address called *A Plea for Captain John Brown*. Because the sexton refused to ring the bell calling the community's attention to the lecture, Thoreau rang it himself—an act highly characteristic of the man as a great dissenter.

[37] On Burritt, one of the most remarkable of nineteenth-century dissenters, see Charles Northend, *The Life and Labors of Elihu Burritt* (1879). On p. 478 of this volume there is a bibliography of Burritt's works.

[38] The Union had its headquarters in Independence Hall, Philadelphia. But its opposition to the war led the city to expel its officers and staff from this historic building.

[39] *Milwaukee Leader*, August 24, 1917.

[40] *The American Socialist*, June 16, 1917.

[41] See Norman Thomas, *Is Conscience a Crime?* (N.Y.: Vanguard, 1927) for an account of objectors in World War I.

[42] Bourne became known for his statement "War is the health of the State," which was the theme of his short essay on *The State*.

The Nuremberg Principles

WILLIAM V. O'BRIEN

ONE of the principal arguments for selective conscientious objection asserts that aggressive war, war crimes, and crimes against humanity are violations both of international and U.S. municipal law. When it appears to an American citizen that his nation is guilty of such crimes in a particular war, he clearly has a moral right, it is argued, and ought to have a legal right, to refuse participation in such criminal activity. I will attempt to assess the validity and relevance of this approach. In so doing I will treat of the following subjects:

(1) The content of the so-called "Nuremberg principles";

(2) The status of these Nuremberg principles in public international law and in the municipal law of the United States;

(3) The degree of relevance of each of the Nuremberg principles to the issue of selective conscientious objection;

(4) The practical issues of defining "participation" in crimes violative of the Nuremberg principles and of the individual's capacity, responsibility, and legal right to make judgments about their interpretation and application to particular wars in which his country is engaged. In this last section I will also evaluate the present status of the laws of war.

The Legal Base for and the Content of the "Nuremberg Principles"

The London Charter annexed to the London Agreement of August 8, 1945, adhered to by the U.S., U.K., France, and the

Soviet Union, as well as nineteen other of the wartime "United Nations,"[1] established the Nuremberg International Military Tribunal to try the so-called "major" German war criminals. The legal foundation for the trial was two-fold:

(1) As belligerents the "United Nations" had the right to try captured enemies for violations of the international law of war.

(2) As conquerors exercising supreme authority in Germany, the victorious Allies in the war in the West had the right to try German nationals and others who would have been under the jurisdiction of the deposed German state.

The Nuremberg International Military Tribunal was established for major war criminals "whose offenses have no particular geographical location."[2] In addition to this tribunal, virtually all of the victorious allies established their own tribunals to try the so-called lesser war criminals either on the grounds that their alleged crimes had occurred within the territorial jurisdiction of the tribunal, now re-established by virtue of the defeat of the Axis powers, or because the individuals charged with war crimes were apprehended within their occupation zones. Thus the United States conducted a series of "Nuremberg trials" of individuals falling into the latter category and it was these trials that inspired the film *Judgment at Nuremberg*. These trials are reported in well-written and carefully edited reports published by the United States government. Overviews of the total number and nature of trials of the lesser war criminals may be obtained by consulting the United Nations War Crimes Commission *Reports* and by Appleman's *Military Tribunals and International Crime*.[3] For the dedicated scholar, a careful perusal of the *International Law Reports*, which covers many of the national tribunal trials of war criminals would be worthwhile.[4]

There are really four major substantive offenses defined by the London Charter and applied by the judgment of the International Military Tribunal. There are, in addition, two overlapping principles prescribed by the London Charter and applied by the Tribunal which are relevant to the issue of selective conscientious objection. Article 6 of the London Charter gives the Tribunal power "to try and punish persons [the major war criminals], acting in the interests of the European Axis countries, whether as individuals or as members of organizations," for the following crimes:

"(a) *Crimes against the peace:* Namely, planning, preparation, initiation, or waging of a war of aggression, or a war in violation of international treaties, agreements, or assurances, or participation in a common plan or conspiracy for the accomplishment of any of the foregoing.

"(b) *War crimes:* Namely, violations of the laws or customs of war. Such violations shall include, but not be limited to, murder, ill-treatment or deportation to slave labor or for any other purpose of civilian population of or in occupied territory, murder or ill-treatment of prisoners of war or persons on the seas, killing of hostages, plunder of public or private property, wanton destruction of cities, towns or villages, or devastation not justified by military necessity.

"(c) *Crimes against humanity:* Namely, murder, extermination, enslavement, deportation, and other inhumane acts committed against any civilian population, before or during the war, or persecutions on political, racial, or religious grounds in execution of or in connection with any crime within the jurisdiction of the Tribunal, whether or not in violation of the domestic law of the country where perpetrated."[5]

To these three categories of crimes—crimes against the peace, war crimes, and crimes against humanity—was added a somewhat ambiguous and controversial fourth count, (d), *conspiracy to commit any or all of the three categories of crimes, viz.:* "Leaders, organizers, instigators, and accomplices participating in the formulation or execution of a common plan or conspiracy to commit any of the foregoing crimes are responsible for all acts performed by any persons in execution of such plan."[6]

It is essential to distinguish between these categories of crimes. The second category, war crimes, was not a new one, although proceedings under this rubric on such a large scale were unprecedented. The novel aspect of the Nuremberg trial of the major war criminals and the real source of the charges of "Victor's Justice" and *ex post facto* condemnations was, on the one hand, the new concept of crimes against the peace, i.e., of illegal aggressive war, and, on the other hand, of individual liability for such crimes. For under older international law concepts such alleged crimes would have been considered "acts of state" for which there should only be corporative or community responsibility and punishment.

The question at Nuremberg, which is still controverted, was whether so-called aggressive war had been legally outlawed by the time of the Nazi invasions. Today there is no question but that unilateral first recourse to armed force is *prima facie* aggression. Today we have also established that, circumstances permitting (and they seldom do), individuals may be tried for complicity in wars of aggression, just as they have long been subject to trial for violations of the laws and customs of war.[7]

The third count, crimes against humanity, is of interest because of its recognition of higher law standards and their relation to an incomplete and developing positive international law. In practice, however, crimes against humanity were usually merged with the category of war crimes, e.g., the new and dreadful concept of genocide, a crime against humanity, also involves gross violations of the traditional law of belligerent occupation.[8]

In order to narrow down our discussion to the real legal and moral issues that are relevant to the selective conscientious objector, I would like first to dispose of three of the "Nuremberg principles" which, I contend, are not of central interest for this discussion, and then to turn to a more detailed examination of the two overlapping principles regarding the defenses of superior orders and of acts of state. The three Nuremberg principles which I consider relatively unimportant to the debate over selective conscientious objection—but which are raised in discussion on this subject—are the following:

(1) The concept of crimes against the peace, or aggressive war;

(2) The concept of genocide as a crime against humanity;

(3) The concept of conspiracy to commit any of the three categories of crimes.

Irrelevant Issues

As regards crimes against the peace ("planning, preparation, initiation, or waging of a war of aggression, or war in violation of international treaties, agreements, or assurances, or participation in a common plan or conspiracy for the accomplishment of any of the foregoing") we must emphasize that the characterization of a war as an illegal aggression does not brand every single participant on the aggressor's side as a "criminal." The contention that all participants in an aggressor's military forces were in principle criminals who might then be granted various excuses was put forth at Nuremberg by the French prosecutor, M. de Menthon. The Court implicitly rejected this approach and it was explicitly rejected by American Nuremberg tribunals.[9] However, either the logic or the propaganda potential or both of this approach has been used by Communist belligerents, notably by the North Koreans and Chinese Communists in the Korean War. All U.N. prisoners of war were declared aggressors and criminals in principle. Extension of normal legal rights to them was portrayed as a generous but legally unnecessary gesture.[10] But the proper view is that the illegal character of a war does not taint all members of the aggressor's armed forces with criminality under international law.

Consequently, I think that for the conscientious objector the real relevance of crimes against the peace lies not in the danger of his being made a war criminal simply by serving in the armed forces of an illegal belligerent but that such crimes reinforce his contention that in positive international law—as well as in individual moral judgments—there are such things as aggressive, illegal wars which ought not to be supported. But the issue of participation, not as a top decision-maker but as an ordinary soldier, in what is believed to be an aggressive, illegal war, is one of individual morality, not of international law.

Concerning genocide: Article I of the Convention on the Prevention and Punishment of the Crime of Genocide approved by the U.N. General Assembly on December 9, 1948, and entered into force on January 12, 1951, states that, "The Contracting Parties confirm that genocide, whether committed in time of peace or in time of war, is a crime under international law which they undertake to prevent and to punish."[11]

Under Article IV of the Convention, "persons committing genocide . . . shall be punished whether they are constitutionally responsible rulers, public officials, or private individuals."[12] Article V obligates contracting parties "to enact, in accordance with their respective Constitutions, the necessary legislation to give effect to the provisions" of the Convention.[13] Under Article VI, "persons charged with genocide . . . shall be tried by a competent tribunal of the State in the territory of which the act was committed, or by such international penal tribunal as may have jurisdiction with respect to those Contracting Parties which shall have accepted its jurisdiction."[14] It should be pointed out that *no* international criminal tribunal exists and none is likely to come into being in the present divided world. Hence the Genocide Convention is essentially dependent for enforcement on individual states which obtain custody over alleged violators of the Convention. Moreover, Article VII asserts that genocide shall not be considered as a political crime for the purpose of avoiding extradition in accordance with laws and treaties in force.[15] (Normally, extradition, i.e., transfer of a fugitive from justice from one sovereign jurisdiction to another, is limited to persons charged with acts which are criminal in both jurisdictions, and does not apply to political refugees.)

The concept of genocide in international law was the most important product of the debates and decisions about "crimes against humanity" that occurred in international and national war crimes proceedings, in the U.N., and in diplomatic and general political discussions following World War II. The term itself was coined by Raphael Lemkin[16] and it has a very definite historic meaning. Quite simply, genocide is what the Nazis and their allies did to the Jews and, to a lesser extent, to the Poles and other occupied peoples, and to such supposedly inferior groups as the gypsies. Genocide involves the systematic destruction of a group of human beings, to use the language of Article II of the Convention, "as such." Such destruction is not based on any argument of military necessity; it applies both in peace and war.

I emphasize the historic meaning of and normative rationale underlying the concept of genocide because the term has been widely, loosely, and most irresponsibly tossed around in the debates over the war in Vietnam which, above all else, occasions our present concern with selective conscientious objection. The term has been used by respected critics of the war as well as by enemy propagandists. Such usage is invalid in terms of law and mischievous in terms of informed public debate and international intercourse.

Killing many people (including noncombatants on a large scale), destroying vast areas of property, perpetuating a war which wears down the material and moral fiber of a nation—all these may be "war crimes" because of the means employed or because of violations of the principle of legitimate military necessity which requires proportionality between admissible political-military ends and the means employed to achieve them, or because of disproportionality between the probable good likely to emerge from a war and the demonstrable and projected evils resulting from it. But all these questions concern the justice of recourse to force in the first place, the reasonableness of continuance of the war in the second place, and the legality and proportionality of the means employed in the third place. In any event, they are questions of "war," not "genocide." In my opinion, however, the present indiscriminate use of the term by critics of U.S. defense and foreign policies is invalid and irrelevant to the SCO issue.

The charge of conspiracy to commit any of the three major categories of war crimes is perhaps the most irrelevant of the Nuremberg principles insofar as selective conscientious objection is concerned. First, it was developed to deal with an aggressive totalitarian state dominated by one man and his omnipotent party and all-powerful, repressive government. Despite all of the wild analogies that have been made between the Nazi society and the much advertised "Military-Industrial" complex, there is simply no way of establishing a plausible "conspiracy" theory with respect to contemporary American society.

Second, the concept of "conspiracy" at Nuremberg was an Anglo-American contribution which the French and Russians apparently either never entirely understood or cared about.

Third, and most important as concerns our subject, the selective conscientious objection problem obviously does not involve Secretaries Rusk or McNamara or Clifford or Generals Wheeler or Westmoreland. Nobody has to volunteer to serve in the government at such a level as to render him guilty of conspiracy in the Nuremberg sense, unless one wishes to argue that the Secretaries of Health, Education and Welfare or Housing and Urban Development are as much to blame for the war in Vietnam and SAC's contingency plans for nuclear deterrence as if they were adjacent to the Pentagon war room. I will return to this theme in my closing observations about "participation" in unjust wars.

The foregoing subjects are comparatively irrelevant to our problem but because they have been raised they had to be considered before they were dismissed.

Relevant Issues

Now let us turn to the real problems raised by the Nuremberg principles for the issues of selective conscientious objection. They are three-fold:

(1) The denial of the fighting man's recourse to superior orders and act of state as legitimate defenses.

(2) The existence of a body of international law governing the conduct of war, much of which is clearly part of the municipal law of the United States, and much of which is notoriously violated in modern wars.

(3) The possibility that an American fighting man may be captured and tried as a war criminal under rules which the United States took the lead in establishing and promulgating; or, alternatively, that he may be tried by a U.S. Court Martial for violations of U.S. and international law.

The Denial of the Defenses of Superior Orders and of Act of State: As we have observed, in contrast to the charge of crimes against the peace, which was a new, controversial, post-1918 concept, the concept of war crimes (violations against the law of war for which a belligerent could punish a captured enemy) was not new. What was new at the Nuremberg Trial of Major War Criminals and the lesser trials that followed was the prosecution of large numbers of individuals for such violations. On the whole, in previous wars sanctions for the law of war had taken one of two forms:

(1) reprisals;

(2) reparations imposed upon the defeated state by the victor.

The classic view in international law tended to be that in the execution of its chosen policies a state's armed forces engaged the corporative international legal responsibility of the state rather than the individual persons executing the policies. If punishment was justified and possible it should be directed against the state *qua* state rather than toward individuals, statesmen, commanders and troops. The efforts of the Allies of 1918 to change this attitude were almost entirely unsuccessful. Indeed, it is interesting to recall that the U.S. delegation to the Versailles Conference opposed the other Allies on the issue of individual responsibility—under international law—for alleged war crimes, basing their objections on classical international law doctrine.[17] Defense counsels at all the Nuremberg war crime trials laid heavy stress on the traditional concept that only the state as an international person is legally responsible for its acts and that, therefore, war crimes proceedings should be limited to cases of individual misbehavior, e.g., pillage, rape, voluntary acts of cruelty and destruction. They did not get very far.

In the first place, the Tribunal was bound by the London Charter of August 8, 1945, and the Charter explicitly ruled out the defenses of act of state or superior orders as a *complete* defense for alleged war crimes. This is one of the disturbing features of the Nuremberg precedent. One is impelled to wonder what would have happened if the judges, in their own minds, had come to a different decision. Could they have violated the rules of the London Charter on the grounds that their own reading of international law was different? In any event, the Tribunal appears to have honestly concluded that law and justice vindicated the Charter's handling of the questions and, as we will show, the precedent was established. Whether it was entirely fair at the time is not relevant to the issue of selective conscientious objection. The precedent is there, it has come to be widely accepted in international law, and it must be taken into consideration in judging the issues of selective conscientious objection.

In summary, then, the Nuremberg principles most relevant to this issue in the debate on selective conscientious objection are:

(1) There are violations of the international law of war, i.e., the so-called *jus in bello* governing the conduct of war, for which individuals may be tried either before international tribunals when such come into existence, or before the national military tribunals of foreign powers which capture an individual serviceman in war or obtain jurisdiction over him in some other manner.

(2) The prevailing view in international law, based upon the Nuremberg precedents, is that neither an act of state nor the plea of superior orders is a complete defense for such violations, but that a fair court, following the Nuremberg precedent, would make a judgment as to the degree of "moral choice" which the accused actually had when, under orders, he perpetrated the illegal acts of which he is accused.

The Status of the Nuremberg Principles in Contemporary International Law and in U.S. Municipal Law: To assess the current legal status of the Nuremberg principles we must first say a word about the relation between public international law and the municipal (i.e., domestic) law of the United States. Under Article VI of the Constitution, treaties are the law of the land and have an effect equal to legislative enactments, executive decrees within the President's competence, and judicial decisions. If there is a disparity between a treaty provision and a legislative or other valid provision of U.S. law, the later in date prevails if the provisions cannot be reconciled. The presumption is that conflict between treaty provisions and legislation is not intended and the courts will attempt to find a construction which will avoid ruling for one provision over another. If a treaty provision is overridden by legislation and/or the judicial or executive branches, U.S law has changed but U.S. obligations under international law have not, and the other parties to the broken treaty have a right to secure remedies under international law.[18]

Executive agreements are made by the executive without the advice and consent of the Senate as in the case of treaties. Nevertheless, the courts have ruled that executive agreements are just as binding in domestic law as are treaties and the same rules of interpretation apply to them in the event of an apparent conflict with domestic law as obtain in the case of treaties.[19] The London Charter of August 8, 1945, was an executive agreement. It laid down legal principles to guide U.S. and Allied prosecutors and judges in dealing with enemy war criminals. It did not, of course, deal with possible U.S. or other United Nations war criminals, but I would hope that it would be unthinkable for any U.S. government to take the position that the legal principles prescribed for accused enemy war criminals ought not to be taken as guidelines for the conduct of U.S. forces. The United States was in the war crimes prosecution business on a very large scale in the immediate postwar years. Moreover, the United States took the lead in obtaining support from the various organs of the United Nations, particularly the General Assembly, for the Nuremberg principles which we have summarized.

It would be clear from even the briefest summary of consideration of the Nuremberg principles within U.N. organs—even before turning to other relevant sources of international law—that the state of the law does not turn on such questions as "victor's justice" and 'ex post facto" judgments. The Nuremberg principles are widely, if not universally, accepted as binding norms of international law. The United States took *the* leading role in producing this state of affairs, so the principles are certainly binding on the United States.

But the issue of the relevance of international state practice, amounting to customary international law, should be touched briefly. In the landmark case, *The Paquete Habana, The Lola,* the Supreme Court of the United States said:

> International law is part of our law, and must be ascertained and administered by the courts of justice of appropriate jurisdiction, as often as questions of right depending upon it are duly determined for their determination. For this purpose, where there is no treaty, and no controlling executive or legislative act or judicial decision, resort must be had to the customs and usages of civilized nations; and, as evidence of these, to the works of jurists and commentators, who by years of labor, research, and experience have made themselves peculiarly well acquainted with the subjects of which they treat. . . .[20]

The force of this statement on the relation of U.S. municipal law to international law may have, in some subject areas, been diminished by the U.S. Supreme Court's decision in the Sabbatino Case.[21] But the position of the *Paquete Habana* decision on the binding quality of customary rules of international law in the realm of the law of war remains relevant and binding to the SCO issue.

The United States has repeatedly gone on record as an adherent to the Nuremberg principles. The most central is the U.S. Army's Field Manual 27–10, *The Law of Land Warfare,*[22] which summarizes and interprets the general principles of the law of war, the conventional law of the Hague and Geneva conventions, and other sources of the law of war. FM 27–10 and its Navy counterpart, Robert W. Tucker's *The Law of War and Neutrality at Sea,* appear to be consonant with the position taken in my study with respect to war crimes, and the defense of superior orders.

In an even more concrete fashion, the U.S. government has recently demonstrated its respect for the Nuremberg principles in two highly controversial cases. In the court martial proceedings against Captain Howard B. Levy at Fort Jackson, South Carolina, concerning Levy's anti-Vietnam war, anti–Green Beret statements and agitation, trial officer (judge) Colonel Earl V. Brown ruled on May 17, 1967, that (in the words of Washington *Post* reporter Nicholas von Hoffman), "if the defense can prove that the United States is committing war crimes in Vietnam as a matter of policy he will acquit the young Army doctor of willfully disobeying an order to train Special Forces medical aides."[23] The burden thereby placed on counsel for the defense proved insuperable and on May 25, 1967, Colonel Brown ruled that:

> While there have been perhaps instances of needless brutality in this struggle in Vietnam about which the accused may have learned through conversations or publications, my conclusion is that there is no evidence that would render this order illegal on the grounds that these men would have become engaged in war crimes or some way prostitute their medical training by employing it in crimes against humanity. . . .[24]

There have, moreover, been court martial trials of U.S. military personnel charged with violations of the laws of war. One of the most recent was the trial in South Vietnam of S/Sgt. Walter Griffen, who was convicted in July, 1967, of unpremeditated murder in the killing of a Vietnamese prisoner although he testified that he had acted on the orders of his commanding officers.

U.S. municipal law, then, has recognized those Nuremberg principles most relevant to the SCO problem, namely, individual criminal liability before international or domestic tribunals for violation of the conventional law of war, of which there is a substantial body, and of the customary international law of war. The U.S. also recognizes the illegality of crimes against humanity, including genocide. U.S. law also rejects almost completely the plea of superior orders as a complete defense but follows the general line of the Nuremberg precedent and the general practice of states as reflected in discussion and resolutions of the organs of the United Nations and in national war crimes legislation and proceedings in holding out the possibility that superior orders may be considered, on a case-by-case basis, as a mitigating circumstance warranting diminishment of and possibly exemption from punishment, for acts which constitute war crimes.

But the record is mixed. While U.S. military tribunals have

heard arguments and evidence relative to alleged violations of the Nuremberg principles and the laws of war by U.S. forces, the federal courts thus far seem to have considered these principles irrelevant to cases of refusal of military service based specifically on the grounds that the U.S. involvement in Vietnam violates the Nuremberg principles generally and, specifically, the Treaty of London of August 8, 1945, as well as other treaties on war to which the United States is a party. In *U.S. v. David Henry Mitchell III*, the U.S. Court of Appeals (2nd Circuit) upheld a District Court's conviction of the defendant for willful failure to report for induction into the Armed Forces.[25] Mitchell "made no claim to be a conscientious objector but sought to produce evidence to show that the war in Vietnam was being conducted in violation of various treaties . . . and that the Selective Service system was being operated as an adjunct of this military effort."[26]

Upholding the District Court's ruling that evidence in support of these contentions was "immaterial," Judge Medina said that, "Regardless of the proof that appellant might present to demonstrate the correlation between the Selective Service and our nation's efforts in Vietnam, as a matter of law the congressional power 'to raise and support armies' and 'to provide and maintain a navy' is a matter quite distinct from the use which the Executive makes of those who have been found qualified and who have been inducted into the Armed Forces. Whatever action the President may order, or the Congress sanction, cannot impair this constitutional power of the Congress."[27]

The Supreme Court denied certiorari without comment, except for a dissent by Justice Douglas. In his dissent, Douglas specifically cites Article 6 (a) of the London Treaty concerning the crime of aggressive war and individual responsibility for participation in this crime. Douglas also quotes the language of Article 8 of the Treaty regarding superior orders.[28] Douglas claimed that the Mitchell case raised five major questions which ought to be considered in the light of the London Treaty which, whatever its constitutionality or fairness in 1945, "purports to lay down a standard of future conduct for all the signatories."[29]

Justice Douglas concluded his dissent by disavowing any opinion on the merits. But he favored certiorari by the Supreme Court, saying, "We have here a recurring question in present-day Selective Service cases."[30] On November 6, 1967, the Supreme Court once more denied certiorari in a case touching in part on the Nuremberg principles. In this case three privates, already in service, sought to bar the Department of Defense and the Army from sending them to take part in "the illegal and immoral Vietnam conflict."[31] This time Justice Potter Stewart joined Douglas in dissenting and urging that the issues raised by the appeal be dealt with by the Court.

This latter case is not clearly based on the Nuremberg principles. It turns mainly on the U.S. constitutional law question of the existence of a state of war. For our purposes the case is of significance because of the support given Douglas by Stewart and the modest prospect that there might be a trend toward reversal, or at least serious reconsideration of, the Court's position that the issues in both cases are political and military and, hence, not within the jurisdiction of the federal courts.

It should be added that although the main point in the most relevant case, *U.S. v. Mitchell*, as discussed in Medina's opinion and Douglas's dissent to the Supreme Court's denial of certiorari, is the legality under municipal and international law of the U.S. involvement in the Vietnamese conflict, Mitchell also charged war crimes and crimes against humanity. But it seems at present unlikely that the federal courts will judge on the merits *either* of allegations that the U.S. is guilty of crimes against the peace or of war crimes and crimes against humanity. This is so not only because of the present attitude of the Supreme Court and other federal courts, but because of the whole history of judicial reluctance to interfere with the Executive's exercise of the war powers, or even with the intricate relations between the Executive and the Legislative branches in determining when war exists and what war powers may be properly exercised by the Executive without explicit Legislative authorization.[32]

The Practical Likelihood That an Individual Soldier May Be Placed in Circumstances Obliging Him in One Way or Another to Commit and Be Tried for War Crimes: This remains the core of our inquiry. I will address this subject in two ways. First, I will summarize the record of the principal war crimes proceedings and report on what happened to ordinary soldiers accused of war crimes after the Second World War. Second, I will discuss in a purely speculative way the subject of "participation" in aggressive wars and wars in which war crimes are allegedly committed.

The 15-volume series edited by the United Nations War Crimes Commission summarizes in its first 14 volumes 89 war crimes cases tried before national tribunals against individuals who had allegedly violated international law and were physically within the territorial jurisdiction of the tribunal and/or individuals who were accused of violations of the law of the forum. In many instances there were numerous defendants, all tried in the same proceedings. The cases therein reported do not begin to reach the total number of such cases, some of which continue, as in the Federal Republic of Germany, to this day. But the series does cover quite well the best known of the so-called lesser war crimes proceedings, i.e., all of those other than the Nuremberg International Military Tribunal's decision and its Tokyo counterpart. I have searched through these fifteen volumes to find specific cases relevant to the issues of selective conscientious objection on the grounds of justifiable fear of trial as a war criminal. It must be said that the results of this inquiry yielded little that is of relevance to the problem of selective conscientious objection. (Note that the "United Nations" commission was an organ of the wartime alliance, not of the U.N. founded at San Francisco in 1945.)

If one begins with Chapter VII of Volume 15 of the series, "Defence Pleas," the prospects for finding arguments relevant to the issues of selective conscientious objection seem promising. After having noted that the Nuremberg International Military Tribunal, following the London Charter, had ruled out "superior orders" as a complete defense but permitted its consideration as a mitigating circumstance, the U.N. War Crimes Commission goes on to analyze the practice of the national tribunals whose decisions were summarized in the preceding 14 volumes. It is noted that three pleas were advanced very frequently, often overlapped, and were sometimes confused. These were:

(1) the plea of superior orders;
(2) the plea of duress;
(3) the plea of "necessity."³³

These three pleas are then described and considered by the United Nations War Crimes Commission as they applied in various trials.

The pleas of superior orders and duress overlapped and they were in fact taken into account in mitigation of punishment. I will summarize some cases on these issues but at this point I will dispose of the third plea mentioned by the U.N. War Crimes Commission: "necessity," or "military necessity." The principal cases in which military necessity is discussed have to do with very high military commanders, not ordinary enlisted men or even junior officers. They are not, therefore, very relevant to the problem of selective conscientious objection. Whatever the moral dilemmas of generals and the intricacies of the concept of total command responsibility set forth in the case considered, our concern is for the "common man" who, out of moral or other scruples, demands the right to refuse military service in a particular war. Therefore I intend to pass over the otherwise interesting and complex plea of military necessity for violation of the normal laws of war.³⁴

This brings us to the further and most basic point which emerges from the citations accompanying the general analyses of the pleas of superior orders and duress. Most of the precedent-making cases involved either or both of the following categories of defendants:

(1) High level commanders or governmental officials;

(2) Persons, at whatever level, who served—presumably by choice—in *élite* organizations or in particular kinds of operations which, whatever their last-minute scruples, predictably put them in positions wherein their commission of the criminal acts of which they were accused was foreseeable and likely. Out of all the 89 cases reported in the fifteen-volume *U.N. War Crimes Law Reports* only ten appear to bear directly on the problem of

comparatively minor persons, whether commissioned or enlisted personnel, being ordered to commit war crimes, and, of those ten, six concern German SS units. No doubt an intensive study of the national tribunal cases reported in the *Annual Digest of Public International Law Cases* and the *International Law Reports* would produce more cases of war crimes proceedings against involuntary war criminals. But certainly a survey of the U.N. War Crimes Commission's reports produces little that is of direct relevance to the issues of selective conscientious objection.

Practical Issues

In order to come down to the practical SCO issues of allegedly illegal wars, war crimes, and criminal participation in either or both, I propose to break this section down into three subjects:

(1) The judgment that one's nation is engaged in a war contrary to binding rules of international law;

(2) The judgment that, regardless of the legal permissibility of one's nation's recourse to force, illegal means are known to be in use to the point that the individual citizen has a right to disassociate himself from a war characterized by substantial recourse to such means;

(3) The judgment that *any* "participation" in a war which is illegal either in terms of the decision to have recourse to force as an instrument of foreign policy and/or the decision to use certain allegedly illegal means places the individual citizen in jeopardy of punishment under the Nuremberg principles and that, therefore, SCO has a valid basis in the Nuremberg precedents.

Judging the Legal Permissibility of Recourse to Armed Force by One's Nation: The state of the law with respect to recourse to armed force in international relations is simple and clear, but subject in practice to violent disagreements over facts and justifications. Today, all states are prohibited from first recourse to armed force as an instrument of foreign policy by virtue of the

U.N. Charter, particularly Article II (4).[35] The only legally permissible bases for recourse to armed force are participation in a U.N. enforcement action under Chapter VII of the Charter or individual and collective self-defense under Article 51 of the same chapter, a natural right which, I would contend, is not granted but merely reiterated by the Charter.[36] Thus it would be as illegal for the U.S. to launch an offensive to "liberate" Cuba from Communist rule as it would be for the Soviet Union to attack West Germany to liberate it from the rule of capitalist-militarist-*revanchist* cliques.

The practical problem, particularly since the Korean War and the establishment of the awful but seemingly effective world order of the nuclear balance of terror, is that international conflict seldom takes a clear-cut, aggressor-defender, invader-resister form. The most common form of modern international conflict is a deadly and complex combination of genuine domestic insurgency and substantial, often essential, support by so-called indirect aggression.

Whereas the rule of thumb in the League of Nations period was that the party which had failed to exhaust the peaceful remedies of the League and of general international law and organization and which had had first recourse to open armed force was the aggressor, the present state of international conflict makes judgments about the legal permissibility of war much more difficult. If for example, we were to eliminate, from the debate over the Vietnamese conflict all those who abhor war in principle on the one hand and all those who reject loss of American lives and treasure without the prospect of "victory" in the "national interest" on the other, we would probably come down to a debate over the facts and implications of the conflict, as to which party or parties did, in a meaningful, legally significant sense, start an international conflict engendering rights of collective self-defense on the other side. I think that it is demonstrable from the disagreements of highly informed statesmen, legislators, scholars, public figures, and concerned citizens that, simply in terms of one's own conscience, this is an extremely difficult decision to make.

Now, if one is then to go on to the legal—as distinct from the moral, political, strategic, or other—judgment about selective conscientious objection to a war on the grounds that it violates the U.N. *régime* restricting recourse to force, the Nuremberg principle condemning aggressive wars, and general contemporary international law, I would have to say that it is relevant to the high-level decision-maker and, perhaps, to high-level military commanders. Scruples about the legality of a war might lead, first, to dissent within the decision-making process and, second, to resignation. But, in terms of international law, this problem is not, in my judgment, very relevant to the plight of the ordinary draftee or even to a junior officer. As has been explained, the law of Nuremberg, and of most of the trials of the lesser war criminals, holds that mere service in the armed forces of a nation which is subsequently found by some authoritative international body or court to have engaged in aggression is—in itself and without the commission of war crimes and crimes against humanity—not a crime under international law.

Prescinding from the possibility of unfair trials of "aggressors" or threats thereof by a detaining power, which would not be considered legitimate by an unbiased third party, fear of punishment as a war criminal for mere participation in the armed forces of an aggressor state is not justified in the light of contemporary international law doctrine and practice.[37] I conclude, then, that the issue of participation in "crimes against the peace" is not the central issue insofar as SCO based on the Nuremberg precedent is concerned.

I will not undertake in this paper to deal with the questions of U.S. constitutional law concerning the existence of "war" and the legality of the Executive's commitment of the nation to armed conflict without a clear-cut declaration of war by the Congress.[38] Selective conscientious objection on such grounds would, I think, provide a stronger case for the objector than reliance primarily on the Nuremberg principle prohibiting aggressive war. Were I counseling such an objector, I would advise him to bring in the Nuremberg principle regarding crimes against the peace as a secondary, in a sense "background" argument, in support of the primary argument based on U.S. constitutional law rather than on international law.

Judging the Means Used in Warfare: In relating the Nuremberg principles to selective conscientious objection, the heart of the matter I believe concerns the possible commission of war crimes and crimes against humanity, either under direct order or out of tactical or individual necessity. In considering this issue I will also raise an additional category which I will describe as "operational necessity." In so doing I hope to meet Professor Paul Ramsey's call for a survey of the relevant laws of war.

If we limit ourselves to international law as a basis for SCO, the problem of judging the means of warfare becomes complicated. Three categories must be considered:

(1) the problem of judging persistent violations of conventional international law (i.e., treaty law, the "law on the books") which violations also run counter to the general practice of states;

(2) the problem of judging persistent violations of the laws of war which appear to be so frequently violated in the practice of states as to render questionable their continued validity and relevance, even if such laws are affirmed in treaties and appear to be the "law on the books";

(3) the problem of judging means of warfare which have been the object of moral, humanitarian, and even utilitarian condemnation or criticism but which are not legally impermissible under existing positive international law, and are at best controversial. Unfortunately, from the legal point of view, this third category includes most of the decisive—and much criticized—means of modern warfare.

The first two categories are highly relevant to the subject of selective conscientious objection, particularly if the "law on the books," the conventional law of war, is binding under the domestic law of the objector's state, as is the case in the United States with respect to every major international convention on the laws of war, except the Geneva Protocol on Chemical-Biological Warfare of 1925 and the Genocide Convention. The third category is the most difficult. When dealing with it one cannot argue that one wishes to avoid violation of clearly established international law and, presumably, of the law of one's own country through the process of incorporation of international law into domestic or, as it is called by international lawyers, "municipal law."[39] One must argue on moral or other grounds about what the law *should be,* not what it is, and such arguments are beyond the scope of this paper.

With these distinctions in mind, I will examine three categories of offenses against the laws of war and humanity:

(1) violations of the law protecting prisoners of war;

(2) violations of the law governing the means of war;

(3) violations of the law protecting civilian populations in war areas.

All three categories overlap. However, this is the breakdown which the principal controlling international agreements adopted. Thus, the second category will deal, *inter alia,* with the limitations on the means of combat arising out of consideration for their effect on noncombatants, whereas the third category will deal with post-combat situations of belligerent occupation or, as is increasingly the case, ambiguous situations where the conventional forces of a belligerent are theoretically in a situation of belligerent occupation but in which indigenous and other resistance elements continue a sub-conventional conflict.

Prisoners of war have the following basic rights:

(1) The right to lay down their arms, surrender, and acquire the status of prisoner of war.[40] This right is reiterated in all of the Geneva Conventions of 1949 even for irregular forces in "armed conflict not of an international character," for soldiers who are *hors de combat,* having "laid down their arms."[41]

(2) The right to "humane treatment," as provided for in a number of treaties culminating in the Geneva Convention Relative to the Treatment of Prisoners of War of August 12, 1949.[42] In terms of the Nuremberg precedent, "murder or ill treatment of prisoners of war," is a "war crime."[43] We will not discuss the detailed rules of the POW *régime.*[44] For the purposes of this paper it is sufficient to mention several provisions of international law which have in fact often been violated and which are fre-

quently raised in criticisms of belligerent behavior in contemporary conflicts.

Common Article 3 of the four Geneva Conventions states in part:

> To this end [that POW's be treated humanely] the following acts are and shall remain prohibited at any time and in any place whatsoever with respect to the above-mentioned persons:
>
> (a) violence of life and person, in particular murder of all kinds, mutilation, cruel treatment and torture;
>
> (b) taking of hostages;
>
> (c) outrages upon personal dignity; in particular, humiliating and degrading treatment;
>
> (d) the passing of sentence and the carrying out of executions without previous judgment pronounced by a regularly constituted court affording all the judicial guarantees which are recognized as indispensable by civilized peoples.[45]

Article 13 of the Geneva Convention Relative to the Treatment of Prisoners of War of 1949 provides:

> Prisoners of war must at all times be humanely treated. Any unlawful act or omission by the Detaining Power causing death or seriously endangering the health of a prisoner of war in its custody is prohibited, and will be regarded as a serious breach of the present convention. . . .
>
> Likewise, prisoners of war must at all times be protected, particularly against acts of violence or intimidation and against insults and public curiosity.
>
> Measures of reprisal against prisoners of war are prohibited.[46]

Anyone who reads newspapers and news magazines, or who watches television, has read about and seen innumerable examples of violations of these rules. A typical catalogue of them is offered by Eric Norden in "American Atrocities in Vietnam" in *Liberation,* an anti-war periodical.[47] Although this is an adversary critique the sources are, for the most part, objective and the charges are, on their face, probably accurate. Likewise, *Vietnam and International Law,* a publication of the Lawyers Committee on American Policy Towards Vietnam—composed of highly respected lawyers and scholars—asserts that:

Numerous reports and photographs published in the American world press indicate violations of international rules of warfare regarding, for example, the mistreatment of prisoners of war. . . .[48]

I take it that no knowledgeable person denies that these charges have considerable objective validity and that, in terms of international legal responsibility, the United States must answer for violations of the POW *régime* committed by U.S. military personnel and, to a lesser extent, by allies under the direction of or in the proximity of U.S. military personnel. I further assume that the fact, also widely acknowledged, that atrocities have been threatened or committed by the Vietcong and North Vietnamese troops against those who are POW's under international law standards, would *not* justify violation of the 1949 conventions and of the customary and conventional law on the subject that developed prior to 1949.

In short, I assume that it is "given" in the war in Vietnam (and in most foreseeable international conflicts including so-called U.N. "police actions" or "peace-keeping" operations wherein combat breaks out)[49] that violations of the international law *régime* of POW's have occurred and will continue to occur. It is at this point that we are obliged to return to the difficult but inescapable distinction between violations of treaty law which are unusual and those which are fairly common in the practice of states. First, it is a simple historical fact that, in modern times, most combatants desiring to surrender were given quarter and POW status; most of them did survive and, ultimately, return to their homes, although there have been millions —out of hundreds of millions—who were denied the rights of surrender, POW status, and protection. But the kinds of violations of POW rights described in Norden's article, and referred to by the Lawyers Committee are quite familiar—lamentably—to war veterans and to military historians. In *every* war there are innumerable instances of denial of quarter. This may result from a risky tactical situation, from outrage against recent enemy atrocities, or simply from frustration and grief over heavy losses recently suffered. Moreover, all armies include vicious and depraved individuals who murder and mistreat POW's.

But, on the whole, it seems highly unlikely that a reluctant participant in a war will be obliged to deny quarter. The exception would be the case of a desperate tactical situation where an individual or an entire unit might be ordered to deny quarter and to kill wounded or unwounded prisoners. Generally speaking, such an order ought to be disobeyed. A moralist would presumably have problems with the extreme case of duress. A lawyer could only say that denial of quarter, for any reason, is legally impermissible and that necessity or duress or superior orders would be no defense but ought to be considered in the category of possible mitigating circumstances. But if we try to link the likelihood of confronting such orders and situations with the issue of SCO on the grounds of the Nuremberg principles, it seems to me we are again stretching rather far to justify SCO. Nevertheless, this is a real issue and should be discussed further as the debate over SCO continues.

The issue of torture is much more central, critical, and intractable. The moral, legal, and practical dilemmas of this subject can hardly be exaggerated. The facts are well known. Most modern wars involve a high degree of sub-conventional, guerrilla warfare. The identity of enemy combatants and terrorists is sometimes almost impossible to establish by normal, legal, intelligence techniques. Fruitful interrogation of captured enemy troops and of persons in civilian clothes suspected of belligerent activities becomes the key to success in the conflict. All of the positive counter-insurgency methods of nation-building and gaining the allegiance of the population are frustrated if the enemy is sufficiently powerful, patient, and ruthless. Enlightened counter-insurgency measures have often failed in the face of guerrilla warfare and terror. If, as Norden and others claim, the United States is fighting in Vietnam the "dirtiest" war in its history, it is not surprising. The theory and practice of wars of "national liberation" are very dirty, by Western and international law standards, and are expressly designed, among other things, to *force* the counter-insurgent forces into "dirty" behavior in self-defense.[50]

But if selective conscientious objection to "particular" wars turns in considerable measure on repugnance to the practice of torture, then SCO will be *very* selective indeed. The selective CO will have to be exempted from virtually all contemporary conflicts, particularly those—which are the most likely—involving guerrilla warfare and terrorism in underdeveloped areas. It seems almost unnecessary to make the point that actual involuntary participation in torture is rather unlikely. Seemingly, in all armies and police forces, there are people who are willing to do the dirty work of torture, for various reasons, some of them very evil. In any case, there is no avoiding the dilemma. Torture of POW's is clearly prohibited by international law. It is practiced almost universally in modern conflicts. The relevance of the Nuremberg precedent would seem to be limited to the case of widespread, indiscriminate, systematic, often pointless and sadistic torture.

I doubt, but cannot prove, that the United States and its allies in the Vietnamese conflict have come so close to such a monstrous system of torture as to warrant SCO on the basis of the Nuremberg and other international law prescriptions regarding the protection of POW's. However, I readily grant that the existence of such practices might well produce conscientious objection, either selective or general. But, as I have indicated, I have a feeling that the more defensible position would be general objection to *all* modern wars, for it will seldom be the case that a modern war will be conducted without recourse to some kind of torture as a standard operating procedure in the interrogation of POW's and civilians suspected of belligerent sympathies or activities.

There are a number of ways of approaching the subject of the law governing the conduct of hostilities. Some authorities and decision-makers operate on the assumption, explicit or implicit, that, in the final analysis, there are no legal restrictions on "military necessity" as defined by the responsible commander or government official.[51] This attitude is clearly rejected by the Hague Conventions on Land Warfare of 1899 and 1907, by the four Geneva Conventions of 1949 mentioned above,[52] and by numerous earlier conventions that were supplemented or replaced by the 1949 conventions[53] and by the Nuremberg principles relative to war crimes and crimes against humanity. Such an attitude has been expressly condemned by every U.S. military field manual on the law of war since 1863.[54] In terms of our discussion, the only relevant question, then, for an American who respects international law and the treaty commitments of the United States, which are the supreme law of the land under Article VI of the Constitution, is, "What is the content of the international law of war with respect to the conduct of hostilities?"

The answer is difficult. Respected authorities have held that everything is permitted in combat which is not clearly prohibited.[55] As will be demonstrated, few of the principal means of modern warfare are regulated by binding international agreements. The practice of contemporary belligerents is notoriously permissive. The content of the law governing hostilities, the *jus in bello*—the law *in* war—is therefore determined, in the eyes of legal authorities, largely on the basis of their own understanding of international law, the manner in which it is made, and the proper techniques of interpreting and applying it. At present, then, the content of the *jus in bello* depends a great deal on the extent to which basic *principles* governing the conduct of hostilities are accepted. These principles may be divided into two categories: (1) negative prohibitions, i.e., principles stating what ought not to be done in war; (2) positive guidelines, principles stating what may be done, i.e., which measures a belligerent has a legal right to take. It should be noted that one of the most difficult problems involved in discussing this area is that it is often controverted, first, whether a prescription is a general principle or an ironclad rule, and, second, whether a principle or a more specific rule which was once widely accepted has survived long and widespread violations.

The most widely discussed prohibitions are the following:

(1) the prohibition against the intentional killing, or otherwise injuring, or attacking the rights, of noncombatants;

(2) the related prohibition against attacks on "non-military" targets;

(3) the likewise related prohibitions against "blind," or "indiscriminate" means of warfare which, by their very nature,

cause indiscriminate injury in populated areas or which "take out" very large populated areas in which, by any standard, significant numbers of noncombatants are known to be present;

(4) the prohibition, under the so-called "St. Petersburg principle" of the use of weapons which cause "superfluous suffering";

(5) the prohibition against "the use in war of asphyxiating, poisonous or other gases, and of all analogous liquids, materials or devices," as well as "the use of bacteriological methods of warfare"; [56]

(6) the prohibition, to use the language of the London Charter of 1945, of "wanton destruction of cities, towns, or villages, or devastation not justified by military necessity."[57]

It is important to point out that principle or rule 6 is distinct from rules one to three. It is derived from Article 23 (g) of the Hague Rules of Land Warfare and, in the practice of the Nuremberg International Military Tribunal and the other war crimes tribunals, applied primarily to the action of *ground forces*, not to aerial attacks. The most frequent charge under this category was indiscriminate recourse to inhumane "scorched earth" policies or retaliatory destruction of whole villages or areas, mainly by ground forces. The importance of this distinction and of the comparative status in international law of the various principles and/or rules will become evident shortly.[58]

There was a time when principles (or rules—authorities differ) were widely held to be binding under customary international law, although they were never explicitly agreed to in a convention of the stature of the Hague Conventions on Land Warfare of 1899 and 1907.[59] The fact is that these first three principles, as positive law, did not survive World War I. What I have called "operational necessity" rendered them impossible of observance. The weapons, the means of transportation and communication, the size of the forces, the difficulty of defining "noncombatant" and "non-military target" in a "total war," as well as the fanatical character of contemporary conflict, all resulted in such widespread violations of the first three principles that they ceased to create valid expectations of observance. Any statesman or military commander relying upon them as standards of behavior by an enemy ought rightly to be deposed and placed in a mental institution.

This does not mean that might—or technical facts—make right. It may mean that modern war is intrinsically immoral, as more and more people have come to believe. But in terms of the universal practice of belligerents of every type the first three principles represent, at best, goals, guidelines, preferred rules of the game to be observed if possible, but not legally binding prescriptions.[60] By the end of World War II the most distinguished authorities were reduced to stating that international law prohibits direct, intentional attack on persons and targets that have no conceivable military significance, an ambiguous and essentially irrelevant prohibition.[61]

Before proceeding to prohibitions four to six, which are to be taken more seriously in terms of binding international law, I would like to turn to the second category of general principles, a category which can be summed up in the concept of *proportion* between ends and means and which I have characterized as the principle of "legitimate military necessity."[62] Many authorities would frame this principle in the negative and make it a prohibition of disproportionate means. Following the tradition of the original U.S. Army field manual and the logic of the concept of the right of self-defense, I prefer to formulate the principle in the following, positive fashion:

> Military necessity consists in all measures immediately indispensable and proportionate to a legitimate military end, provided that they are not prohibited by the laws of war or the natural law, when taken on the decision of a responsible commander subject to judicial review.[63]

The latter part of that definition was strongly influenced by the vast accumulations of war crimes proceedings following World War II. Since the Korean and other conflicts revealed that the conditions of "victory" requisite to conducting war crimes trials were seldom present and since hopes for international criminal tribunals have so far proved vain, I have broadened my concept of review to mean review by a commander's superiors, by his allies, and by unbiased third-party opinion.[64]

The Nuremberg Principles / 169

No matter what one thinks about wars such as that in Vietnam, it seems to me quite clear that they are more limited than they might otherwise be because of the moderating influence of domestic criticism, enlightened policies of self-restraint by responsible statesmen and commanders, the attitudes of co-belligerents and political allies, and by "world opinion," which, whatever its content, dynamics, and objectivity, patently exists as a major factor in international politics to which all participants in the world arena pay a great deal of attention.

It is my belief that the interaction of policies and claims regarding their legal permissibility in the area of regulation of combat practices produces customary international law. The efforts of responsible statesmen and commanders to give content to the concept of legitimate military necessity may well produce prohibitions, or at least legal presumptions, against attacks involving the killing of large numbers of noncombatants or of whole populated areas. Indeed, I believe an argument can be made that there are emerging a number of tacit "rules of the game" as between the nuclear powers, the most important of which may be a prohibition of *first* recourse to nuclear weapons in *any* form.[65] I would further argue that this rule applies to so-called "counter-city" attacks on population centers with conventional means and that the "city-busting" air-raids of World War II are now viewed in retrospect with remorse and with a feeling that they were not justified in terms of military utility much less in terms of normative standards.

Still, the fact is that there was, during World War II, no adequate, binding international law prohibiting such raids. Ironically, although many *ground* commanders were tried and convicted as perpetrators of war crimes for "wanton" destruction (usually in extremely desperate strategic or tactical situations where the destruction was carried out in the interests of survival) there appear to have been no convictions of *Luftwaffe* or other enemy officers or their superiors for illegal air-raids.[66] It remained for a Japanese court, in a totally domestic litigation, to rule that the U.S. atomic attacks on Hiroshima and Nagasaki were contrary to international law.[67]

Judging Any *Participation in "Illegal" War:* In any event, this discussion recalls our earlier problem of relating SCO to the Nuremberg principles, war crimes trials, and international law. If an individual believes that the development of ever-more effective and terrible weapons and their intrinsic incompatability with the first three principles protecting noncombatants and population centers makes all modern war immoral, then he is a CO, not an SCO. If he believes that serving in the same armed force with troops who mount counter-city air attacks—or, as we have discussed, torture prisoners—is contrary to his conscience, he is really a CO, not an SCO. As concerns modern weapons systems, willingness to employ them and the abandonment of moral scruples appear to change in proportion to their availability and the exigencies of foreign and defense policy, as both the Egyptians and Indians, for example, have amply demonstrated. If, on the other hand, the issue is true apprehension that military service may require close collaboration with those who order and execute policies violative of the former immunity of noncombatants and non-military targets from direct, intentional attack, I would reiterate my earlier argument that one can avoid service in the Air Force, one need not become an officer or even a noncom. This still leaves us, however, with the man who faces the draft and possible combat service in which he may very well be required to employ means violative of prohibitions four to six. We shall now examine these issues which are very close to the heart of SCO.

The fourth prohibition of classical international law relevant to our inquiry is that prohibiting the use of weapons which cause "superfluous suffering" and render death "inevitable." The legal basis for this principle, endorsed by the Declaration of St. Petersburg of 1868[68] and Article 23 (e) of the Hague regulations of 1899 and 1907 Respecting the Laws and Customs of War on Land which provides:

> . . . it is especially forbidden—. . .
> e. To employ arms, projectiles, or material calculated to cause unnecessary suffering.[39]

The principal contemporary authorities on the law of war have emphasized the vague and subjective character of this principle.[70]

The main weapon discussed in current SCO debates is napalm, protest against which is almost the symbol of anti-war criticism of the Vietnam conflict.[71] In the light of this controversy it is instructive to consult the instructions of the U.S. Army's FM 27-10. Regarding "Employment of Arms Causing Unnecessary Injury," it is said:

> . . . [Hague Regulations, art. 23 (3)]
> b. *Interpretation.* What weapons cause "unnecessary injury" can only be determined in light of the practice of States in refraining from the use of a given weapon because it is believed to have that effect. The prohibition certainly does not extend to the use of explosives contained in artillery, projectiles, mines, rockets, or hand grenades. Usage has, however, established the illegality of lances with barbed heads, irregular-shaped bullets, and projectiles filled with glass, the use of any substance on bullets that would tend unnecessarily to inflame a wound inflicted by them, and the scoring of the surface or the filing off of the ends of the hard cases of bullets.[72]

Turning to "Weapons Employing Fire," the Army's Manual maintains:

> The use of weapons which employ fire, such as tracer ammunition, flame-throwers, napalm and other incendiary agents, against targets requiring their use is not violative of international law. They should not, however, be employed in such a way as to cause unnecessary suffering to individuals.[73]

It is known that napalm was used by Israeli forces in the Middle East war initiated June 5, 1967.[74] It is believed that a survey of the world's armed forces would demonstrate that virtually all of them have used or are prepared to use napalm or other "weapons employing fire" (e.g., flame-throwers) if such means are available to them. If this belief is correct, by the reasonable standards of the U.S. Army's Field Manual 27-10, such means, terrible as they may seem, are *not* considered "superfluous" in the practice of states. On the contrary, they are considered necessary and not generally disproportionate to the ends for which they are normally used. Of course, if used indiscriminately or cruelly they would violate the basic principle of legitimate military necessity, just as indiscriminate use of firearms, artillery, or any other means of warfare would become legally impermissible if that principle were violated.

Unless there is a more definite and conspicuous abstention from the use of napalm, and other weapons employing fire, by belligerents and by armed forces in training throughout the world, it would seem that objection to military service based in part on the prospect that it will involve complicity in the use of such weapons ought to be based, not on SCO and on regard for the Nuremberg principles, but on CO on the grounds that modern war exceeds all normative limits. This is not to dismiss the very real moral and human arguments and explanations for a revulsion against the use of napalm and similar means of war but, again, we are talking about international law, not morality or humanitarian impulses.

Much more serious, in terms of international law, are the proscriptions against "the use in war of asphyxiating, poisonous or other gases, and of all analogous liquids, materials or devices," as well as "the use of bacteriological methods of warfare." In view of the broad scope of this study it will be necessary to compress the alternative analyses of these rules into rather clear-cut formulations of issues which doubtless do violence to a highly complex and controversial subject. But the following would seem to be the issues and the main alternative positions regarding so-called "CB" warfare (chemical-biological, taken from the formulation "ABC" warfare, i.e., atomic-biological-chemical):

(1) A very sweeping prohibition of the use in war of "asphyxiating, poisonous or other gases, and of all analogous liquids, materials or devices," as well as of "the use of bacteriological methods of warfare" is binding as conventional international law on all adherents to the Geneva Protocol of June 17, 1925. The United States and Japan are the only major powers which are not adherents to the Protocol.[75] *Question* (1): Does such a widespread, formal, and long-standing prohibition carry such weight

as to engender obligations under international law for non-adherents?

(2) Upon analysis it appears that the prohibition of the Geneva Protocol of 1925 is really only against the *first* use of the proscribed means and that retaliation in kind against their first use would be permitted. It is also known that all serious military establishments are prepared to use CB warfare and train with a view to defense against CB warfare.[76] *Question* (2): Do these legal and practical limitations on the broad prohibitions of the Geneva Protocol lessen its importance, particularly as regards non-adherents?

(3) The practice of states since 1925 has seen virtually *no* use of CB warfare.[77] *Question* (3): Has the practice of states, by such a lengthy abstention from CB means, some of which became standard in World War I, produced a rule of *customary* international law, justifying expectations by statesmen, military commanders, and civilian populations that CB warfare will not be used, at least not in any circumstances other than as retaliation for similar or equally impermissible means?

(4) If there is a customary international law rule against the use, or at least the first use, of CB warfare, a question is raised as to the application of that rule with regard to a state, such as the United States, which is not a party to any conventional limitation on CB means. Yet, as we have noted, "international law is part of our law," according to the Supreme Court.[78] *Question* (4): Is the U.S. bound by a rule of customary international law not to use CB means, or to use them only as lawful reprisals after their first use by an enemy; and is this international legal obligation, if it exists, enforceable as a matter of municipal law and, therefore, relevant to the defense of a SCO that his nation is utilizing illegal means in the Vietnam war?

(5) On the other hand, it is argued that non-lethal gases are used almost universally to maintain internal order and that defoliants and crop-destroyers such as are being used in Vietnam are essentially domestic farm products. *Question* (5): Regardless of the status of lethal gases and controversial forms of biological warfare, is there not a valid exception to any alleged rule, name-

ly, that non-lethal gases and other materials permitted within the domestic public orders of the world should not be included in any general prohibition against CB warfare?

Before attempting to answer these five questions, one basic point should be made. The underlying issue (perhaps we should make it issue 6) is whether there is a definable category of "CB" means which are legally impermissible and whether use of *any* means within that category, no matter how reasonable in the abstract, is legally impermissible. In other words, does recourse to CB warfare in any form represent the crossing of a normative and practical threshold which has not hitherto been crossed, except by belligerents whose behavior was generally condemned? I would argue that, whatever the difficulties of defining CB warfare, there *is* a prohibited category of means, that these means were not in fact used by the major belligerents in World War II or the Korean War, and that the legal presumption is against their legal permissibility, no matter how "humane" or "proportionate" they might be.[79]

If this perspective be valid, one must say that the use, for the first time, of non-lethal gases "in war" by the U.S. in Vietnam represents a crossing of a legal threshold which, at best, is dangerous, and at worst may be illegal and highly dangerous to the hard-earned little corpus of law which governs this subject. In the light of this conclusion, I would answer the five questions posed as follows:

With respect to the first two questions,

(1) The Geneva Protocol of 1925 is a vulnerable document which is subject to a number of criticisms and abuses which need not concern us here. Alone, it would not bind a non-adherent such as the United States. It is also questionable whether it should prejudice all weapons developments after 1925 regardless of other considerations.

(2) However, concerning the third question, which seems to be central, it seems quite clear that, say, by the end of the Korean War, if not by the end of World War II, there was a rule of customary international law prohibiting CB means. The combination of *intent,* expressed in the Protocol of 1925, and *practice,*

in the form of general abstention from the use of CB, even in major wars, has produced, I believe, an international law rule prohibiting the use of such means.

(3) Accordingly, the legal presumption is *against* the U.S. policies regarding non-lethal gas in Vietnam, the more so since such means were previously available to the U.S. and other belligerents and were, in fact, not used. The use of defoliants is a very marginal case which could go either way. The use of crop-destroyers probably falls within the general prohibition of CB means.

In the interests of brevity, it may be concluded that all of the U.S. policies in Vietnam involving possible violation of the ban on CB means are at best controversial and at least some of the means being used are probably not legally permissible. If this statement offends those who find these means innocuous if not positively humane as compared to means which are more destructive and which are not specifically regulated by international law, one can only say that the imperfect law of war which has developed must be taken as it is, not as it ought to be either in terms of higher values on the one hand or military necessity on the other. Since this paper is concerned with international law, not morality or public opinion, I can only state that, whereas the use of napalm for example is accepted, not specifically prohibited, and therefore not assimilable into the general rule of customary international law prohibiting CB means (even though it might have been and might be in the future), the use of any means, no matter how mild, which can reasonably be included in the forbidden category of CB warfare, is legally impermissible and will remain so unless the practice of states countenances exceptions.

The draftee infantryman may very well be obliged to use tear- and nausea-gas grenades and dispensers that are technically illegal under international law. A draftee might very well get involved in preparations for delivery by air of non-lethal gases as well as defoliants and crop-destroyers, in large quantities, perhaps in a rather indiscriminate fashion. He may thereby become, technically, a war criminal or an accomplice to acts that a war crimes or other tribunal might deem to be contrary to international law. Just how important this prospect would loom in the total calculation by the individual as to the propriety of his serving in a particular war where such means were known to be in use must be left to the reader's judgment.

Finally, there is the international law proscription against "wanton destruction of cities, towns, or villages, or devastation not justified by military necessity." There is no question whatever about the validity and binding force of this rule in conventional international law, particularly in the Hague Conventions of 1899 and 1907, and it is one of the principal specific rules that make up the content of "war crimes" as defined at Nuremberg.[80] There is, further, no doubt that members of the armed forces at all levels, from high commanders to privates, may be held legally accountable for violation of this rule. It is, therefore, perhaps the most relevant of all those which we have considered in connection with the Nuremberg basis for SCO.

Moreover, participation in measures of wanton destruction—burning, dynamiting, bulldozing, and otherwise destroying a population center or area of a countryside—is just as likely to be the lot of a serviceman in a combat zone as any other "detail." Naturally, the principal responsibility for controversial acts of destruction falls upon the commander. In many cases the ordinary serviceman will have little or no way of knowing whether the destructive acts in which he is engaged are legitimate or not. Some destruction is clearly permitted by military necessity, i.e., clearing a field of fire, or destroying dangerous cover which the enemy could use to approach one's lines. On the other hand, retaliatory destruction of whole villages because of guerrilla activity in the area is, generally speaking, considered to exceed legitimate military necessity. War crimes tribunals have given mixed, but, on the whole, lenient treatment to commanders and forces employing "scorched earth policies" as a means of delaying pursuit by a superior enemy. The latter category of cases involves a considerable balancing of prudential judgments, even in retrospect, for which the ordinary soldier ought not to be held too closely accountable.[81]

Anyone who has an ordinary familiarity with recent conflicts in the Third World is aware that there is a comparatively high incidence of the kinds of destruction by ground troops which we have just termed generally unjustified by legitimate military necessity. Since guerrillas and regular forces using guerrilla tactics often blend into the indigenous society and utilize the population for all manner of vital functions and resources, the temptation is great for counter-insurgency forces to destroy entirely insurgent-held villages or even whole areas. The *rationale* may range from eliminating a source of persistent sniper fire to a systematic denial of food and shelter to the insurgents and their allies, willing or unwilling. We lack sufficient authority, I think, from the vast reports of war crimes trials and commentaries thereon after World War II adequately to judge this modern phenomenon of war. The problem was dealt with after World War II but it was always secondary to the basic problems of conventional military behavior. Now so-called sub-conventional war, or conventional war in a basically guerrilla warfare context, has become the central form of contemporary armed conflict and the definition of means of destruction "justified by military necessity" is extremely difficult. I can only conclude that there is a very real problem here that needs more clarification in positive international law on the one hand and more imagination and restraint on the part of belligerents on the other.

As to the individual who includes this important part of the Nuremberg concept of war crimes in his objections to a particular war and his arguments for SCO, it seems to me that we are back to the point made in discussing involvement in controversial behavior toward POW's and hostages. If the individual wants even general assurance that military service will not involve him in the war crime of wanton destruction unjustified by military necessity, in the kinds of wars which are presently being fought and which can be anticipated, I am inclined to think that it would make more sense to claim CO rather than SCO.

The international law relative to the protection of civilian persons in time of war (to use the language of the Geneva Convention of 1949) is summarized in Articles 42–56 of the 1907 Hague Convention on the Laws and Customs of War on Land and on the provisions of the 1949 Geneva Convention. There is, then, a very substantial body of conventional law on this subject; more than on any other part of the law of war except that dealing with prisoners of war. There is, moreover, an enormous body of case law, international and national, arising out of World War II which deals with this subject. Accordingly, one might expect that it would furnish us with a great number of issues relevant to SCO based on the Nuremberg principles. In my opinion, however, this is not the case.

The reason, I think, for the comparative sparseness of provisions concerning the protection of civilians in war areas relevant to our inquiry is as follows: The law as codified in 1907 and again in 1949 is focused almost exclusively, with the exception of Article 3 of the 1949 Convention previously discussed, on international, i.e., *interstate* wars, not on civil wars or on mixed civil-international wars. The basic concept underlying both conventions is that of sovereign responsibility. When a territorial sovereign is displaced from part of its domain by an enemy invader, the (sovereign) invader assumes, so the traditional law runs, a temporary but significant responsibility under international law to act somewhat as a sovereign with respect to the civilian population and resources of the area under belligerent occupation.[82]

Everything in the traditional law flows from this concept of replacement of sovereign responsibility. The belligerent occupant is granted rights commensurate with the military necessities of continuing hostilities. There is a price, however, which the civilian population in the occupied areas must pay for this protection and assistance. The traditional law required that, when the regular forces of the territorial sovereign were displaced, the civilians should obey the orders of the belligerent occupant so long as they were consonant with international law. In a very real sense, the occupied population was *hors de combat,* much in the same manner as prisoners of war. The occupant's legal obligations rested on the assumption that most of the occupied population would, as far as possible, not contribute significantly to the continuation of the war effort by their own state or its allies.[83] The Second World War showed beyond doubt that this assumption is not valid in most modern war situations. One of the most conspicuous features of that war was the activity of resistance movements within occupied territories. Resistance activity ranged from spontaneous revolt to organized guerrilla operations by troops either left behind or infiltrated into occupied areas, or both. It is remarkable, and unfortunate for those who confront contemporary conflicts, that these developments were not adequately considered at Geneva when the 1949 Convention on this subject was drafted.

In the post-Korean conflict period, when conventional war directly involving any of the great powers became unlikely, the typical war has been a combination of a civil war and interventionary indirect aggression and counter-intervention involving, overtly or covertly, forces of foreign powers. It is obvious that these changes imply factual and doctrinal dilemmas which render unhelpful, if not irrelevant, international law rules based on past assumptions about war and its principal actors. Thus, if a joint U.S.–South Vietnamese–Korean force overruns and holds an area that was formerly a Vietcong stronghold and has more recently been jointly defended by the Vietcong and elements of the army of North Vietnam, the number of possible legal arguments as to legal title to and responsibility for the territory and the status of the occupants is too great to encumber these pages. Under these circumstances, the most sensible and humane approach to the law protecting civilian populations in war areas is to play down arguments about legal title and legitimacy and look to the practical needs of the civilian victims of war.

This involves, on the positive side, all and reasonable measures to maintain order, provide the basic necessities of life, and to protect the population from involvement in hostilities. In terms of limitations on the occupants of areas formerly held by an enemy—whether insurgents, alleged foreign "aggressors," or whatever—it would seem that the basic requirements of the traditional international law should serve as guides, if not as binding rules of conduct according to the conventional international law "on the books." Of these rules, only the most relevant and controversial will be mentioned here.

In the light of contemporary experience with mixed civil-international counter-insurgency conflicts it would seem that these limitations, accepted in treaties to which the U.S. and most powers are parties, fall into three categories: (1) rules which ought to be observed regardless of the demands of military or political utility and convenience and which are not unreasonable even in terms of such utility; (2) rules which are so frequently and widely violated as to cast doubt as to their binding character and practicality; (3) rules which fall in a gray area between the first two categories.

Unfortunately, it appears to me, there are not many rules that fall in the first category. Pillage, for instance, is prohibited. It is not only unjust and illegal, it is contrary to true military and political utility, *particularly* in counter-insurgency wars. At this point, I am afraid, we exhaust the first category of rules which are clearly binding and which are reasonable, even from the standpoint of the belligerent occupant.

When we contemplate the other basic rules of conventional international law limiting belligerent occupants we are dealing with subjects which are difficult and controversial. Certainly this is the case with many in the second category, for example, the rule prohibiting the occupant from forcing the inhabitants of an occupied area to furnish information about the army of the other belligerent. As observed in our discussion of prisoners of war, interrogation, and torture, information about the enemy is by all odds the most important element both in insurgency and counter-insurgency operations, particularly in underdeveloped countries with difficult terrain.

A number of rules seem to belong to the third category of controverted and unclear provisions of the existing conventional law. For example, the rule protecting the occupied society from radical and purportedly permanent changes in social, economic, and political institutions has been dated since at least 1917.[84] Western "democratic," Communist, Fascist, and other occupying powers have undertaken immediate fundamental changes in territories under their control. On the other hand, it may be argued that *real* change in institutions is difficult in counter-insurgency conflicts where the fortunes of war ebb and flow and that the *appearance* of change often may be all that a temporary occupant can achieve. Accordingly, the practical importance of this rule is probably quite variable and at times marginal. Observance of the rule requiring due process of law in the passing of sentences and carrying out of executions is also subject to a number of qualifications and probably to be considered in the third, gray area.

I have deliberately left one rule to be considered separately. It is the rule that the "taking of hostages" is prohibited. I will conclude this survey of the law regulating hostilities with some comments on this rule because, first, it raises important and difficult issues in modern war and, second, it could be highly relevant to the service of an individual in a typical modern conflict and, therefore, to the issues of SCO.

If we were to review the other basic rules limiting occupation forces, I think that it would be apparent that, with the possible exception of the rule about forcing the inhabitants to give information, it is rather unlikely that the ordinary soldier, or even junior officer, would be forced to break them in a way for which he would be responsible under the laws of war.

The rule prohibiting the taking of hostages, however, does reach down to any and all troops in an occupied area. It concerns the seizure of members of the population in an occupied area, often persons of power and prestige, and holding them for the purpose of threatening and/or actually carrying out their execution both as a deterrent to and punishment for acts hostile to the occupying power.

Three things should be said about the "taking of hostages." *First,* the prohibition of the Geneva Convention of 1949 is aimed ultimately at the *execution* of hostages even though the sole verb in the rule is "taking." Unless hostages are occasionally executed in the course of a conflict the taking of hostages would be no more than an injustice and inconvenience rather than a major war crime. *Second,* international law was not clear on this subject until the 1949 Convention. There is no prohibition of the practice in the Hague Convention of 1907. We have a significant history of recourse to this sanction of occupation rights by belligerents in modern history. Moreover, the most elaborate judicial treatment of the subject, the U.S. military tribunal's decision in the "Hostage Case," condoned the taking and execution of hostages in extreme situations where all law and order and all respect for the legitimate exercise of occupation powers had disappeared.[85] *Third,* to confuse the picture further, the history of contemporary military occupations leaves unanswered the question whether, on the whole, the taking and execution of hostages is an effective means of deterring and punishing opposition to an occupying power or whether it is rather a source of spiraling reprisals and counter-reprisals which incite the population and encourage resistance.

Rather than speculate on the various forms of participation in the taking and execution of hostages which might prove the lot of an individual soldier, I would prefer to leave the subject in this unsettled and ambiguous state as a final example of the practice and legal complications involved in determining: (1) the content and validity of the Nuremberg principles and the law of war; (2) the responsibility under municipal and international law for participation in acts regulated by these principles and rules of law. In this case, it would be easy for the individual SCO and his lawyer to look up the Geneva Convention of 1949 Relative to the Protection of Civilian Persons in Time of War and read the clear language of Article 3 prohibiting the taking of hostages and the related language of the same article requiring due process of law before sentencing and carrying out sentences of members of an occupied area, even in armed conflicts "not of an international character" (thus, *a fortiori* in armed conflicts of a mixed civil-international character).

To the best of my knowledge, taking and executing hostages in the manner of World War II practice by Germans, for example, has *not* been charged against the United States and its allies in the Vietnamese conflict. Very possibly the U.S. experts in counter-insurgency have learned the lessons ignored by the Germans in World War II and have decided not to try to win "The Other War" for the loyalty of the indigenous population by threats and reprisals against hostages. But desperate circumstances, such as an intense campaign by the enemy based in large measure on the taking and threatened execution of hostages, might well drive the South Vietnamese, the United States, and other allies to contemplate retaliation in kind. If this were to occur—or if it could be shown that something like a hostage policy has already been employed in Vietnam—an additional legal argument could be raised for SCO based on the Nuremberg principles and the international law of war.

Conclusions

If this analysis seems inordinately inconclusive for a comparatively detailed treatment of the subject of SCO and the Nuremberg principles, the author will deem his effort successful. For the purpose of this study has been neither to encourage nor discourage SCO generally or SCO on the basis of regard for international law as interpreted and applied by the United States. It has been concerned with penetrating facile rhetoric and purported statements of law on all sides of the controversy to demonstrate the limits, possibilities, and ambiguities of appeals to international law as a basis for SCO.

On the basis of this study the following conclusions appear to be warranted:

(1) The claim that a war is illegal under international law and that, therefore, any participant in such an illegal war risks treatment as a war criminal is not a good basis for SCO, either under international or United States law.

(2) Objections to allegedly illegal military, political, and other policies not directly involving the individual soldier are not very relevant to claims for SCO since they fall within the legal responsibility of high-level decision-makers who have voluntarily assumed their positions and participated in the making of these policies.

(3) The really relevant portion of the Nuremberg principles and of the law of war, insofar as the SCO in or out of the armed forces is concerned, is eminently that of "war crimes and crimes against humanity," i.e., the law governing the conduct of hostilities and belligerent occupation. Although there is a substantial body of conventional law on these subjects, each rule must be carefully considered in order to determine its meaning, its present validity in the light of the practice of states, and its practical feasibility in the mixed civil-international conflicts, mainly in the difficult

terrain of underdeveloped countries, before serious consideration should be accorded claims that it is violated and further claims that these violations justify refusal to participate in the war with respect to which the violations are alleged.

(4) There appears to be such a widespread tendency to violate some of the most definite laws of war—e.g., concerning denial of quarter; torture to obtain vital information; extremely broad interpretations of "military necessity" as justification for widespread destruction of inhabited towns and whole areas; and, possibly, reprisals against rebellious civilian populations such as the taking and execution of hostages—as to create a troublesome gap between the "law on the books" in international conventions and the usage of belligerents. This gap vastly complicates the task of the SCO whose principal objection to a particular war is its illegal conduct.

(5) Many of the most controversial methods of war, e.g., napalm, are not explicitly regulated by the law of war except by the broad principles of legitimate military necessity and proportionality. Hence SCO based on objections to means must be primarily moral and humanitarian rather than legal.

(6) Virtually all of the objections based on the Nuremberg principles and the law of war generally tend to apply across the board to most recent and foreseeable wars, thus raising the question whether the more persuasive claim might not be for CO on the grounds that all modern warfare exceeds permissible legal and moral limits, rather than that a *particular* war exceeds those limits.

However, I must say that the foregoing conclusions are reached with reluctance and a feeling that something is very definitely wrong with the present relationship between U.S. municipal law and international law. For, notwithstanding the many difficulties which I have mentioned, a dilemma remains for any American who takes seriously international law and official U.S. pronouncements supporting it. There is something wrong with a system which acknowledges the binding effect of international law, particularly conventional law, but which, apparently, manages to exclude most of this law from cases involving individual citizens who claim the right to invoke it as the basis for SCO. If the federal courts will not rule on "crimes against the peace" on the grounds that the claim involves "political questions," this is perhaps regrettable but understandable. But for the federal courts to refuse, as they apparently have, to consider international law "part of our law," and to apply it—particularly when it is formulated in treaties to which the U.S. is a party—directly in cases involving individual charges that United States policy concerning conduct of a particular war is illegal under both international and domestic U.S. law, is to leave a situation which would seem to require a restatement of the U.S. position on international law.

With respect to the law of war, international law is part of the law of the United States, *if* the Executive and/or the Legislative branches waive the preeminence which they have and which the Judiciary has accepted. In other words, the courts apparently are relatively powerless to protect individual SCO's from forced participation in violations of the law of war ordered and/or acquiesced in by the Executive and the Congress.

Yet it is axiomatic that the municipal laws of a state and the peculiarities of its internal constitutional processes do not release it from its responsibilities and obligations under international law. Nor, under the Nuremberg precedent, do the pleas of "act of state" or "superior orders" absolve the individual from responsibility for acts violative of international law. It would seem that the federal Judiciary will have to confront the issues raised by those who claim SCO on the basis of Nuremberg and international law, or else add another chapter to the record of judicial retreat before the determined advances of the Executive in the pursuit of its broad powers to conduct foreign relations and national security affairs. If this is to be the case, perhaps a somewhat more charitable note might be taken with respect to those defeated enemies of World War II who, also, were often caught up in the domestic laws, practices, and personal dilemmas of wartime and who were treated as war criminals.

NOTES

[1] U.S. Department of State, *Trial of War Criminals*, 13; Department of State Publication No. 2420 (1945), 39 AM. Jl. Intl. Law Supp. 257 (1945).

The other wartime "United Nations" which adhered to the London Agreement in conformity with Article 5 thereof were: Greece, Denmark, Yugoslavia, the Netherlands, Czechoslovakia, Poland, Belgium, Ethiopia, Australia, Honduras, Norway, Panama, Luxembourg, Haiti, New Zealand, India, Venezuela, Uruguay, and Paraguay.

See the United Nations War Crimes Commission, *The United Nations War Crimes Commission and the Development of the Laws of War* (London: Published for the United Nations War Crimes Commission by His Majesty's Stationery Office, 1948), p. 457, for the text of the Agreement of August 8, 1945, to which the London Charter was annexed. (Hereinafter cited as *UN War Crimes Commission.*)

The most convenient source document is Office of United States Chief of Counsel for Prosecution of Axis Criminality, *Nazi Conspiracy and Aggression, Opinion and Judgment* (Washington: U.S. Government Printing Office, 1947). Portions of the *Judgment* quoted on pp. 1–4 summarize the basic provisions of the Charter. For convenience this source, hereinafter cited as *Nuremberg Judgment*, will be cited and quoted as the principal primary source on the trial of the major war criminals before the Nuremberg International Military Tribunal.

The basic source document for the Nuremberg trials of major war criminals is Nuremberg International Military Tribunal, *Trial of the Major War Criminals Before the International Military Tribunal*, Nuremberg, 14 November, 1945–1 October, 1946 (published at Nuremberg, Germany, 1948), 42 volumes. The Judgment of the Tribunal appears in Vol. XXII, pp. 411–589. (This source will be cited hereinafter as NIMT, *Trial of Major War Criminals.*)

[2] *Nuremberg Judgment*, p. 1.

[3] *U.N. War Crimes Commission, op. cit.;* John Alan Appleman, *Military Tribunals and International Crimes* (Indianapolis: Bobbs-Merrill, 1954).

The Nuremberg Trials held by the United States are extremely well reported in a carefully edited series, *Trials of War Criminals Before the Nuremberg Military Tribunals Under Control Council Law No. 10*, at

Nuremberg, October, 1946–April, 1949 (Washington: U.S. Government Printing Office, 1951), 15 volumes. (Hereinafter cited as *U.S. Trials of War Criminals—Nuremberg.*)

These trials are also covered in part in an invaluable series of reports and analyses of virtually all international and national war crimes proceedings of note by the United Nations War Crimes Commission, *Law Reports of Trials of War Criminals* (London: Published for the United Nations War Crimes Commission by His Majesty's Stationery Office, 1947), 15 volumes. Volume 15 contains an analytical summary of all of the principal charges, issues, and defenses involved and the law on each as it emerged from the practice of the tribunals.

4 See Hersch Lauterpacht, ed., *Annual Digest and Reports of Public International Law Cases* (London: Butterworth), for the years 1945–1949; the same and succeeding editors under the title *International Law Reports*, since the 1950 edition.

5 *Nuremberg Judgment,* pp. 3, 4.

6 *Ibid.*, p. 4.

7 See Herbert W. Briggs, ed., *The Law of Nations, Cases, Documents and Notes,* 2nd ed. (New York: Appleton-Century-Crofts, 1952), pp. 96–98 and authorities cited therein; William W. Bishop, Jr., *International Law, Cases and Materials,* 2nd edition (Boston/Toronto: Little Brown, 1962), pp. 266, 267. The basic provisions of the U.N. Charter prohibiting first recourse to force as an instrument of foreign policy are found in the Preamble, in the Purposes set forth in Article 1, and most definitely in Article 2, paragraph 4, which states: "All Members shall refrain in their international relations from the threat or use of force against the territorial integrity or political independence of any state, or in any other manner inconsistent with the Purposes of the United Nations." Sanctions in support of this rule are provided for in Chapter VII of the Charter and Chapter XVII.

8 In the Judgment of the Nuremberg International Military Tribunal only Streicher and von Schirach were found guilty of crimes against humanity but not of war crimes. Admirals Doenitz and Raeder were the only defendants found guilty of war crimes but not of crimes against humanity. The following were found guilty of what were characterized as "war crimes and crimes against humanity": Goering, Hess, von Ribbentrop, Keitel, Kaltenbrunner, Rosenberg, Frank, Frick, Funk, Sauckel, Jodl, Speer, Fritzsche, and Bormann. See *Nuremberg Judgment,* pp. 108–166. Seys-Inquart was, in effect, found guilty of "war crimes and crimes against humanity." See *Nuremberg Judgment,* pp. 54–55.

A typical linking of the two counts is demonstrated by two of the best-known of the U.S war crimes proceedings at Nuremberg. In U.S. v. von Leeb *et al* ("The High Command Case"), Count One was "Crimes Against the Peace," Count Four was "Common Plan of Conspiracy." Count Two was "War Crimes and Crimes Against Humanity: Crimes Against Enemy Belligerents and Prisoners of War." Count Three was "War Crimes and Crimes Against Humanity: Crimes Against Civilians." *U.S. Trials of War Criminals—Nuremberg*, Vol. X, "The High Command Case," pp. 13-48.

Likewise, in U.S. v. List *et al*, "The Hostage Case," all four counts charged "War crimes and crimes against humanity" of various kinds. *Ibid.*, Vol. XI, pp 765-776.

9 I have analyzed the International Military Tribunal's handling of this approach in "Military Necessity in International Law" 1 *World Polity* 109, 142-147 (Institute of World Polity, *World Polity, A Yearbook of Studies in International Law and Organization:* Utrecht/Antwerp: Spectrum Publishers, 1957) wherein the relevant passages of M. de Menthon's position are quoted, the silence of the International Military Tribunal on this position interpreted, and the rejection of this approach by the U.S. Military Tribunals at Nuremberg in the "High Command" and "Hostages" cases noted, with appropriate quotations. Relevant commentaries are cited therein. For the relevant passages of the "High Command Case," U.S. v. von Leeb *et al*, see *U.S. Trials of War Criminals*, Vol. XI, pp. 485-491: "The Hostage Case," U.S. v. List, *Ibid.*, pp. 1246-1248; see also the account of the latter disposition of this question in U.N. War Crimes Commission, *Law Reports of Trials of War Criminals, op. cit.*, in the commentary on the Hostage case entitled, "The Irrelevance to the Present Discussion of Illegality of Aggressive War," Vol. VIII, pp. 59, 60. M. de Menthon's presentation may be found in NIMT, *Trial of the Major War Criminals Before the International Military Tribunal, op. cit.*, Vol. V, pp. 368-391. In an article criticizing de Menthon's approach Paul de la Pradelle notes that it was abandoned by the French prosecutor Dubost in his final statement and that the Tribunal did not discuss it in the Judgment. See his article, "Le Proces des grands criminels de guerre et le developement du droit international," extrait de la *Nouvelle Revue de droit international privé* (Paris: Les Editions Internationales, 1947), pp. 15, 16.

10 This attitude has been examined by Martin O. Milrod in his unpublished M.A. dissertation of June, 1959, at Georgetown University, "Prisoners of War in Korea: The Impact of Communist Practice Upon International Law." At the time of the Korean War neither North Korea nor the Chinese People's Republic were parties to the several

Geneva conventions of 1949 relative to treatment of prisoners of war and other wartime problems. Milrod observes that:

> The USSR and its "bloc" (there perhaps was a "bloc" in those days) entered a reservation to Article 85 of the Convention, which relates to war criminals. Extending what was originally a French proposal, they adopted at Geneva the following approach: "Some delegations maintained that those who transgress the laws of war forfeit their benefits by placing themselves outside of the law. Prisoners condemned under the regulations established at Nuremberg did not come under international law, it was argued, but should be treated as common law criminals." See Angenor Krafft, "The Present Position of the Red Cross Geneva Conventions," 37 *Grotius Society Transactions* 131 (1951), p. 138. Quoted in Milrod, *op. cit.*, p. 136. Milrod cites the de Menthon arguments at Nuremberg, *Ibid.*

The communist belligerents further manipulated the Nuremberg principles by sweeping interpretations of the concept of war crimes and crimes against humanity, in addition to crimes against the peace, so that the basic protection of U.N. POW's was placed in question. See Dept. of State, *General Foreign Policy Series 34*, Conventions of 12 August, 1949 (Pub. No. 3938) (Washington: U.S. Government Printing Office, 1950); also reproduced in Dept. of the Army *Pamphlet No. 20–150* (Washington: U.S. Government Printing Office, 1950) p. 252; as cited in Milrod, *op. cit.*, p. 137.

[11] For the text of the Genocide Convention see Res. No. 260 (III) A, U.N. Gen. Ass. Off. Rec., 3rd Sess. (I), Resolutions, p. 174; U.N. Doc. No. A/810; U.S. Dept. of State Publ. No. 3416 (1949); 45 *American Journal of International Law* Supplement 6 (1951). The source quoted here is Bishop, *International Law, op. cit.*, p. 476.

[12] *Idem.*

[13] *Idem.*

[14] *Idem.*

[15] *Idem.*

[16] Raphael Lemkin, *Axis Rule in Occupied Europe* (Washington: Carnegie Endowment for International Peace, Division of International Law, 1944). Raphael Lemkin, "Genocide as a Crime Under International Law," 41 *American Journal of International Law* 145 (1947).

[17] See Commission of Responsibilities, Conference of Paris, *Violations of the Laws and Customs of War*, Reports of Majority and Dissenting Reports of American and Japanese Members of the Commission of Responsibilities, Conference of Paris, 1919 (Carnegie Endowment for International Peace, Division of International Law, Pamphlet No. 32; Published for the Endowment; Oxford: At the Clarendon Press, 1919),

190 / A Conflict of Loyalties

Annex II, Memorandum respecting Reservations by the United States of America, pp. 53–79; U.N. War Crimes Commission, pp. 39, 40.

[18] The two landmark Supreme Court decisions are Whitney v. Robertson, 124 U.S. 190 (1888); Cook v. U.S., 288 U.S. 102 (1933).

[19] See U.S. v. Belmont, 301 U.S. 324 (1937); U.S. v. Pink, 315 U.S. 203 (1942).

[20] 175 U.S. 677 (1900) as quoted in Bishop, *International Law, op. cit.*, p. 27.

[21] See Banco Nacional de Cuba v. Sabbatino, 376 U.S. 398 (1964); Lyman M. Tondel, Jr., ed., *The Aftermath of Sabbatino*, Background Papers and Proceedings of the Seventh Hammarskjold Forum, Richard A. Falk, Author of the Working Paper (Published for the Association of the Bar of the City of New York by Oceana Publications, Dobbs Ferry, N.Y., 1965); Ulf Goebel, *Challenge and Response* (Portland, Oregon: University of Portland Press, 1964).

[22] Department of the Army, July, 1956, FM 27–10, Department of the Army Field Manual 27–10, *The Law of Land Warfare* (Washington: U.S. Government Printing Office, 1956).

[23] Nicholas von Hoffman, "Nuremberg Defense Allowed in Levy Trial," Washington *Post*, May 18, 1967.

[24] Colonel Brown was quoted in Nicholas von Hoffman's story, "Levy Is Dealt Trial Setback," Washington *Post*, May 26, 1967.

[25] U.S. v. Mitchell, 369 F. 2nd 323 (1966).

[26] *Ibid.*, p. 324.

[27] *Ibid.*

[28] 386 S 972, 87 S. Ct. 1162 (1966).

[29] *Idem.*, p. 153

[30] *Idem.*, p. 154

[31] 88 S. Ct. 282 (1967). Dissents by Stewart and Douglas at 282–285. See Fred P. Graham, "Stewart Bids Court Weigh Legality of U.S. War Role," *The New York Times*, November 7, 1967, pp. 1, 15.

[32] Edward S. Corwin, *Total War and the Constitution* (New York: Knopf, 1951); Clinton Rossiter, *The Supreme Court and the Commander-in-Chief* (Ithaca, New York: Cornell University Press, 1951).

[33] U.N. War Crimes Comission, *Law Reports of Trials of War Criminals, op. cit.*, Vol XV, p. 156.

[34] See William V. O'Brien, "The Meaning of 'Military Necessity' in International Law," 1 *World Polity* 109–176 (1957); William V. O'Brien, "Legitimate Military Necessity in Nuclear War," 2 *World Polity* 35–120.

35 "All Members shall refrain in their international relations from the threat or use of force against the territorial integrity or political independence of any state, or in any other manner inconsistent with the Purposes of the United Nations." Art. II, paragraph 4 of the U.N. Charter.

36 See J. L. Brierly, *The Law of Nations*, Sir Humphrey Waldock, ed. (6th ed.; New York/Oxford: Oxford University Press, 1963), pp. 416-421.

37 See *supra*, p. 159 and note 9.

38 See *supra*, p. 159.

39 See D. P. O'Connell, *International Law*, 2 vols (London: Stevens; Dobbs Ferry, N.Y., 1965), Vol. I, pp. 37-88 on the question generally; pp. 67-71 on U.S. law and practice.

40 Article 23 of Hague Convention IV of 1907 Respecting the Laws and Customs of War provides:

"In addition to the prohibitions provided by special Conventions, it is especially forbidden—

". . . c. To kill or wound an enemy who, having laid down his arms, or having no longer means of defense, has surrendered at discretion.

"d. To declare that no quarter will be given; . . ." DAP 27-1, p. 12.

41 Common Article III of the Geneva Conventions of August 12, 1949, for the Amelioration of the Condition of Wounded and Sick in Armed Forces in the Field, for Amelioration of the Condition of the Wounded, Sick and Shipwrecked Members of Armed Forces at Sea, Relative to the Treatment of Prisoners of War, and Relative to the Protection of Civilian Persons in Time of War, provides:

In the case of armed conflict not of an international character occurring in the territory of one of the High Contracting Parties, each Party to the conflict shall be bound to apply, as a minimum, the following provisions:

(1) Persons taking no active part in the hostilities, including members of armed forces who have laid down their arms and those placed *hors de combat* by sickness, wounds, detention, or any other cause, shall in all circumstances be treated humanely, without any adverse distinction founded on race, colour, religion or faith, sex, birth, or wealth, or any other similar criteria. . . . *(Ibid.,* pp. 24-25, 49, 67-68, 135-136.)

42 See *Ibid.*, pp. 67-134.

43 *Nuremberg Judgment*, p. 4.

44 See DAP 27-1, *op. cit.*, pp. 67-134; FM 27-10, Chapter 3, pp. 25-82.

45 See the texts of the four conventions, *Ibid.*, pp. 24-25, 48-49, 67-68, 135-136.

46 *Ibid.*, pp. 72-73.

192 / *A Conflict of Loyalties*

47 Eric Norden, "American Atrocities in Vietnam," *Liberation* (February, 1966), pp. 14–27.
48 The Lawyers Committee on American Policy Towards Vietnam, *Vietnam and International Law* (Flanders, N.J.: O'Hare Books, 1967), p. 62.
49 William V. O'Brien, "The Prospects for International Peacekeeping," James E. Dougherty and J. F. Lehman, Jr., eds., *Arms Control for the Late Sixties* (Princeton: Von Nostrand, 1967), pp. 213–230.
50 Norden, *op. cit.* pp. 116, 119–20.
51 See O'Brien, *The Meaning of Military Necessity, op. cit.* (see n. 73, p. 25) and authorities cited therein.
52 See Hague Convention IV, Respecting the Laws and Customs of War on Land, of 18 October, 1907, in DAP 27–1, Preamble, pp. 5–6, and, in particular, Articles 22 and 23, pp. 12–13.
53 See *supra*, pp. 206–207.
54 FM 27–10, pp. 3–4.
55 See H. Lauterpacht, "The Problem of the Revision of the Law of War," 29 *British Yearbook of International Law* 361 (1952).
56 Protocol Prohibiting the Use in War of Asphyxiating, Poisonous or Other Gases, and of Bacteriological Methods of Warfare, June 17, 1925, 3 Hudson, *International Legislation* 1670–72 (1931). (Hereinafter cited as *Geneva Gas Protocol, 1925.*)
57 *Nuremberg Judgment*, p. 4.
58 See *infra*, p. 167.
59 See William V. O'Brien, "Legitimate Military Necessity in Nuclear War," 2 *World Polity* 35, 83–86 and authorities cited therein (1960).
60 *Ibid.*, pp. 85–86.
61 See Myres S. McDougal and Florentino P. Feliciano, *Law and Minimum World Public Order* (New Haven & London: Yale University Press, 1961), pp. 71–80. They quote Lauterpacht's statement from the Article cited *supra*, n. 126, that:

> ... It is clear that admission of a right to resort to the creation of terror among the civilian population as being a legitimate object *per se* would inevitably mean the actual and formal end of the law of war. For that reason, so long as the assumption is allowed to subsist that there is a law of war, the prohibition of the weapons of terror now incidental to lawful operations must be regarded as an absolute rule of law. (*Op. cit.*, pp. 364–365.)

62 O'Brien, *Legitimate Military Necessity in Nuclear War, op. cit.*, pp. 35, 43–57.
63 William V. O'Brien, "The Meaning of 'Military Necessity' in International Law," 1 *World Polity*, pp. 109, 138 ff.
64 O'Brien, *Legitimate Military Necessity in Nuclear War, op. cit.*, pp. 63–65.

65 I develop this line of thinking in William V. O'Brien, *Nuclear War, Deterrence and Morality* (Westminster, Md.: Newman Press, 1967), pp. 77–80.
66 See U.N. War Crimes Commission, *Law Reports of Trials of War Criminals*, XV, 110.
67 Richard A. Falk, "The Shimata Case: A Legal Appraisal of the Atomic Attack on Hiroshima and Nagasaki," *American Journal of International Law*. Vol 59, pp. 789–793. This article discusses a decision of the District Court of Tokyo. See *Japanese Annual of International Law* for 1964, pp. 212–52; digested in *American Journal of International Law*, Vol. 58, p. 1016, 1964.
68 The Netherlands Government. *Documents Relating to the Program of the First Hague Conference.* (New York: Oxford University Press for the Carnegie Endowment for International Peace, 1921), p. 25.
69 DAP 27-1, p. 12.
70 M. W. Royse, *Aerial Bombardment* (New York: Vinal, 1928). McDougal and Feliciano, *Law and Minimum World Public Order, op. cit.,* pp. 615–618 and authorities cited therein.
71 Clergy and Laymen Concerned about Vietnam, *In the Name of America* (New York, 1968), pp. 269–270.
72 FM 27-10, art. 34, p. 18.
73 *Ibid.,* art. 36, p. 18.
74 See, for example, Randolph S. Churchill and Winston S. Churchill, *The Six Day War* (Boston: Houghton Mifflin, 1967), pp. 171, 173, and 182.
75 Protocol Prohibiting the Use in War of Asphyxiating, Poisonous or Other Gases, and of Bacteriological Methods of Warfare, Manley O. Hudson, *International Legislation* (Washington/New York, Carnegie Endowment for International Peace, 1931–1950), Vol. III, pp. 1670–1672 (1931).
76 William V. O'Brien, "Biological/Chemical Warfare and the International Law of War," 51 *Georgetown Law Journal* (1962), pp. 28–32.
77 *Ibid.,* pp. 32–37, 56–57 and authorities cited therein.
78 See *supra,* p. 173.
79 O'Brien, "Biological/Chemical Warfare and the International Law of War," *op. cit.,* pp. 57, 63.
80 See *supra,* p. 176.
81 See United Nations War Crimes Commission, *Law Reports of War Criminals, op. cit.,* Vol. XV, pp. 175–176, for a summary of war crimes law on this subject. The best-known and most-cited cases are the "High Command" and "Hostage" cases tried before the U.S. Military Tribunal at Nuremberg. See *U.S. Trials of War Criminals—Nuremberg, op.*

cit., Vol. XI. The Judgments and relevant passages are to be found on pp. 462, 541, 609 for the "Hostage Case" 1230, 1232-1233, 1253-1254, and especially, the comments on the German scorched-earth tactics in their retreat from Finnmark, Norway, in 1944, 1295-1297 153.

[82] Ernst H. Feilchenfeld, *The International Economic Law of Belligerent Occupation* (Washington: Carnegie Endowment for International Peace, 1942), pp. 10-11.

[83] Julius Stone, *Legal Controls of International Conflict*, 1st ed (New York: Rinehart, 1954), pp. 723-732.

[84] Feilchenfeld, *International Economic Law of Belligerent Occupation*, op. cit., pp. 17-29

[85] *U.S. Trials of War Criminals—Nuremberg*, op. cit., Vol. XI, pp. 1209-1222, and in the Judgment, pp. 1230, 1232, 1244-1253.

Selective Conscientious Objection and Political Obligation

QUENTIN L. QUADE

THE question of selective conscientious objection has become a significant political problem for this nation. Articulate persons and groups are seeking it as a policy for the United States; other articulate groups wish to prevent its becoming a policy. Free men, following free consciences, in a society that calls itself free and proclaims freedom its goal; the primordial and intrinsic need of government to govern and in governing to bind universally the governed—such are the generic ingredients of the present conflict. Reconciliation of these values-in-conflict is possible if we perceive that one *depends* upon the other, and one *exists* for the other.

It is my contention that the question of selective conscientious objection is, in its essentials, a modern form of a classic and recurring political problem; that despite this, much discussion on both sides of the issue has lacked political awareness; that the result has often been irrelevant argument, true to the American tradition of non-political discourse about politics; that it is necessary to attempt a reconstruction of the argument in fully political terms; that it is possible to do so, and once done that the problem is susceptible to rational and tolerable resolution.

Proponents of selective conscientious objection in effect ask the government to adopt a policy which would allow some individuals under certain circumstances to be exempted from other policies of the government—in this case, some wars. But war is a thing nation-states do. When a nation through its regular channels of decision decides to go to war, this decision is a national policy, not essentially unlike other policies established through legislative processes, judicial decrees, or executive order. As such, the policy of war is usually thought of as a policy with much the same character as other policies, i.e., universally binding on all citizens. In this traditional view, the citizen is obliged to follow the policy (which has about it at least a procedural legitimacy) even while he may be trying to change it. Implicit in this "accepting even while opposing" is a prior, more fundamental judgment that the political system is itself a value worth supporting.

Advocates of selective conscientious objection say that in war, at least, procedurally legitimate policy need not always be followed, that indeed citizens have a *right* to diverge from it, to avoid its repercussions. In this form the present debate is an absolutely basic one, for it demands that we once again examine root issues of politics: what is the character of political decision, particularly in a democratic situation; what is the meaning of political obligation; how does individual conscience relate to societal value judgment?

A classic political problem it is. Yet, as I have suggested and, hopefully, will demonstrate, much of the discussion surrounding it has been relatively unproductive. This is so largely because both sides have tried to strip the problem of its political character, and to carry on the argument at the level of pure, sharply contradictory, yet seldom intersecting abstractions. Differing in the values they have chosen, each side has tended to identify a single value as not only prime but exclusive. Where values are exclusive, politics does not exist. Politics serves to find resolution among conflicting values. Selective conscientious objection needs to be seen as a problem involving multiple values, none of which should be ignored or destroyed but, rather, all of which should be integrated into one acceptable decision.

1. SCO—*Some Problems with Its Friends*

I think the beauty of the Gospel story of the Pharisee and the Publican is that no one except the Lord Himself can call another man a Pharisee without automatically becoming one himself. Accordingly, I certainly will not brand as Pharisees those who contend that the issue of war and military service is practically the only anguish- and virtue-generating political issue which ever arises; and, in this view, because anguish- and virtue-generating, not even truly a political issue. But I do propose that many of these commentators seem to think that their concern over this matter gives them some sort of monopoly on indignation. No such monopoly exists. It depends on what and whose ox. . . .

A number of responsible journals have published articles and editorials strongly favoring selective conscientious objection that will serve as illustrations. *Christianity and Crisis* is justly considered a leading Protestant journal of opinion. But in an editorial otherwise marked by considerable prudential strength, Roger L. Shinn slips into two common and related difficulties. First, he portrays the responsibility for military service as a somehow unique burden, and a burden somehow more ethically charged than others. Second, and companion to the first, he tries to distinguish between politics involving moral choices (and thus pregnant with the possibility of conscientious objection) and politics involving non-moral choices (and thus not susceptible to conscientious objection).

Acknowledging the fact that not all who disagree with this or that policy can be permitted to act out this disagreement, Shinn writes:

> Everybody finds himself in the minority on some public questions, but he conforms. We [proponents of selective conscientious objection] are asking for the right to reject governmental policy on the grounds not simply of opinion but of conscience.
>
> We think it is possible to make some distinctions between moral and political judgments. If a man says, 'I think this war is not the most effective way to serve the national interest,' he would not be a conscientious objector. If he says, 'I profoundly believe that this war is morally evil,' he probably is a conscientious objector.[1]

There are genuine distinctions to be made, but in each case Shinn makes the wrong one, in my view. What is the difference between "grounds of opinion" and "grounds of conscience"? Conscience reflects on "opinions" or judgments one makes and brings forth new opinions and judgments. One can properly differentiate degrees of intensity with which opinions or convictions are held, and the degree of diligence displayed in arriving at a position, but the opinion on a policy's rightness is a judgment of the conscience in any case.

When someone says the policy in question is "not the most effective way . . . ," is he really saying something different from the man who says the policy is "morally evil"? Again, the genuine distinction, if there is to be one at all, is in the intensity of the critique. Both statements are in fact and inescapably statements about the morality of the policy. The question of "effectiveness" in pursuit of "national interest" has indeed two clear moral dimensions: effectiveness concerns the utility of means; the content of national interest speaks of the value ends or goals.

Thus the man (if he is himself conscious) who says "I think this war is not the most effective way . . ." is stating a conscientious objection quite as surely as his verbally more impassioned counterpart. The relevant distinction, therefore, is not that one speaks "morally" and the other "politically"—speaking politically is always to portray some vision of the human good—but precisely that one may be speaking with much greater passion, intensity, and subjective need.

This is itself of crucial importance politically, and an enlightened political system will be more sensitive and responsive to the more anguished voice. But it is not true, seemingly, that one voice is the voice of morality and the other some kind of non-moral, "political" expression.

Commonweal, a journal published by Catholic laymen, succumbs to a similar analytic malaise:

> If a political draftee objects to a particular war on the grounds that it involves widespread torture or genocide, his decision seems clearly a moral one, even if he should have to make some elementary political judgments to define or ascertain the facts. If a potential draftee objects to a particular war on the grounds that it is causing evil disproportionate to whatever good might emerge from it, then he is probably applying a somewhat sophisticated political analysis to the situation; and locating the specifically moral element in his objection becomes much more difficult.[2]

This seems passing strange from a journal which on the same page champions members of "... religious traditions whose moral teachings on warfare are based on the distinction between just and unjust wars, *and whose normal method for reaching moral conclusions involves a prudential examination of the actual circumstances of any action."* (Emphasis added.) The confusion runs very deep. Again, a true distinction seems to be portrayed in the lengthy quotation above, but it is not the one sought by the editorialist. While he seeks a non-existent distinction between moral and political (thus conscientious and non-conscientious) objection, what he actually portrays is a distinction of moral methods, a distinction between ways of judging the right, a distinction probably best described as that between a deontological ethic and an ethic of consequences.

Commonweal also states, in the same editorial, that "Participation in warfare is clearly recognized as ultimate and exceptional among the many demands a nation puts on citizens. It would be easy to draw the line between exemptions from this particular obligation [military service] and exemptions from obligations such as payment of taxes." "Clearly recognized" by whom? Ultimate? Exceptional? Indeed, by degrees. And like any class of obligations, "exceptional" from any other. Is it really so easy to draw the line, even between apparently easy cases such as military service and taxes? J. Bracken Lee appeared not to think so, when he sought to hold back the portion of his tax liability destined to be used for foreign aid. And Joan Baez appears to agree that it is not so easy, as she seeks to subtract from her taxes those monies that would go for war.

Even if it were easy to draw the line between what seem to be easy cases, what of the countless matters of principle (somebody's principle) which crop up in politics every day? Not all men who oppose racial desegregation are simply expedient cynics. To believe in essential racial superiority is, in my judgment, flatly wrong. But it is a position that can be truly, if wrongly, held. And, as this country painfully knows, it is a position which can and does generate truly conscientious objection to national policy. Nor are all men who oppose welfare legislation just selfish beings spewing out smokescreens of moral indignation behind which to clip their coupons. I believe that Social Security is a work of social justice. But some men truly believe it to be a corruption of human existence, and their opposition to it is a matter of conscience in the most complete sense.

War, though grievous, is not the only cause of grief. And there are not political choices which are moral choices and then political choices which are just—well, "political" choices. Political choosing —what should be done, here, now, for the human community—*is* moral choosing. The choice may be good or bad, enlightened or blind, on important or trivial matters, socially disruptive or inoffensive, based on intense conviction or clouded uncertainty—but a moral choice it is. Indeed, there is something peculiarly self-defeating in a *Commonweal* or *Christianity and Crisis* attempt to put matters of war in a separate category. For this tends to rob them of moral force when they turn their attention to other issues of equal significance, such as distribution of wealth internationally or civil rights domestically. If war is a uniquely moral matter, how do they claim to enunciate moral guidelines in other areas?

By portraying the case of war and military service as unique, the proponents of selective conscientious objection are able to dismiss easily one of the major criticisms: that to provide for selective conscientious objection would be to invite general disobedience to laws. Because in the advocates' eyes the case is unique, it would not constitute a precedent for others in society. As I have suggested above, the claim for uniqueness is a weak one, and the notion that it would not serve as a precedent is highly questionable also. Those who reject the possibility of selective conscientious objection serving as a precedent for other types of selective exemption could take a lesson in logic and straightforwardness from Gordon Zahn. Professor Zahn characteristically entitles an essay on selective conscientious objection "An Explosive Principle." After endorsing the principle completely, he proceeds to draw what to him is an obvious corollary: "conscientious objection to taxation," i.e., to that part of one's tax liability which would be devoted to the war from which one had already been exempted.[3]

Another major problem in the political thinking among selective conscientious objection advocates is this: they repeatedly indicate that the nation should adopt selective conscientious objection as a policy simply because, in the abstract, it is so clearly a good in itself. Men should follow their consciences—therefore, let there be selective conscientious objection; just-war theory teaches that some wars may be unjust—therefore . . . ; men should be men before being Americans—therefore . . . One may agree profoundly that conscience should be obeyed, that some wars (including ours) may be unjust, and that men should not succumb to national egomania. But none of these points is an integral basis for a national policy. Each of the points is a value which is abstractly good, but which is only a *part* of the total social equation that goes into policy. An abstract value does not constitute an imperative for society, even though it may for the individual. What are the other values which might be impacted upon by implementing this one? What would be the cost (in terms of values) if this provision were enacted? These are questions which political society legitimately asks before deciding on any policy's desirability.

Gordon Zahn illustrates this direct movement from one value to policy, in the essay mentioned above, when he says that anyone who is convinced the war in question is unjust ". . . must refuse active and direct participation in the injustice. If this nation is sincere in its democratic pretensions . . . the right of the individual to make such a refusal must be respected *and supported,* even by those who do not share that adverse moral judgment concerning the war." Grant that the individual should obey his conscience—but how does his decision serve as a directive to "this nation," which while properly concerned with the objector's conscience must necessarily have other concerns simultaneously?

In an editorial entitled "The Selective Conscientious Objector" the Jesuit journal, *America,* evidenced a similar confusion. "Every man is obliged to follow his conscience. Yet, under current legislation, there is no legal protection for the young man who, though not an absolute pacifist, is forbidden by his conscience to fight in the Vietnam war."[4] Again, the presumption is that the individual's need to follow his conscience is equivalent to a directive to society to enact a selective conscientious objection provision. The individual's need *should* clearly serve as advisory to society as it considers policy, but society cannot be *bound* by it. Following conscience is a recognized good in this society, indeed a good of a very high order, related to other values such as freedom of speech and religion. But even goods as basic as these are not translatable directly into policy. We weigh, balance, and judge them, we constrict and expand them in their action dimensions according to circumstances—and we do this because we understand that each of them is a *good among goods*.

Other attempts to demonstrate the policy validity of selective conscientious objection by straight deductions from an abstract premise are equally problematical. In another *Christianity and Crisis* editorial, one of America's most prominent theologians, Harvey G. Cox, stated: "Also, it is now time for our draft procedures to recognize the rights of conscientious objectors who, although they are not pacifists, nevertheless have moral objections [is there some other kind of objection?] to fighting in some particular war. As Roger L. Shinn has argued in these pages before, '. . . selective objection would be a natural extension of our present recognition of the rights of the [universal] conscientious objector. . . ."[5] It is a natural extension in the logic of conscience, I would agree, but it is certainly not a natural or automatic political extension. Selective and universal conscientious objection are alike, or naturally related, in one respect: they both involve negative moral judgments of a relatively intense kind. But in this they are like serious objections to any national policy.

They are quite unlike each other, however, in a crucial respect: the universal conscientious objector's opposition to war is not a critique of his own government in any specific respect, but is a general rejection of one proclivity of all nation-states. In that sense, it is almost a pre-political judgment. But the selective conscientious objector by definition is criticizing *his* government on *this* policy *now*—and whatever else this may be, let us understand that it is indeed a political judgment. One may advocate a policy of selective conscientious objection, as I do, but not simply on the grounds that it would be a logical and natural extension of present protections for the universal objector.

In looking over these points, the central problem is fairly

clear: many of the commentators have not reconciled themselves to a political framework for thinking and speaking on political matters. In his essay "As Freedom Is a Fantasy" [6] Everett E. Gendler states that the present requirement for conscientious objection—that the objection be to all wars—represents ". . . an absolutist demand which strikes me as a denial of full freedom of conscience to religious Jews, religious Catholics . . ." and others who believe ". . . that the essence of respect for their conscience is precisely a *sometime* nay-saying." "Denial of full freedom of conscience"—in terms of acting out the dictates of private conscience, that is in the nature of political existence. There are no "full freedoms" in this sense, and there are no abstract values the logic of which can be taken to infinity in the realm of action.

Another set of arguments for selective conscientious objection made by its supporters is drawn by analogy from two historical situations which are presumed to be instructive to the present circumstances of the United States. The first of these is the Nuremberg War Tribunals precedent, which many people see as logically demanding a selective objection law. Typical of such views are those expressed by Graham R. Hodges, Pastor, Emmanuel Congregational Church, Watertown, N.Y. As quoted in *Commonweal*, he said, "In the Nuremberg convictions we contend that the individual, not the state, is final arbiter of conscience. Now, by refusing selective conscientious objection we are saying to American youth, 'The state, not the individual, is the final arbiter of conscience.' "[7] And Michael Harrington has written that "It has even been asserted by the United States Government in the Nuremberg trials that, in certain cases, murderous orders are so obviously immoral as to create a universal obligation of disobedience with the force of positive law."[8]

Leaving aside the large and real question of whether Nuremberg ultimately made sense, what is its meaning, its instruction for the present problem in the United States? If Nuremberg taught that in some situations men should say no to their governments, this was hardly new or news. One can conceive of countless cases in which the individual should refuse to act, even if martyrdom is the alternative. Concretely, Dachau, for example, would seem clearly to be an instance where individuals should have refused to implement the extermination orders. But note: this is an instruction to the individual to disobey the most inhumane commands; it offers no clear lesson to a society on how it should treat the disobedient. Its lesson to society is a systematic one: do not let madness achieve institutional control.

Moreover, Dachau, and all of Nuremberg for that matter, is too easy and obvious a case to be very useful for present purposes. Its analogic relevance to current or likely future wars of the United States seems to me radically limited, despite the Bertrand Russell Tribunal's attempt to equate the two (which strikes me as somewhat comparable to the recent Soviet comparison of Israeli and Nazi policies). Individual American field commanders may order or countenance clearly heinous acts, but is overall policy likely to order or condone them? If that possibility seriously exists, the task of conscience is to permeate the policy structure *before* decision, for it will certainly be too late after. We need to note that most Germans so instructed did carry out the orders we so readily and rightly condemn; we need to note that Stalin had no difficulty recruiting thousands and thousands of OGPU and NKVD operatives to carry out similar policies of liquidation.

When one looks at Nuremberg in this manner, it is easier to see its meaning. That meaning surely was not simply to tell us that conscientious men should refuse orders in some situations. Nuremberg's central message, in my judgment, is one for society at large: there are no limits on the evil possible under a regime which has gathered total control as the modern totalitarian systems have been able to do. Nuremberg is, in short, a plea to maintain the strength of non-authoritarian systems.

Nuremberg is used to show that there *ought* to be a selective conscientious objector provision. But the British exemption from military service of selective objectors during World War II is offered as evidence of the *feasibility* of such a policy for the United States.

The *Commonweal* editorial to which I have referred typifies the use made of British experience: "The British, even during the bombardment by Nazi Germany, managed to exempt from military service those men who admitted they might fight in certain wars but could not morally fight in this one." [9] On its face, the British case proves nothing except that under some conditions *a* nation might be able to allow selective conscientious objection. Even preliminary analysis indicates that attempts to draw much more meaning from it in order to apply it to the United States would be rather dubious: of all wars in which a nation might try selective objection, World War II would certainly be among the easiest, especially for Britons. Of all the nations that might try it, Britain was probably ideal in terms of political homogeneity, lawfulness, martial tradition, and so forth. This suggests to me, at least, that Britain's policy is of limited relevance to present-day United States, engaged for the foreseeable future in conflicts intrinsically blurred, and with ample evidence of internal political incoherence far greater than Britain, circa 1940–41.

While an argument can be made for selective conscientious objection as a policy for the United States, it should be clear that the argument has been inadequately developed by most of its friends so far. They have wrongly portrayed the case as unique in the political order; they have distorted the relationship of politics and morality; they have failed to confront and accommodate satisfactorily the values which conflict with the value of conscience-following; and they have relied on quite doubtful analogies to support their case.

With friends like these, selective conscientious objection may well need no enemies. But it has some, nonetheless.

2. SCO—*Some Problems with Its Enemies*

Perhaps the most important direct attack upon the wisdom of selective conscientious objection was that contained in the *Report of the National Advisory Commission on Selective Service,* issued in February, 1967. The reasoning expressed in this statement is, in its own way, as lacking in a sense of the political as are most of the pro-selective exemption positions examined above.

The Commission considered two recommendations for selective conscientious objection provisions offered by minority elements within the Commission. The first of these is like most such proposals, in that its essence is simply to remove objection to "war in any form" from present requirements for conscientious objection, and let objector status be sought on the basis of conscientious objection to a particular war.

It argued that the traditions of this country recognize that the justice of war and its prosecution are always in question—may or may not be just; and that the individual citizen, in addition to policy-makers, is obliged to judge the justice of particular war. This citizen obviously may judge conscientiously contrary to his government and if he does he should not be forced to violate his conscience by bearing arms. For the rest, the selective objector would do as the universal objector presently does: convince a panel that his judgment was "truly held," and accept alternative service.

The second minority recommendation was significantly different. Those who sought exemption from combatant service should be quite automatically excused, but only after accepting a very rigorous option: service ". . . in a noncombatant military capacity, under conditions of hardship and even of hazard, and perhaps for a longer period (for example, 3 years)."[10]

These two recommendations for a selective conscientious provision are both seemingly policy conclusions drawn from explicit or implicit just-war theorizing: since wars or their conduct could be unjust, and since the responsible individual might conclude on this question differently from his government, therefore provide for that individual the conscience or integrity safeguard of selective conscientious objection status.

The Commission's majority rejected both proposals. As the Report states, "The majority of the Commission did not agree with either the premise or the conclusions of the minority."[11] The majority put forth five arguments against selective conscientious objection.

First, they state that the status of conscientious objector ". . . can properly be applied only to those who are opposed to all killing of human beings. . . ." Either the Commission here means that a person could not conscientiously object to killing in a particular situation (which seems analytically false, for most of us who can conceive acceptable grounds for killing would certainly object conscientiously to killing in general) or the statement is a simple tautology. In either case, it lacks persuasiveness. "It is one thing to deal in law with a person who believes he is responding to a moral imperative outside of himself when he opposes all killing. It is another to accord a special status to a person who believes there is a moral imperative which tells him he can kill under some circumstances and not kill under others."

Indeed, as I argued above, they are quite different things. But nowhere does the Commission explain what differences they are alluding to and, most importantly, nowhere do they tell us what in the difference constitutes a refutation of the validity of selective conscientious objection.

"Secondly, the majority holds that so-called selective pacifism is essentially a political question of support or nonsupport of a war and cannot be judged in terms of special moral imperatives. Political opposition to a particular war should be expressed through recognized democratic processes and should claim no special right of exemption from democratic decisions." This clearly illustrates the failure of the Commission to maintain analytic rigor and to sustain a political framework. There is a sense in which the Commission's first point here is correct: conscientious objection to a particular war *is* a political question in a way the universal pacifist's rejection of all war is not. The universal pacifist's critique, as we saw earlier, is not distinctively aimed at his own nation's policies, and his claim to exemption is not in that sense a political question. The selective objector just as clearly seeks his exemption because of a critical judgment he has made about his nation's policy, and this is a political question. But in no way does this lessen the fact that the stance of the selective conscientious objector is a position of moral force equal to that of the universal pacifist. In no way is the internal moral imperative any less for this man.

Thus the Commission falls prey to the standard confusion: that somewhere, somehow there are *political* postures, and then there are *moral* postures. The real truth illustrated here, of course, is that the political conviction (on anything of significance) is itself an ethical position, a judgment about human values. This confusion pervades the entire debate on selective conscientious objection, and is significantly responsible for the nonproductiveness of the argument thus far.

The second part of this second point is absolutely correct—but it yielded the wrong conclusion and illustrates once again the non-political context of the Commission's thinking. I submit that it is transparently true that opposition to a particular war should use regular democratic processes, and that such opposition can "claim no special right" to be exempted from political discussions. But this does not constitute an argument against selective conscientious objection either. It is an argument only against proclaiming that selective conscientious objection is a *right* deriving from some self-defining source. As such, it in no sense refutes the possible *policy desirability* of granting selective conscientious objector status on the political grounds of its being, on balance, a social good. The advocates, as we saw earlier, have tended to call their policy recommendation a right, and thereby have distorted the argument. Then, with something approaching absolute predictability, the opponents use the distortion as the basis of discussion and declare that there is no such right. Their declaration is correct; it is also politically irrelevant.

"Third, in the majority view, legal recognition of selective pacifism could open the doors to a general theory of selective disobedience to law, which could quickly tear down the fabric of government; the distinction is dim between a person conscientiously opposed to participation in a particular war and one conscientiously opposed to payment of a particular tax."

In the second half of this sentence the Commission displays a truer political insight than most selective objection supporters have demonstrated. As shown previously, there are simply no grounds for asserting that the only political matters which pose serious conscience problems are those involving war. *Laissez-*

faire proponents of yesterday and today did and do believe that government involvement in the economy is not only tactically questionable but morally wrong. To many people, miscegenation creates not just a burden for the offspring but is additionally a sin against God. If the test of conscience is that a belief be sincerely held—rather than objectively right—there is indeed a dim distinction between conscientious objection to a particular war and a similar objection to any other policy judged to be abominable.

But all of this, while true enough, is only an analytic, abstract point. If selective conscientious objector status were granted, and *if* a person who conscientiously objected to another policy— e.g., taxation for Social Security—stated that he, too, should be exempted from these taxes in view of the selective objection precedent, he would be on good logical grounds. And if in fact the selective objection provision were seized upon by large numbers as a precedent for selective exemption from many kinds of policy, as could in fact happen, *then* one could argue against selective objection that it threatened the "fabric of government" and was accordingly invalid because too dangerous.

But that is the point. In its third argument, the Commission used as a conclusive political consideration the totally abstract *possibility* that selective conscientious objection *might* lead to general disobedience to law. Indeed, it might. But if selective objection advocates are mistaken in dismissing out of hand the question of anarchic potential—and they are—the Commission is equally wrong in using this anarchic potential as if its dimensions were an established fact, a fact from which conclusions can readily be drawn. Both sides are confusing abstract logical possibilities with political reality. Analytically, all one can possibly say is that a selective objection provision is not essentially different from selective exemption to any class of policy to which people seriously object, and that therefore it *could* constitute an anarchic precedent. But there is no intrinsic reason for saying that it would constitute such a precedent, and the *would* is the politically relevant category.

As I will suggest, one can recognize the abstract potential of a selective conscientious objection law, and then do a variety of things to test the likely repercussions of its adoption. What *could* happen? This is relatively lacking in political significance. What *would* happen if it were adopted? This is a pertinent question.

"Fourth, the majority of the Commission was unable to see the morality of a proposition which would permit the selective pacifist to avoid combat service by performing noncombat service in support of a war which he had theoretically concluded to be unjust." If the alternative service offered the selective conscientious objector is entirely military and would thus in some sense be directly supporting the combatants, this point probably has considerable validity. But it excludes for no stated reason other forms of alternative service, with no direct military connections, which would recognize the moral depth of one's objection.

And the fifth argument suffers from the ills of the third and fourth. "Finally, the majority felt that a legal recognition of selective pacifism could be disruptive to the morale and effectiveness of the Armed Forces." *Could* be? Well, certainly it could be. But would it? The point is that it is possible to gather some data on what the repercussions would be. It is not necessary to rely simply on intuitive estimates of abstract possibilities. "A determination of the justness or unjustness of any war could only be made within the context of that war itself." If the individual had to determine the justice of the war, this ". . . could put a burden heretofore unknown on the man in uniform and even on the brink of combat, with results that could well be disastrous to him, to his unit and to the entire military tradition."

If you want to destroy a suggestion, reduce it to its absurd conclusion, even though you know not all ideas have to be pushed to their conclusions. This is essentially what the Commission has done here. One need only conjure up a vision of a Marine platoon, twenty yards from the enemy, the platoon sergeant shouting "Charge "—and five members of the platoon reply "Sorry, we conscientiously object to this war, or this phase of it, at this moment." But to see the impossibility of tolerating such a situation as this does not in itself show the impossibility of selective conscientious objection for persons at some moment prior to combat or, more likely, prior to entrance into the service.

Summarily, it may be said that the Report is something less than a model of prudential, political judgment. Its authors saw fit to issue a judgment on a political question without thinking seriously in a political sense. They did not, for example, remark on the multiplicity of values involved in the issue, they did not note the very real societal good that would be achieved if it were judged possible to grant selective conscientious objection status in this country. They did not articulate the value of preserving conscientious integrity *in action* if feasible. They saw clearly the primary possible social evil that could result from a selective objection provision. And because they saw this essentially in isolation—that is, without the competition of contrary values—they were able to move quite easily, because abstractly, to a rejection of selective conscientious objection.

They were able to move easily, but ineffectively, and unpolitically.

3. Toward Reconstruction and Resolution

The problem of selective conscientious objection should be seen for what it is: a recurrence in contemporary dress of the inherent political problem of man with limitless aspirations confronting the necessary reality of political limitation. When the current problem is viewed in categories as old as political man himself, one can begin to see the path to a tolerable resolution of the conflict also. This kind of difficulty triggers the beginning of the political process, not the end of society or any segment of it—unless the segment in the dispute so alienates itself or is so alienated from the rest of society as to become irreconcilable. This could happen if the segment were to become completely egoistic, refusing to perceive the other values present and refusing to see the necessity for society reigning through its political agencies. Or this could happen if those same agencies were to become completely frozen in their posture and failed to see also the values proposed by the disenchanted element. It is a central function of the democratic process to avoid this kind of apocalyptic development and find the way toward political reconciliation. The first and in a way most important step is to reconstruct the terms of the argument. What are the values placed in conflict by the selective conscientious objection proposal? What are the rewards and costs of alternative actions?

Wars may be just or unjust. In a democratic nation and in an age of personalism, not just the formal policy-makers but each citizen has the opportunity and obligation to judge matters of national policy, including war. But clearly, the individual may judge differently from the majority or the government. Further, there is, of course, no guarantee that the majority or the government will be right in its judgment. If the nation goes to war, should it provide military exemption for the citizen who conscientiously judges the war to be unjust?

The abstract good proposed is obvious enough: to relieve this person from the unhappy choices of serving a cause he considers immoral or going to jail for following his conscience. But the problem is this: in its essence, war is a national policy akin to other policies. It is in the character of political society that decisions (policies) made by the legitimate authorities are binding on all men in society. Indeed, looked at from one point of view, the state exists precisely to bring uniform social action to areas in which conflicting values are at issue. To war or not, and how to war if doing so—these are political questions which demand *an* answer, in the same sense that to have Medicare or not demands *an* answer, not an infinite series of individual responses which constitute no policy at all.

This, then, is the second and competing value which all but the anarchist will recognize: it is good to maintain the health, vitality, and effectiveness of the state itself, which brings order and stability to its society, and frees its members by so doing. If, therefore, a selective conscientious objector statute would in some clear and significant sense endanger this government's ability to do what governments exist to do, one would have to weigh the values in some either/or relationship—that to choose one would be practically to exclude the other. To choose a selective conscientious objection statute would be to abandon political stability; to opt for political stability would be *ipso facto* to exclude selective conscientious objection. If the only choices before us were those, the choice for me would be easy (as it was for the Commission): in no sense do I think the value of selective conscientious objection comparable to the value of political effectiveness and order.

But this is a Hobbesian view of the alternatives and, I think, a wrong one. Not every conflict need become Armageddon. Genuine either/or situations do arise, but in general it is an objective and a responsibility of democratic politics to avoid them, to find a hierarchy among competing values rather than reduce all to one, to harmonize multiple goods rather than mute one in the name of the other. And this objective is possible in the present case, it seems. We need to begin by asking if the good of a selective conscientious objector provision can in some manner be achieved without introducing an unacceptable probability of anarchistic repercussions.

That the individual is or should be conscience-bound is not a part of the dispute. What is a part of the dispute is the role political obligation *perceived as a human value* should play in forming that conscience. If an individual concludes that a policy of his nation—a war, let us say—is absolutely untenable; and if all the available means of changing it have been fruitless and give promise of fruitlessness in the future; then presumably he must withdraw from the existing situation, and accept the consequences of so doing. He ought only to be sure that a recognition of his obligations to society was part of his conscientious make-up in coming to his conclusion. He must understand also that his decision was *his*, and will not likely serve as an instruction to his society. Nor is there any reason why it should, if the government has been as careful in its judgmental process as he was.

But presumably this conscientious person, like Socrates, even if driven to the extreme of some form of political martyrdom over the disputed policy, would not seek to sunder his society simply on the grounds of *this* policy dispute. For what he took to be horrendous error on this policy would not in itself mean that the political system itself was erroneous. If, then, his complaint was confined to a particular policy, he presumably would do nothing to endanger the health of political society.

He would seek to do this momentous thing—sunder the political fabric—only if he concluded, again circumspectly, that the system itself had become irretrievably corrupted. And even then, if he were fully conscientious, he would judge the system's corruption only comparatively, only, in a word, with an eye to the alternative: he would ask, as Carl Lotus Becker once asked, "How *new* will the better world be?" Destroy a system if you wish—neither I nor anyone can say that this should never be done. But be honest enough to explain the future, and demonstrate its superiority.

And what of political society? What are its obligations to those within itself whose consciences are deeply troubled by policy? Clearly, it has no obligation to be tyrannized by the objecting voices in its midst. But it is obliged to strive for that same circumspection of judgment which the objector must seek. It is obliged to see that serious criticism of its political actions is a warning signal itself, a signal to re-examine, re-think, and re-evaluate the policy it has espoused.

And more important, even if that policy should be reaffirmed, it is obliged to seek avenues of accommodation and reconciliation with those disenchanted elements in its body. This it should do both because the political good ought to be insofar as possible a good for all, and because in its own interest it needs to understand the destructive potential of alienated parts of the political community.

The present problem is a case of this type. Multiple goods are in conflict and priorities must be established among them. But even if the priorities are set, and set as I see them, with society's prerogatives recognized as prime, the point is that priority does not mean exclusivity.

Even if there is no right to selective conscientious objection from military service (any more than there is a right to conscientious objection to civil rights laws), perhaps society should grant it as a privilege. Maybe selective conscientious objection *could* be adopted because it is possible to do it without establishing a serious precedent for general disobedience of the law. Maybe, under these circumstances, it *should* be done because it can be without great disruption and because, as we have seen, there is a real good to be achieved by such a policy.

To say these things is only to say that it is time to move the question of selective objection from its seeming apocalyptic dimensions into what in fact it is: a prudential question, posed to a democratic system, which asks that system to appraise the goods and bads and to decide, on balance, *whether it should be done.*

If the selective objection problem is approached in this way, significant progress can be made. First, regarding the value it would have for society, these points are fairly clear: a serious source of community disgruntlement would be removed; a segment of society would find the area of its self-definition expanded; society would provide itself and the world at large a new demonstration of American belief in self-specification.

But what of the costs, or counter-values? Clarity does not exist here, as the earlier critical sections have indicated. Some argue that there would be no real cost; but we have seen that within the notion of selective objection there is a potential for social disruption. Others assert that the cost is clearly too high—that selective objection would unleash and aggravate ever-present anarchistic tendencies within society. But we have seen that while this exists as a possibility, there is no compelling reason for believing that it would inevitably transpire. In short, on the matter of costs, there seems to be an analytic and argumentative impasse.

What needs to be done, accordingly, is to probe empirically these various possibilities, to better ascertain the likely costs in order to better judge the real costs of such a program. The tools exist: public opinion surveys have considerable utility for identifying future actions. Within the national pool of service-eligible men, surveys could seek answers to such broad questions as these: how many young men would be likely to apply for selective objector status; more important, what would be the impact (in terms of morale or esprit) of such a provision on those in service and those likely to serve in the future? With this kind of data available, one could judge more rationally whether selective objection would have a seriously debilitating impact on the services, and whether it would impair the capacity of the services to perform their functions.

Using a national sample representative of all adolescent and adult citizens, surveys could then turn to another and perhaps more important series of questions: what would be the effect of selective objection to military service on people with other, nonmilitary conscientious complaints against national policy? To what extent, if any, would such a provision constitute a precedent-at-large for disobedience to law? How many Negroes, for example, would respond to it in this way? Or how many Southerners would feel justified by it in trying to exempt themselves from the strictures of civil rights legislation?

These are the kinds of questions one needs to answer in order to judge with reasonable intelligence the costs of the selective conscientious objection proposal. And it is not necessary to rely simply on intuitive judgment. The devices for obtaining relatively hard knowledge exist, and we have some obligation to use them.

My own intuitive judgment would be that selective objection could be adopted by this nation without serious social disruption, and therefore, given the values which can be obtained by it, I would urge that such a provision be enacted. But first there should be the kind of attitude surveys suggested here. If these bear out the presumption that expected repercussions would be tolerable, then appropriate legislation should be adopted. If the point is to influence Congressional and Administration thinking before the next review of draft legislation, then perhaps private groups and foundations should undertake the opinion surveying suggested above.

What have I suggested? Fundamentally, that the question of selective conscientious objection has become a political problem: should the United States adopt such a practice? Further, that, like any political question, no rational answer for this one exists *a priori*, despite the fact that most commentators on both sides have acted as if the matter were self-evident.

In the absence of a self-evident (one-value) resolution, it is necessary to identify and assess the several values which are in conflict, and to establish priorities among them. In the case at hand the values are clear enough, and for me at least the priorities are clear also. But it is not enough to identify the prime value and simply snuff out the secondary one. It is necessary to try to maintain them both, and to gauge the intensity of their conflict. In this case it seems likely that the secondary value can be supported without seriously endangering the higher one. If this be the case, the prudent polity will do so, even at some price of social turbulence.

The foregoing points are essentially analytic: they can be seen simply through reflection on the character of the problem in the context of democratic politics. Before moving to adoption of the proposal, however, the prudent polity will inform itself empirically regarding likely repercussions.

Such a formula is a political response to a real problem confronting society. Its logic is not the logic of spinning off the abstract implications of a single value. Rather its logic is the logic of politics, in which several values must be interwoven and harmonized even while recognizing and articulating the fact that not all values are of equal importance. It presupposes some considerable wisdom on all sides: wisdom in the polity inclining it to accommodate its estranged elements; and wisdom on the part of the estranged inclining them to see the value of political order (the very cradle of justice *and* freedom) and its corollary of political obligation. It is easier, I think, for society to harden and suppress; just as it may be easier for the disenchanted to go the distance to complete alienation and irreconcilability. But it would not be wiser, nor more virtuous.

NOTES

[1] *Christianity and Crisis*, April 3, 1967, p. 63.
[2] "The Draft and Conscience," *Commonweal*, April 21, 1967, p. 140.
[3] *worldview*, March, 1967, p. 6.
[4] *America*, July 22, 1967, p. 73.
[5] *Christianity and Crisis*, April 17, 1967, pp. 73–74.
[6] *worldview*, February, 1967, pp. 7–8.
[7] *Commonweal*, June 2, 1967, p. 306.
[8] "Moral Objection and Political Opposition," *worldview*, March, 1967, p. 6.
[9] *Commonweal*, April 21, 1967, p. 140.
[10] *Report of the National Advisory Commission on Selective Service* (Washington: United States Government Printing Office, 1967), p. 50.
[11] *Idem*.

Politics, Morality, and Selective Dissent

MICHAEL HARRINGTON

THE war in Vietnam has given rise to more agonies of conscience than any conflict in which America has participated during this century.

The reason for this moral anguish is not hard to find. In the First and Second World Wars and in the Korean War, the overwhelming majority of the American people believed that their country was acting in self-defense against German, Japanese, or North Korean aggression and was therefore justified in the use of violence. There was a tiny minority of pacifists who refused service. In World War I, some of them were political opponents of American participation, but in World War II most maintained their position on the basis of a transcendental commitment to abjure the use of force under all circumstances.

With the tragic intervention in Vietnam, however, popular opposition against the war became widespread. It went far beyond the ranks of the religious pacifists and was widely prevalent among the most intelligent and idealistic of the young. (What empirical data we have on the campus activists of the Sixties indicates such a correlation between scholarly attainment and political concern.) At this writing, it has spread to the majority of the best students on the finest campuses.

These deeply held, but un-pacifist, attitudes toward the Vietnam war could not be contained within the traditional categories which the society had established for conscientious objection. In some cases—the simplest to deal with—this was a legal matter, for the Federal statute permitted exemption from military service only to those conscientious objectors who professed a belief in a "Supreme Being." In other, and more complex, instances, students and intellectuals asserted an obligation, under the doctrine proclaimed by the United States in the Nuremberg trials, to refuse any form of support to the military effort, such as paying taxes. Finally, some asserted a right to disrupt the prosecution of the war through non-violent civil disobedience.

These various issues are obviously related to one another, yet it is extremely important to understand the different questions which they pose and to treat each in its turn. What is at stake in all of them is a definition of the relationship between politics and morality in that extreme situation when the state proclaims its right to take life and orders the citizen to execute, or cooperate with, its command. Hopefully, this larger point will become clarified in the course of analyzing the specifics of protest.

My own analysis is based on the following premises: First, I reject the proposition that a society's decision to employ violence against its alleged enemies cannot be questioned. That is the conclusion of some absolute forms of judicial pragmatism; it is the faith of the super-patriots. In this context, I take it as a gain for the entire nation that the young have insisted upon the necessity of making a conscientious decision about the political use of violence. As the late John Courtney Murray, S.J., put it, "the student community is to be praised for having raised a profound moral issue that has been too long disregarded in American life."

But, secondly, I also oppose the notion that one can easily violate the law in a democratic society. I believe that democracy is an excruciatingly imperfect method of political organization— and the very best there is. In its present form, where legal equality before the law is systematically contradicted by economic and social inequality, the democratic structure must be radically transformed. In my opinion the best way to do that is through democracy itself, and this requires that the losers abide by the political victories of the winners. If the democratic structure collapses under the strain of its tensions, then politics will take to the street, but probably not in non-violent form. And from the point of view of human freedom, a tragedy will have occurred. And, I also believe that, in Reinhold Niebuhr's terms, it is "blasphemous" when an individual casually pretends to be the voice of God, and thereby places himself above his fellow citizens.

In short, I hold that, even in a manifestly inadequate democracy, the individual is normally obliged to obey the laws but may, under extreme and limited circumstances, be required to break them. In what follows I propose to apply this dialectical principle to the very difficult task of defining some important relationships of politics and morality as they have been posed by the horrible war in Vietnam.

1

The present Selective Service statute should be both reinterpreted and revised in order to provide atheist and agnostic objectors with the same legal status as members of peace churches and to permit exemption on the basis of moral opposition to a particular war. This would grant Federal protection to peace activists, the bases of whose actions are now wrongly considered to be only political and who are therefore excluded from the exemptions provided by the present law.

When the courts and the Selective Service system originally interpreted the present statute, they did so in a literalist, undemocratic, and anti-libertarian fashion. Congress' language demanded (wrongly, I believe) that the objector base his claim on belief in a Supreme Being. The government proceeded to insist upon a narrow, textbook definition of that Being and, in effect, restricted the protections of the law to members of the historic peace churches. Atheists and agnostics whose positions were rooted in deeply held convictions about the nature and destiny of man were sent to prison.

This interpretation of the law was, I believe, unconstitutional and, even though the courts have thus far rejected this assertion, I hope they will eventually come to recognize it. Simply put, the First Amendment should apply to religion in a completely non-sectarian way. Definitions of the religious spirit by thinkers like William James and Paul Tillich have already made a persuasive case for extending the concept to any transcendent commitment, earthly as well as heavenly, and this should be the rule of the courts. The effective establishment of theistic religion which has prevailed for more than two decades should be ended as soon as possible.

In recent years there have been some signs that the judiciary is moving in this direction. In the Seeger case, an agnostic objector had been denied even a hearing on the grounds that his lack of religious affiliation *a priori* excluded him from any consideration under the law. The Supreme Court responded favorably to a due process appeal but not to the substantive issue of whether the "Supreme Being" proviso was constitutional. It held that the question of belief in a Supreme Being was complex and that it was therefore wrong to assume without a hearing that an "agnostic" could not possibly qualify. The local board then gave Seeger an exemption.

The Court's strategy in *Seeger* was to work within the limits of the present statute and to duck the more basic issue of the constitutionality of the "Supreme Being" test. Given the hallowed American tradition of repealing bad laws by intelligent judicial re-interpretations of them, the very phrase, Supreme Being, could eventually be taken as symbolic Congressional language for any deeply held, ultimate principle, and atheists would thus be qualified as objectors under the present rules. It would, of course, be infinitely preferable to have a clear declaration on the unconstitutionality of the current language. But, in any case, it is imperative that the society accept the claims to conscientious objection of agnostics and atheists as well as of Quakers and Mennonites.

But such a reform of the law does not resolve the issue of politics and morality. It is only a first step. For it does not deal with the citizen who, on formal religious or philosophical grounds, refuses to serve because he is against a particular war. Here, I would argue that anyone who can show that he is opposed to all wars *or all wars of a certain type* should be granted objector status.

In making this last point, I would distinguish between moral objection to war, or a war, and political objection to a war. The moral objector invokes a principle which requires him not to kill at all, or only to kill when certain conditions of a "just war" are present. In the course of coming to his decision, he may well take political considerations into account, i.e., a major Christian tradition requires that the war itself be "just," and a judgment on this criterion will inevitably intermingle politics and morality. But even then, the obligation being stated is a transcendental one in the sense that it requires the objector to refuse combat in any and all situations which fail to meet his criteria. It is not that he is simply politically opposed to the war, but that he maintains a moral position in which such political opposition makes it conscientiously impossible for him to be a participant in that war.

Such an attitude can be distinguished from one of political opposition pure and simple. Here I would take the figure of Lenin as an illustration of my point. Lenin was against Russia's case in World War I, heart and soul—he was a "revolutionary defeatist." Yet he did not believe that his political stance required him to refuse military service. Exactly the opposite. Since he believed that the only way to end this war, and war itself, was by the revolutionary overthrow of the existing order, he urged his followers to go into the army precisely because they were anti-war. For, he argued with some prescience, it was in the army that the upheaval would begin.

A relatively small minority of the anti-war young in America today adhere to this Leninist position. I cite this case, not because it is at all typical, but rather to show that political opposition to a war, and moral objection to serving in it, are not the same thing.

But most young political opponents of the war today are, I believe, in a heart-rending dilemma. On the one hand, they are horrified (rightly I would say) by this particularly ugly, futile combat in Vietnam; on the other hand, they are not absolute pacifists and yet they do not have the Leninist hope that being drafted is a worthwhile step toward revolution. They have the worst of all possible worlds.

Under these circumstances, the Selective Service law and administrative practices should be changed so as to allow for principled moral objection to a specific war. Here again, as in the case of atheists and agnostics, it would be possible to sneak into a decent position by juggling with the current phraseology. For that matter, this writer was granted full objector status by a St. Louis draft board in 1951 after clearly enunciating a "just war" position. But it would be much better if American society made an honest, candid decision to broaden the scope of its respect for conscience. For that is what is at issue: whether this nation is going to insist that an entire category of individuals should be under legal compulsion to violate the dictates of their own conscience.

The National Advisory Commission on Selective Service took up this question and, by a majority vote, decided to urge that objector status be reserved to absolute pacifists. I think they were wrong.

John Courtney Murray, S.J., was a supporter of the American presence in Vietnam—and an advocate of the rights of "selective conscientious objection" in that war. As he said about the "just war" position: "It is not exclusively Roman Catholic; in certain forms of its presentation, it is not even Christian. It emerges in the minds of all men of reason and good will when they face two inevitable questions. First, what are the norms that govern recourse to the violence of war? Second, what are the norms that govern the measure of violence to be used in war? In other words, when is war rightful, and what is rightful in war? One may indeed refuse the questions, but this is a form of moral abdication, which would likewise be fatal to civilization."

The majority of the National Advisory Commission voted against Murray's lucid presentation. "It is one thing," they said, "to deal in law with a person who believes he is responding to a moral imperative outside of himself when he opposes all killing. It is another to accord a special status to a person who believes there is a moral imperative which tells him he can kill under some circumstances and not kill under others." The law, in other words, will provide exemption for a conscience formed in the

Quaker tradition but not for one educated to traditional Catholic norms. And the Commission apparently believed that a simple statement of the distinction between the two positions was one justification for it. Yet in both cases even the Commission's language admits that the individuals are responding to "moral imperatives." Why honor the one and send the youth obedient to the other to jail?

But there are other reasons asserted beyond this *ipse dixit*. "Moreover," they continue, "the question of 'classical Christian doctrine' on the subject of just and unjust wars is one which would be interpreted in different ways by different Christian denominations and therefore not a matter upon which the Commission could pass judgment." But the Commission is not being asked to pass this judgment on the various advocates of the "just war" position any more than it has to choose between, let us say, Protestant and Jewish versions of absolute pacifism. It is being asked to suggest a public policy toward those who, for whatever serious and deeply held reason, feel themselves morally compelled to refuse service. Indeed, it is precisely the Commission's negative attitude toward selective objection which takes it into the area of making theological judgments. It is in favor of the selective protection of conscience and it uses religious criteria to determine which conscience shall be respected and which shall be outraged.

The Commission also says that "selective pacifism is essentially a political question." In view of the fact that it had held, in the previous paragraph, that this position is taken on the basis of a "moral imperative," I do not take this point very seriously.

Indeed, the one substantive rationale for the majority decision which I found—and with which I disagree—is this: ". . . legal recognition of selective pacifism could open the doors to a general theory of selective disobedience to law, which could quickly tear down the fabric of government; the distinction is dim between a person conscientiously opposed to participation in a particular war and one conscientiously opposed to payment of a particular tax." I will postpone commentary on the second part of this objection (tax refusal and conscientious objection) until I have considered the first point about tearing down the fabric of government.

In societies where the political majority supports a war—and since this issue is raised within the framework of democratic principle, we can base our discussion on that presumption—the number of conscientious objectors will, I am convinced, be small. The basis of this opinion is sociological, not ethical. It merely states the fact that, under non-revolutionary conditions of a majority democratic consensus, the emotions of patriotism and conformity are alas usually stronger than those of individual defiance on the basis of morality.

To be sure, there can be mass resistance to war under certain circumstances. I am told that a significant number of French Canadians avoided service out of nationalist convictions during World War II and effectively kept their government from sending draftees overseas. In World War I, there were well-known cases of desertion and revolt by the enlisted ranks in the Russian, German, and French armies. The Russian and German examples show what is possible in a pre-revolutionary situation; the example of the French, whose uprising was brutally suppressed, what can happen under conditions of military defeat, though only regional and temporary.

Note that these rents in the "fabric of government" were not made because the Tsar, the Kaiser, or the French President recognized a principle of selective objection but because those societies were undergoing great upheavals in which "normal" obedience to law no longer made sense to great masses of people. Were such social conditions to occur in the United States, there would be similar disaffections from the society, no matter what the Selective Service law. However, the discussion is not really over how to maintain stability during revolutionary times but as to what kind of protections a stable democratic country should afford to a conscientious minority. And all the evidence indicates that such minorities will, in the absence of great transformations, be quite small.

Indeed, if there is any real danger of injuring the fabric of government in this Vietnam war period, it comes from *not* recognizing the rights of selective objection. For it is precisely this policy which has caused so much anguish of conscience, made youthful opposition more and more frenzied, and even driven some to voluntary exile in Canada. No political situation in my memory has occasioned so much despairing discontent with the society, and a sophisticated pragmatism should have impelled the National Advisory Commission to provide some honorable alternative for young people who are now required to choose between jail and self-betrayal.

But my own advocacy of selective objection is not based on such pragmatism. I am convinced that, as Father Murray said, there is a principled "just war" position involving transcendental moral obligations which can impose itself upon the conscience of religious, agnostic, and atheistic citizens. I believe that a democratic society should not require its citizens to violate their deeply held principles. And I am convinced that it would be a relatively simple administrative problem to distinguish the committed from the frivolous, the evaders, and so on.

There is in all this, let it be freely admitted, more of a political dimension than is found in absolute, unconditional pacifism. Yet the basic justification for the policy advocated here is the respect that a democratic society owes to the moral convictions of its members.

In denying, or severely hedging that respect, the government has been led to follow a dangerously anti-libertarian logic. In accusing Dr. Spock, the Reverend Coffin, Mitchell Goodman, Michael Ferber and Marcus Raskin, and convicting the first four, the Justice Department revived two of the most pernicious doctrines of the McCarthy era—the equation of advocacy, even of allegedly unlawful deeds, with the commission of the deed itself; and the use of a vague concept of "conspiracy" to implicate an entire group—and thus undermined the Anglo-American legal insistence upon the individuality of crime and criminal guilt. The defendants in that case have various attitudes on the issues treated here, but every one of them certainly deserves the support of any partisan of democracy, and not just of those of us who oppose the war in Vietnam.

2

Legal reform to grant objector status to atheists and agnostics and to permit selective objection on a moral basis can easily be justified within the present legal framework of the United States. But the question of tax refusal, on grounds that the government is engaged in an immoral exercise and payment would implicate the citizen in this guilt, is something else again. For there are indeed those who have accepted the logic of the National Advisory Commission on Selective Service and, with radical intent, defended a "general theory of selective disobedience to law." This extends the primacy of the individual moral judgment into political spheres where it has not been recognized in the past. So in terms of the general theme of this essay it is a case eminently worth examining in some detail.

First of all, it is important to distinguish between the compulsion directed against a soldier, or even a protestor enjoined from marching, and that exercised against a taxpayer.

The soldier is being drafted into a situation in which his support of what he regards as an immoral cause will be personal and immediate. He can be ordered to kill or to facilitate killing; and he may himself be executed if he refuses, particularly at the front line. He is therefore being told to give the utmost cooperation to an action which he regards as profoundly wrong. If he does not make his stand before induction, then the price of obeying his conscience, which now includes the possibility of his own death, has risen so high that only the most heroic person will, or can be expected to, accept martyrdom.

A less dramatic, but somewhat analogous, case occurs when a march is enjoined by a court. It may well be, as Martin Luther King, Jr., obviously believed in Birmingham in 1963, that to obey such an order would constitute an irreparable loss to the movement. The precise moment for action may come only once, and a retreat would mean that the group is not simply being asked to postpone a demonstration but to sacrifice its cause. This element of immediacy is made all the more acute when there is a very real possibility that higher courts will reverse the decision of the lower tribunals, or that a Federal appeal will overturn a state decision. For all these reasons, deliberate disobedience of the law may become necessary even though those involved are working within the democratic process.

A similar situation arises when the law is being used as a hypocritical instrument of injustice. The use of "trespass" statutes to enforce a *de facto* segregation is a case in point. In the sit-in decisions, the Supreme Court of the United States effectively admitted that normal democratic process had so broken down in the South—or rather, had become an instrument of anti-democratic tyranny—that Negro youth were justified in anticipating a higher Federal legality by disobeying a local ordinance. But this retrospective justification of the non-violent campaign in the lunch rooms and department stores depended partly on the fact that the youth had *correctly* anticipated the Federal law.

Now all of these cases are, I submit, much more immediate than the act of paying taxes. But even more to the point, the taxpayer who believes the war to be immoral has a clear alternative open to him, one that he can pursue without heroic courage and through the exercise of normal democratic rights. In this he differs from the soldier, marcher, or sit-in activist. He can organize politically and change the government which administers the taxes. During the time that he is involved in this campaign he will not be commanded to do anything as decisive as taking another life; he will not be, through paying taxes, subjected to irreparable harm like the protest marcher; he will not be victimized by a mockery of the democratic process like the sit-in student of 1960.

Secondly, the rationale for tax refusal usually rests upon the old economics.

Here is how Gordon Zahn puts the case: ". . . we must now introduce a new principle of 'conscientious objection to taxation' whereby the individual whose refusal to kill would be respected must now also be permitted to refuse to subsidize and underwrite the killing. Along with this would have to go some arrangement for 'alternate payments' to support governmental activities which do not so violate the conscience of the individual." (*worldview*, March, 1967.)

In the pre-Keynesian days, governments did indeed use tax bills as a means of raising revenues for specific purposes. But even then, there was more than a little deception involved: The bonds which Americans purchased to "buy" tanks, planes, hospital supplies, etc., in World War II were primarily useful in controlling inflation. The military goods would have been produced whether the people purchased the bonds or not. Now, however, Washington has become more frank about its general tax strategy, though it still resorts to patriotic appeals and old-fashioned economics when that is politically convenient (as it has become for Mr. Johnson on the Vietnam question).

The size of the Federal budget is now dictated by the general state of the Gross National Product. If the economy has excess capacity, Washington increases its spending in one way or another (through direct public investment, through a tax cut, etc.); if it is operating at full, or over full, capacity, in theory the government is supposed to hold down demand either through cuts in spending (the favorite solution of the conservatives) or through an increase in taxes.

In this context, President Johnson's 1967 proposal of a tax increase was, despite his politically motivated statements to the contrary, only tangentially related to the war in Vietnam and certainly not "necessary" to the prosecution of that conflict. If there is one certainty in American politics it is that Congress, in a united front of hawks and doves, will send sufficient military supplies to Americans in a shooting war. The real purpose of the tax increase was to act as a damper on the inflationary trends which the Administration economists have discerned.

Now it may rightly be said that these inflationary tendencies were given a considerable impetus by the war in Vietnam—but so was the employment of Negroes, and one would not oppose that. More to the point, if the Congress had refused the tax increase, presumably to the cheers of at least some in the peace movement, the result would not have been to bring the end of the war in Vietnam any closer but to place the main burden of that conflict upon the black and white poor.

For in the political realities of 1967, the real debate over the tax increase was a liberal-conservative antagonism over which groups should be required to sacrifice most in the fight against inflation. The Right proposed to deal with the problem through cut-backs in social welfare spending, the Left through the utilization of a highly imperfect tax instrument which, for all of its faults, is the most progressive means of fighting inflation the society possesses. Should the anti-war movement, having not yet succeeded in winning a political majority to put an end to the killing, adopt a tactic whose actual effect would be to tax the ghettos and the rural slums?

What is involved here is one more manifestation of the increasing complexity of government. For under the new economics, a consistent "conscientious objector to taxation" would have had to oppose the tax *cut* in 1963–64, for that policy made it more possible for the government to spark the economy and thus increase the tax base to raise the actual revenues which it received and devoted, in part, to Vietnam. Under those circumstances would the principled pacifist have insisted upon paying his tax? For, according to our present economic logic, that would have been the only way to make it more difficult for the government to carry on its immoral war.

Most of the people who have been attracted to the notion of tax refusal during the course of the Vietnam war would regard all the foregoing as mere sophistry. Their point of departure is not rational or political, but it is substantial and understandable. Tax paying is one of the few "personal" relationships which the middle-class citizen has with the government. Rightly outraged by a horrible war, many people seek desperately for some way that the individual can communicate his distress to the politicians and the IBM machines. And tax refusal is one of the few means at hand. I sympathize profoundly with those who have taken this position—but I cannot agree with them, and not simply for reasons of economic theory.

One should be careful, particularly in a democratic society, of proclaiming too many "Nuremberg" obligations. The court of the victors which sat in judgment of the Nazis asserted a natural-law duty of resistance, and even heroic resistance, to clearly immoral military orders. But, and this is a very important point, the country at issue was Nazi Germany, i.e., a fascist dictatorship. Under such circumstances, I would certainly affirm the right of all citizens to civil disobedience and, for that matter, to the violent overthrow of their own government; and the duty of the citizen to refuse monstrous commands, even if that meant sacrificing life itself.

But the United States of the Sixties is hardly Nazi Germany; the taxpayer is not really being ordered to do anything more specific than to help in maintaining a boom; and there exist alternate methods of bringing the war to an end. Furthermore, once that war in Vietnam is over I could see Gordon Zahn's principle of "conscientious objection to taxation" put to the most reactionary use. With peace it will be necessary to provide a substitute for more than $30 billion a year in Federal spending. It is possible that at least some of this money will be channeled into the economy through direct social investments (if the reactionaries prevail, it will come in the form of a tax cut maximizing individual, rather than social, consumption and commercial, rather than collective, priorities). The committed racists of the South could, under a conscientious objector clause, refuse to pay their taxes, or that portion of them which would go to the abolition of poverty. And as a matter of principle, Zahn would have to recognize their right to express themselves in this way. In the doing, he might unwittingly help to create a fine instrument for the states' righters.

Finally, the central problem is political. The only way one can affect the purposes which the economy and the tax system serve is to gain control of the government. Tax refusal may well be personally therapeutic, morally exhilarating, but it does not pass the supreme test, for it contributes little or nothing to ending the immoral war in Vietnam. If an individual feels conscientiously compelled to take this course, I would defend all of his civil liberties, but I cannot agree that he has either enunciated a binding obligation or formulated an effective tactic for bringing the killing to an end.

3

It is a paradox that, in the fall of 1967, as public opinion polls suggested that a majority of the American people were coming to oppose the war in Vietnam, a minority of protestors turned to desperate, anti-political tactics. At the precise moment when the possibility of winning a majority through democratic action became quite real, these activists chose to move outside of the democratic framework. Their primary rationale was that the immorality of the government's action was so patent and urgent that the individual was obliged to take direct action to prevent Washington from carrying out its policy. So in this case—the most extreme one to be discussed here—a transcendent ethical duty is assumed to justify, not simply opting out of the normal political process through tax refusal, but a form of non-violent sabotage.

As *The New Republic* described this mood in a sympathetic account of a demonstration in October, 1967, aimed at closing the induction center at Oakland, California: ". . . *Stop the Draft Week* represented the transition from 'dissent to resistance.' It was a recognition not only of a previous failure to change the Johnson Administration's war policy—that was to be expected—but a deeper recognition of a loss of momentum and a failure of nerve in the face of an exhaustion of tactical possibilities. The new technique is political disruption, an attempt to 'stop the war machine,' entailing a renunciation of violence while still shrinking from a positive recommendation of violence."

In dealing with this strategy and the philosophy which justifies it, one is not confronting any of the traditional cases for pacifist civil disobedience. In Oakland during that week, the first protest was made according to accepted non-violent rules. Joan Baez and a group of people appeared at the induction headquarters, made no attempt to resist arrest, and went peaceably with the police when they were taken into custody. *They were disobeying the law as a witness to the outrage of their conscience but they were not interfering with those who felt otherwise.*

This form of civil disobedience does not disrupt the democratic process. It allows protestors to manifest the intensity of their convictions and in this way to reach out to the consciences of their fellow citizens. It means that the individual is ready and willing to pay the legal price for making his point. (This writer was twice arrested in the course of such demonstrations and is thus obviously sympathetic to the tactic.)

But it is an entirely different matter when it is claimed that the alleged immorality of a government allows the citizen of an imperfect, but still functioning, democratic society to obstruct that government in carrying out its policies and to disrupt the activities of those who agree with that government. This is the right which was being claimed in the fall of 1967. It is not only a rationale for an attack upon civil liberties but could open up an era of intolerance which will victimize the protestors more than those protested against.

Part of the philosophical underpinnings of this position was revealed at a debate at Oberlin College. Students had trapped a Navy recruiter in a car for four hours until police broke them up with tear gas and water hoses. At a discussion of the incident, as reported in *The New York Times*, one participant said that there was no "moral right" to recruit people to fight in an immoral war. Although put forth by a member of the New Left generation this was, of course, a reiteration of the classic, conservative Catholic argument for refusing civil liberties to non-Catholic faiths. "Error has no right," it was said, and is still said in Franco Spain. What the conservative Catholics and the Oberlin student fail to understand is that, although there is indeed no "moral right" for one who is aware of the immorality of a war to recruit fighters for it, there is a *civil* right for a Navy recruiter to state his point of view freely even if those more ethically sensitive than he know that he is objectively acting in an immoral cause. Error has, in short, civil rights, and particularly when it is honest, sincere error. (It also has them when it is insincere, but I am quite willing to grant the *bona fides* of Navy recruiters.)

Consider, for instance, this statement of Jerry Rubin, one of the organizers of the October, 1967, demonstration at the Pentagon. In talking about the coming Democratic Party convention, Rubin was quoted by *Newsweek* as saying, "Can't you see it—100,000 hippies all around the hall, smoking pot, faking delegates' cards, tossing smoke bombs." The intention of such words is clear enough. It is not to mount a protest, as was done at the Democratic Party conventions of 1960 and 1964 by the civil rights movement, but to disrupt a public meeting. (The middle-class, *épater la bourgeoisie* sources of this fantasy are revealed by the fact that "smoking pot" is put on a par with "tossing smoke bombs.")

The theoretical and practical dangers of this attitude are enormous. In the name of morality, a sort of pacifist, and not so pacifist, *putschism* is justified. And indeed at the Students for a Democratic Society anti-war march in Washington in 1965, Staughton Lynd specifically argued for the desirability of a nonviolent *coup d'état* in which the marchers would, on their own nomination, represent the supposedly voiceless majority of a democratic society and take over the buildings of government. The poetic imagery which Lynd had used at that time was to inspire at least a wing of the protestors when some tried to rush the Pentagon in October, 1967.

But this is not simply a repudiation of fundamental, and precious, democratic principles contained in the Bill of Rights. It is also an invitation to the American reactionaries to answer in kind. And in response to this challenge, former governor George Wallace of Alabama did indeed propose taking the "bearded professors who tell students they are for victory for the Vietcong" and putting them in jail. Thus, as so often happens, the violation of civil liberties in a "just" cause provokes the "unjust" to violate even more civil liberties.

In a letter to *The New York Times* (October 27, 1967), Staughton Lynd, one of the leaders of the movement, defended this new tactic, in a frank, honest, and inadequate attempt to deal with the problem. In terms of the movement, his arguments are significant and worth considering at some length.

First of all, Lynd candidly admits the criticisms of his position. "Perhaps the commonest objection," he writes, "is this one:

Who gave a handful of peaceniks the authority to shut down the United States Government or any part thereof?" And secondly, he recognizes this issue: "When left-wing demonstrators impatiently abandon traditional political methods, do they not create precedents for right-wing direct actionists who, given the present temper of the country, would prove far stronger in any foreseeable confrontation?"

Lynd responded by defending "non-violent obstructive tactics" as a "form of democratic dialogue." He asserts that he would have no objection if the hawks or segregationists would practice them. This attitude shows, I think, a failure to distinguish between those forms of civil disobedience which deny the civil liberties of others and those which make a witness, whether in political terms or not. The latter case can be contained within the democratic framework; the former cannot. For it is precisely the point of the "democratic dialogue" that its rules and laws are a means of protecting the physical and spiritual integrity of the citizen. It is understood in this philosophy that when issues are to be settled in the street—even if the initial intentions are non-violent—passions and *force majeure* take over. That this *force majeure* may be non-violent does not change the essential situation, for it embodies an extra-legal compulsion.

Significantly, Lynd does not really answer his own question about the creation of "precedents for right-wing direct actionists who, given the present temper of the country, would prove far stronger in any foreseeable confrontation." He is undisturbed by this possibility so long as the Rightists will stick to some pacifist rules. That is, to put it mildly, a hopelessly optimistic assumption. They will crack heads and those attacked will fight back.

Secondly, Lynd asserts that "We who burn draft cards, refuse induction and block doorways believe that we act in response to an executive branch which is out of control." Now three different acts are lumped together in this sentence. Refusing induction may well be an obligation imposed upon an individual by a conscience, or a "witness" form of political protest; burning a draft card can be a form of opposition to a foolish, anti-libertarian law and also an anti-war witness; but neither of these acts involves obstructing the rights of the government or of other citizens. And that is not what is at issue here. But can doorways be blocked by a minority in order to dictate to the political process what its majority decisions must be? That is the central question.

For if the executive branch is indeed "out of control," there are many ways of correcting this situation through democratic process. As of the middle of 1968, the Senate of the United States had not repealed the Tonkin Bay Resolution which the President uses as his legal mandate for the war in Vietnam. But, as Mr. Johnson himself taunted the lawmakers, the Senate could move to reconsider at any time. I would certainly agree with Staughton Lynd that it is a tragedy that they have not done so. But the response to this fact should be to organize a movement to force them to do so *through the democratic process.*

It is significant that one of the precedents which Lynd cites to justify his position is that of the European resistance movements of World War II. He thus confuses a conquered continent under fascist military rule where the only possible form of opposition was armed struggle and sabotage with a democratic society in which civil liberties and the rights of political opposition remain quite intact. Yet it seems obvious to me that the right of the European *resistant* is as clear as the wrong of the American disrupter of democracy.

In an aside, I referred earlier to the middle-class mood of much of this protest. I would deepen the point. There is, in this assertion of the duty of a righteous minority to repeal the (to me wrong) decisions of the majority, an element of elitism and snobbery. These protestors show little faith in a democratic people even though the number of citizens opposed to the war was increasing dramatically throughout 1967. At that very moment when the political strategy was becoming more practical, these young people turned their backs upon it. One reason is that they were rightfully horrified at the monstrous war itself. But I suspect that another was that some of them were having a middle-class tantrum. But whatever the motivation, the assertion of a moral right and duty to disrupt the democratic process is, on philosophical and practical grounds, wrong and dangerous.

4

In summary, the Vietnam war has posed a number of different questions relating to the boundaries of the political and the moral and the inter-relationships between the two spheres.

In terms of present American premises, it is intolerably antilibertarian to exclude atheists and agnostics from exemption as conscientious objectors on the grounds that they are not motivated by belief in a "Supreme Being." The courts could, using the prevailing legislative language, make a definition of Supreme Being in the tradition of William James and Tillich and thus bring any deeply held fundamental principles under the operation of this clause. It would be infinitely preferable, however, if this reform were to be a conscious act of the Congress, for that would give the firmest possible foundation to a non-sectarian reading of the First Amendment to the Constitution.

Secondly, the National Advisory Commission on Selective Service erred when it refused to grant moral validity to the position of a particular-war objector. In point of fact, the government's denial of this right is doing much more serious damage to the social fabric than its recognition of it possibly could. In point of principle, the state does not have the philosophical-theological competence to decide that consciences formed in one religious tradition are deserving of respect while those from another religious, or non-religious, tradition are not. So it would be a gain for the entire society if the political order guaranteed fundamental rights to such principled, selective conscientious objection.

Thirdly, the "Nuremberg" analogy, whereby participating directly and personally in the genocidal activities of a fascist dictatorship is equated with paying taxes for a tragic war undertaken by a relatively democratic society, is too loose to be compelling. Moreover, the very structural evolution of modern government, particularly on questions of fiscal policy, undermines the assumption that there is any relationship between a particular tax and a war policy. Therefore, there does not seem to be a good case for a *duty* of tax refusal, although individuals may make the *tactical* decision to engage in this form of protest as a form of witness. In the latter case, the debate over tax refusal is not principled, but rather will be concerned with the effectiveness of the witness. I personally do not think it is a very useful form of opposition mainly because it is almost inevitably restricted to the middle class.

Finally, I would make a sharp distinction between these three forms of protest and the assertion of an obligation, and right, to disrupt the activities of a democratic government through *force majeure*, whether violent or not. Such a policy will threaten the very institution of the democratic dialogue, it will invite savage Rightist reprisals, and it will open up the way to violence. Given the fact that many legal political alternatives are available to the protest movement, there is no justification for such an extreme position. And, perhaps most important of all, this is an elitist stance which justifies an attack upon the civil liberties of citizens, and government itself, on the basis of the presumed moral superiority of a minority.

As a last generalization, it seems to me that anyone concerned with morality and politics should be wary of facile claims that the former must prevail over the latter. For as long as there is a democratic process through which laws can be changed, the presumption is in its favor. There are extreme situations—the pacifist ordered to kill, the selective objector commanded to fight in this war—when the individual must place his conscience above the state. But it would be intolerable if this procedure were made the norm. That would not only overburden the conscience of the individual; it would disintegrate the structures of freedom as they are now known.

Those of us who are against this terrible war are, I think, under a special obligation not to claim privileges from the society, not to tear it down because it has the gall not to agree with us, but to change it. And the fact that we can change it is not something to be lightly dismissed.

The Selective Service System: Actualities and Alternatives

ARNOLD S. KAUFMAN

1. Present Injustice

THE American government is presently inflicting agony on its most conscientious young men.

About a year ago a youngster I know returned his draft card to his selective service board. In an accompanying letter he explained that he could not, in conscience, implicate himself in a selective service system that compelled men to fight in an unjust war. He could easily have avoided making his challenge by securing an undergraduate deferment. Having placed himself on society's chopping block, society chopped. He was eventually forced to choose between up to five years in prison and two years in the army. He accepted induction.

His fight had become a spiritual rallying point for many in his small community. When he chose compliance with the selective service system, supporters felt betrayed. Those who thought him wrong in the first place treated his "weakness" with contempt. About his own feelings one can only guess; but they were probably not gentle toward himself.

As any college teacher knows, the torment inflicted on my young acquaintance is not exceptional. Hundreds of thousands of our best young Americans suffer a similar anguish of conscience. That relatively few of them are confronted by the same terrible choice he had to make is beside the point. For they are squeezed by the knowledge that they are implicated in a system that exercises an extraordinary power over their lives—the power to compel them either to fight in a war they loathe or to accept imprisonment.

Wretchedness due to the war is intensified by knowledge that the selective service system's distribution of burdens is grossly unjust. Skeptics need only read the Report to the President prepared by the National Advisory Commission on Selective Service[1] to have their doubts laid to rest.

Without citing all the Report's relevant facts, a few highlights make very clear the contours and depth of injustice within the selective service system. Though comprising only 11% of the entire population during the first eleven months of 1966, 22.4% of Army men killed in action were Negroes. Though only 18% of whites who qualify for service are actually drafted, 30% of qualified Negroes are compelled to serve. Only 1.3% of all local draft board members are Negro. 50.5% of all draft board members are proprietors or professionals or salaried officials of one sort or another; only 21.3% are wage earners—many of them at supervisory levels. (24.9% are farmers, farm laborers, and farm managers, but no breakdown within this group is given.) The Report does not provide a statistical breakdown by income of draftees, fatalities, or draft board members. But it seems reasonable to infer that the poorer one is, the more likely it is that he will be compelled to serve and become a war casualty. As always tends to happen, to him who has, more is given, and the devil take the hindmost. Whether the larger class of poor fare as badly as the Negro poor is not easily determined. But the poorer youngsters in our society obviously fare very badly. The built-in bias in favor of high-status, high-income, Caucasian people is reinforced in two additional ways.

First, college undergraduates receive automatic deferments as long as they retain good academic standing. The result is that scions of white, affluent families are virtually assured of escaping the draft for at least four years. After graduation they become eligible for the draft. But if drafted, as college graduates they are more likely than those who lack education to secure the kind of job or military training that keeps them away from battlefields.

Second, if someone who is able to command influence should, despite prevailing probabilities, find that he is draft-board prey, he has an alternative way out. He can join the Reserves. In an article titled, " 'Big Shots' Find Draft Escape Hatch," this way of avoiding conscription is candidly described:

> Unlike previous wars of this nation, there has been a noticeable lack of prominent young men fighting in Vietnam. Influential people can now escape combat and still fulfill military obligations.
> The escape hatch is the six months' reserve program. . . .
> This reserve tour has become the legitimate "way out" for hundreds of draft-age athletes, entertainers, and others with either financial or social leverage.
> A case in point is basketballer Bill Bradley. At 24 Bradley is getting on for an NBA (National Basketball Association) rookie. Were he to be drafted for two years' military duty at this time any chance of a professional career might be ended.
> So he will spend six months of active duty in the Air Force Reserve. Such a tour in today's air service is next to impossible to obtain, but Bradley made it. He'll come out in time to play half the coming NBA season.
> All of this is no reflection on Bill Bradley. The six months' program (followed by 5½ years in active reserve) is there to be used.[2]

If, by chance, the "big shot" still finds that he is under draft-board pressure, he can do what actor George Hamilton did: plead hardship on grounds that he is his mother's main support. Like other Americans, draft board members are impressed by status, power, and celebrity. A sufficiently high-class petitioner is likely to discover sympathetic ears.

But it must be admitted that not all white, affluent, well-educated youngsters find it so easy to escape the draft. My young acquaintance did not. Nor did those young men from the University of Michigan who, because they sat in and disrupted local draft-board business, found that state and national officials were eager to strip them of their social immunity to the draft.

In short, the selective service system as it presently functions is one of the most class-biased sets of institutional arrangements in America. Whatever progress may have been made toward classlessness in other areas, the system which compels American youngsters to fight wars for "freedom" and "democracy," which forces them to oppose "Communist tyranny" with their bodies, is an almost paradigm instance of what Marx called "a system of class exploitation."

On the basis of its devastating exposure of existing injustice, the President's Advisory Committee proposed a truly excellent set of reforms. Among other things, they advised that student deferments be eliminated, that the selective service system be reorganized so as to reflect more accurately existing social interests, that rules and procedures be made uniform throughout the country, that individuals be barred from gaining exemption through enlistment in the forces of the Reserve or National Guard. How did our Government respond to these admirable proposals?

Virtually the entire package was rejected. Indeed, the previous provision for undergraduate deferment, which made it at least theoretically possible to draft students, was strengthened in a way that eliminates all possibility of drafting those undergraduates who meet minimal college standards. Only one significant concession was made to justice. A provision depriving graduate students of automatic exemptions was enacted. But as all the loopholes and advantages previously described persist, this concession is something less than a giant step toward genuine equity.

Now it is true enough that the bill the Administration actually sent to Congress was vastly superior to the bill eventually enacted. But the Administration's efforts to get its own measure passed left much to be desired. For example, James Reston describes Administration attitudes toward proposals to eliminate undergraduate deferments:

> This was opposed high in the Administration on two grounds. First, it might create undue interference with the education of the high school graduates, and second, it might inflame opposition on the university campuses into a national crisis.
> Officials discuss this latter point very cautiously, but it is a factor. The opposition in the universities to the Vietnam war is already an

embarrassment and an irritation to the Administration. But there is genuine fear that abolition of all or most college deferments might lead to massive defiance among undergraduates. One estimate here is that if college students were called like any other nineteen-year-olds, as many as 25 percent of them might refuse to serve.[3]

And those who follow Reston's columns know that when he reports the opinions of "high officials" he usually knows whereof he speaks. Whether or not the estimates made by "high officials" are accurate is beside the point. The important things are the calculations and moral concerns that went into the political judgments actually made. In any event, it is not likely that the Administration's estimates of the extent and intensity of student disaffection err on the conservative side.

For political reasons the Administration betrayed its professed commitment to elementary justice in the distribution of military sacrifice. It is not surprising, then, that it offered little resistance to the additional rape of justice perpetrated by the House Armed Services Committee, especially its Chairman, South Carolina's L. Mendel Rivers. The outrageous selective-service bill eventually enacted was steered through Congress by Rivers. He evidently proceeded with skill, determination, passion, energy. And, as Marquis Child points out, "Because of its inherent inequities and the brutal way it was shoved through, conscientious men could only sit by with a sick sense of helplessness."[4]

2. Selective Conscientious Objection and the President's Commission

The problem of conscientious objection to particular wars agitates thoughtful Americans as never before. In its report to the President, the National Advisory Commission on Selective Service unanimously sustained the present system of granting exemptions to absolute pacifists, but by majority vote overruled proposals to exempt selective conscientious objectors. My aim is to show that neither in logic nor morality is there a basis for this judgment. Either legal exemption ought to be widened to embrace *all* who conscientiously oppose killing in a given war, or the legal right ought to be abolished altogether.

This conclusion will not satisfy those who, like myself, believe that *all* conscientious objectors ought to be exempted. Though I suggest a general defense of this position, I do not develop the argument in this essay. Yet something is gained if those already convinced that absolute pacifists ought to be legally recognized will admit that there is no reasoned basis for refusing the same status to selective conscientious objectors.

The Commission Majority's Arguments

The Commission's majority offers four basic arguments against legal exemption of selective conscientious objectors:

1. The majority says:

> It is one thing to deal in law with a person who believes he is responding to a moral imperative outside of himself when he opposes all killing. It is another to accord a special status to a person who believes there is a moral imperative which tells him he can kill under some circumstances and not kill under others.[5]

While the meaning of this is not entirely clear, the operative expression seems to be "moral imperative outside of himself." The most plausible interpretation of the majority's intention is that it tries to distinguish between principles that, because they are *outside*, could be *objective*, and those that can only be subjective. Only principles, it is suggested, whose validity can be established by appeal to external authority or evidence can be objectively known.

Assuming this interpretation is correct—and no other makes much sense—then the majority seems to believe that only those who are opposed to all killing, absolute pacifists, can base their conviction on such principles. Moreover, their remarks also seem to suggest that if an absolute pacifist *does not* appeal to "a moral imperative outside of himself," he ought not to be granted exemption from military service. But these views are indefensible.

First, there is no reason at all to suppose that a selective conscientious objector is unable to base his conviction on moral imperatives that are "outside" and objective. For example, suppose a selective conscientious objector sincerely believes that a class of wars—unjust wars—can be objectively established to be unjust by an appeal to objectively valid moral imperatives. Suppose he also sincerely believes that an objective and absolute moral prohibition against fighting in unjust wars exists. Nor are these mere conjectures. I am describing the sincerely held beliefs of tens of thousands of young Americans who today actively oppose the Vietnam War. Consideration of moral imperatives or objective principles provides no rational basis for distinguishing between absolute pacifists and selective objectors. As far as the *first* argument goes, the majority ought to have joined the minority in recommending legal recognition of selective conscientious objectors.

The majority does make one comment that can be intended as a counter to the position defended above. They say that "the question of 'classical Christian doctrine' on the subject of just and unjust wars is one which would be interpreted in different ways by different Christian denominations and therefore not a matter upon which the Commission could pass judgment." Let us assume that the majority had not only Christian doctrine in mind, but any comparable doctrine—Muslim, Jewish, Humanist, etc. In any case, the cogency of their argument escapes me.

For if the majority must accept the interpretation of doctrine proposed by a conscientious objector, then it should recommend that the exemption for absolute pacifists be rescinded. For the majority quite plainly *does not* agree with, say, the Christian absolute pacifist's interpretation of scriptural test—for example, "turn the other cheek." But it is really inconceivable that the case for or against conscientious objection, either absolute or selective, should be made to rest on the vagaries of exegesis performed by members of a Presidential Advisory Committee.

Second, there is no justification for restricting the exemption of absolute pacifists to those who believe that their views are objectively valid. The appropriate test is the *conscientiousness* of their belief. While conscientiousness has much to do with thoughtfulness, sincerity, and authenticity, it has nothing to do with objectivity. At least, the majority offers no reason to suppose that it does; and I can think of none that would help their argument.

Some absolute pacifists are conscientiously committed because they think their moral principle can be objectively established. Others believe with equal conscientiousness that, though objectivity in moral matters is not possible, still, all killing is wrong. As between the two forms of absolute pacifism, no moral basis for drawing a legal distinction exists—a position the Supreme Court acknowledged when, in the Seeger case, it held that absolute pacifists need only have a belief "that is sincere and meaningful [and] occupies a place in the life of its possessor parallel to that filled by the orthodox belief in God of one who clearly qualifies for exemption." Many believe in God on the basis of faith and reject the idea that their belief is objectively provable.

2. The majority argues that:

> ... so-called selective pacifism is essentially a political question of support or nonsupport of a war and cannot be judged in terms of special moral imperatives. Political opposition to a particular war should be expressed through recognized democratic processes and should claim no special right of exemption from democratic decisions.

This sharp distinction between moral and political questions, though frequently made, is baffling. I suppose it is equally true that the following questions are political: support of the Mississippi Freedom Democratic party at the last Democratic National Convention, of World War II, of fair housing ordinances, famine aid to India, urban renewal, the use of a nuclear deterrent, and of the War on Poverty. Each of these political issues is plainly also a moral one. For sound judgment in any of these cases requires appeal to "special moral imperatives." Indeed, it can safely be claimed that all important political questions are also moral questions. For each requires judgments about what *ought* to be done, to which principles of morality are relevant. The claim that selective pacifists ought (morally) to be exempted from military service cannot coherently be dismissed on the grounds that support of a particular war is (merely) a political question.

The tendency to ignore the moral dimensions of political questions is one of the most repugnant aspects of one of the most characteristic American political styles; the style of those whom I elsewhere call "pseudo-realists."[6] For in the name of greater *realism* and *responsibility* the pseudo-realists actually abandon their deeply serious responsibility to assess the *morality* of political acts and policies. And in their irresponsible flight from moral issues, they sabotage realistic efforts to achieve values to which they give lip service on Sundays and on ceremonial occasions.

Perhaps, however, the majority's distinction between the moral and the political is simply designed to call attention to the appropriateness of political opposition to the war—to its being permissible, even obligatory, to express opposition "through recognized democratic processes." But it does not follow from the fact that someone may or should express opposition through political channels, that one may not also claim exemption on grounds of conscientious objection. As American citizens, absolute pacifists quite properly express political opposition to the Vietnam War; but as morally sovereign human beings they claim a special right of exemption as well. The two, political action and the claim of special right of exemption as a conscientious objector, simply do not preclude one another.

3. The majority feels

> that a legal recognition of selective pacifism could be disruptive to the morale and effectiveness of the Armed Forces. A determination of the justness or unjustness of any war could only be made within the context of that war itself. Forcing upon the individual the necessity of making that distinction—which would be the practical effect of taking away the government's obligation of making it for him—would put a burden heretofore unknown on the man in uniform and even on the brink of combat, with results that could well be disastrous to him, to his unit, and to the entire military tradition.

No such problem arises for the conscientious objector, even in uniform, who bases his moral stand on killing in all forms, simply because he is never trained for nor assigned to combat duty.

The majority's reasoning is, to put it mildly, extraordinary.

Their argument rests on the validity of two central claims. First, they simply assume that the government is obligated to decide *for at least certain individuals*, those in military service or eligible for military service, which wars are just, which unjust. Second, they believe that if people are, perforce, compelled to decide for themselves, *or even encouraged to do so,* the results could prove militarily disastrous.

The idea that the government has an obligation to decide *for anyone* which wars are just, which unjust, comes as a revelation to anyone who supposes that our system is predicated on the conviction that *every* citizen has the right and the obligation to make reasoned judgments about most matters of public policy, and certainly about all fateful public issues—such as issues affecting war and peace. Once someone has made the reflective judgment that a particular war is unjust, then, provided the government has acted in a constitutionally legitimate way, the citizen has a problem. His problem is intensified if he is draft eligible. It *may* be right for the government to circumscribe the dissenter's sphere of action so that he does not collide with established public policy. But the point at issue in this discussion is precisely whether the government has a right to interfere with an individual's sincere determination to refuse service in a particular war. To argue that the government has the right to forestall such conflict by making sure that draft eligibles and men in service do not question the justice of the war is profoundly subversive of democracy as most Americans should understand it.

The majority's suggestion does indeed conjure up an even more sinister possibility. How can the Government effectively discourage draft eligibles from exploring the issues of war and peace without going some way toward destroying the general right of dissent? For how can a highly integrated portion of the population be made the target of the necessary manipulations without also making many others the targets of the same manipulations? It is a practical impossibility—as, perhaps, officials of government are discovering.

A partial solution to the problem, but only a partial one, is to isolate those inducted into military service and attempt to brainwash them. According to certain service men who retain a capacity for autonomy, this is precisely what does happen. For example, Paul W. McBride, a former army officer and Vietnam war veteran, summarizes his "educational" experience in the Army in the following terms:

> I came to realize that one of the reasons for the stultification and even danger of the military mind is the closed system in which it is molded. The training at the M.P. school for officers and troops alike is hardly training at all. It is certainly not education which implies a free flow of ideas. It is propaganda, indoctrination, brainwashing. The films on geo-politics and communism shown *today* in the Army training system anachronistically stress the existence of a Sino-Soviet conspiracy to dominate the world.
>
> What is worse, the narrowness of the military approach to world problems is forced upon the college student in ROTC. The manual 145–45 used now at the University of Georgia still refers to the danger of the "Sino-Soviet conspiracy." It is pardonable to be wrong, but when error is forced upon the civilian college system, and when the military instructors are forbidden to vary from doctrine, then the situation is intolerable in the educational context. The University must not force propaganda down the students' throats. It is bad enough when they, like me, volunteer to be brainwashed.[7]

Ultimately, the majority's stand on the issue of military indoctrination is downright undemocratic. If a democratic system is one in which those most affected by a given policy have at least some opportunity to participate reflectively in the making of that policy, then it is abhorrent to suggest that the very men who are compelled to lay their lives on the line should be systematically excluded from intelligent participation in the process. The majority's earlier contention that "political opposition to a particular war *should* be expressed through recognized democratic processes" is simply betrayed by their subsequent qualification. (Author's emphasis.)

The majority's second claim, that legal recognition of selective pacifism could prove militarily disastrous, is either harmless or absurd. For the probability of such a consequence is miniscule. In this country, belief that the President is contemptuous of full and fair democratic process undermines morale. Belief that the selective service system operates inequitably undermines morale. Belief that the country is committed to an unjust war undermines morale. Military morale is most effectively maintained by creating an equitable system for recruiting men, and committing them to battle in just wars that have been adequately debated before they are begun. If demonstrable failure in all these respects has not already destroyed the spirit of our troops in Vietnam, exempting selective conscientious objectors is most unlikely to do so.

In any event, the general opinion of Vietnam veterans who today oppose the war is that once one is in the battle area, he performs the tasks he is required to perform. Donald Duncan, one of the heroes of the Special Services (Green Berets), and a militant critic of the war, has written extensively about his war experiences. Nothing he has written about his military life in Vietnam suggests that his effectiveness was impaired.

Perhaps, however, the majority's views do raise a deep constitutional issue that ought to be considered—for the problems involved deserve much more extensive treatment.

During time of war fundamental tension is produced by the potential conflict between the requirements of a successful war effort and the imperatives of a free society. This is the "Nervous Nellie" problem, or, more recently, the "Quisling" problem, to adopt the terms of President Johnson. But surely the case for denying civil liberties in favor of efficient war-making is no stronger than the extent of real danger to national security. It is, however, universally agreed that defeat in the Vietnam War poses no short-term threat to national security, and the nation is deeply divided about whether defeat would result in a long-term threat. The simple-minded formula, "If we don't fight them in Southeast Asia, we will have to fight them in Honolulu and San Francisco," is accepted only by the most mindless elements in the populace. The point is that however agonizing the tension described might be in other wars, in this war there is little basis for alarm.

4. The majority holds that:

> legal recognition of selective pacifism could open the doors to a general theory of selective disobedience to law, which could quickly tear down the fabric of government; the distinction is dim between a person conscientiously opposed to participation in a particular war and one conscientiously opposed to payment of a particular tax.

It is in this argument that the majority manages to hit their stride; they commit three textbook fallacies of logic. The majority, in their desperation to find persuasive arguments, try to force open the Pandora's Box of anarchism. Men armed with even minimal intelligence and a small number of facts can force the lid firmly down again.

From the claim that legal recognition of selective conscientious objection *could* open the doors to a general theory of selective disobedience to law (which can be accepted as a logical possibility) it does not follow that it has any tendency to do so at all. And, indeed, no plausible general theory is even suggested, as a careful analysis of the majority's own analogy quickly makes clear. The disanalogies between paying taxes and fighting in wars is so great that the majority's suggestion cannot stand a moment's critical examination.

When a man is compulsorily inducted into the army he is put in a position where he can be ordered to kill another human being. When he is compelled to pay taxes, he is not put in that position. Christian Bay states the underlying moral issue, and the principle of difference, cogently:

> In general, a democratic government may be entitled to obedience, but there are limits to its justifiable demands on citizens. If it orders citizens to kill or die, it comes close to the limits that even Hobbes put down around the authority of the Leviathan. Even in a proclaimed national emergency the individual's right not to kill or die for a cause he considers unjust should be respected by the government.[8]

The distinction between killing and paying does not seem dim to Bay, nor, I warrant, to any morally sensitive human being who reflects carefully on what he is saying. Certainly, many of the Nuremberg trials or the Eichmann trial would have seemed ludicrous had the Germans who were tried been charged with failing to reject Nazi orders to pay their income taxes. This is not to deny that those who pay taxes they know will be used to facilitate killing are normally implicated in the resulting deaths. But one of the fundamental achievements of human civilization is the development of criteria which enable us to grade the culpability of individuals implicated in transgression, and to allocate penalties accordingly.

Let us suppose, for purposes of argument, that a generally accepted theory of selective disobedience does emerge and is widely accepted as a result of legal recognition of selective pacifism. From this admission it does not follow that the fabric of government would quickly, or even slowly, be torn down; nor even that such an outcome is likely. In general, anarchical tendencies are the result of perceived injustice. And perceived injustice is normally the result of actual injustice. A society composed entirely of principled civil disobedients like Henry Thoreau would be the most stable imaginable, *provided* the laws and institutions were perceived as just. Those who spend energies worrying about the threat of anarchy would normally be better advised to spend their time remedying injustice. Alarms about the danger of anarchy often conceal the moral indifference that is principally responsible for whatever threat may actually exist.

The majority's third fallacy of logic is a *reductio ad absurdum*. Consider carefully the relationship between conscientious objection to a particular war and conscientious objection to a particular tax. If we accept the majority's claim that the distinction between these is "dim," then it seems to follow that the distinction between conscientious objection to *all* wars and conscientious objection to *all* taxes is not less dim. Yet the majority favors granting those who are conscientiously opposed to fighting in all wars exemption from fighting in any war. Hence, they should favor granting those who are conscientiously opposed to paying all taxes exemption from paying any taxes. But the conclusion is absurd. Nothing would be more likely to "tear down the fabric of government" than to follow the majority in all the vagaries of its reasoning on the subject of selective conscientious objection.

On the basis of these criticisms of the majority's arguments it seems fair to conclude that the majority abandoned almost all of reason and retained precious little of morality. In a college logic class they would have been given F's, and dismissed with an admonition to try to do better. But the sphere they chose for their muddled thinking was not a classroom; it was the arena in which issues of war and peace, life and death, are debated and decided. Many parts of the Commission's report are excellent; most of the reasoning is sound. But in their discussion of selective conscientious objection, the Commission's majority seemed to become tools of higher political powers.

3. The Case for Legal Recognition of Selective Conscientious Objection

I have shown only that the Commission's majority failed to make even the beginning of a case for differential treatment of absolute and selective conscientious objectors. I now want to show that there is no basis for legal distinction. In the course of my discussion, I shall appeal to principles which provide a basis on which exemption of all conscientious objectors can be defended. But this is not my main concern. The full case for exemption of conscientious objectors, absolute and selective, deserves separate and more extended treatment.

Assume that one arrives, by some route or other, at the conviction that human life is specially sacred. Belief in the sacredness of life would quite naturally be expressed as commitment to the right to life. Assume also that this right is accorded high priority in the moral scheme of things. Finally, assume that *conscientious thought and conduct* are among the central values of civilized society. I have described my own deep convictions. But

The Selective Service System / 255

they are important here only because they are premises that are widely accepted, and on the basis of which legal exemption of absolute pacifists can plausibly be defended. Given these assumptions, the strongest kind of obligation to avoid killing others, the strongest kind of case against forcing anyone to kill against his will, can be made. If these assumptions are effectively challenged, the case for legal recognition of absolute pacifists cannot help but be weakened. If they are sustained, the case for extending recognition to selective conscientious objectors cannot help but be strengthened. I can think of no plausible defense of one that does not support the other, no plausible attack on one that does not throw doubt on the other.

Killing may be justified. But in a good society, government will never compel someone to become a killer unless a catastrophic threat to all values exists. But under these conditions there is no moral reason why legal distinction should be made between absolute and selective conscientious objectors.

Underlying much resistance to this basic conclusion is the suspicion that absolute pacifists are more credible and authentic than selective pacifists. But just the reverse seems generally to be true. For it is almost impossible that someone would refuse to kill in any and all conceivable circumstances—for example, if the lives of those he loves best are threatened by a marauder. Though an absolute pacifist may affirm his position with perfect sincerity, there is psychological basis for suspecting that he deceives himself—by contrast to the selective conscientious objector.

Moreover, as all who favor legal recognition of conscientious objection should acknowledge, the strongest possible basis for exempting an individual from military service is that he regards killing, or direct involvement in killing, as morally repugnant. But there is no reason at all to suppose that selective conscientious objectors need be less sincere than absolute pacifists when they express such repugnance during a particular war.

Though I disagree with people who insist that the conscientious objector's beliefs must have a religious basis, or be shaped by religious training or its equivalent, they are wrong if they suppose that this conviction enables them to make the distinction between absolute and selective conscientious objection. For there is no doubt at all that individuals can have religiously based objection to fighting in particular wars—wars they believe, on religious grounds, to be unjust.

The argument that everyone is equally obligated to fight in wars that protect common social values has a hollow ring, given the inequities and injustice of our present military system. Nevertheless, this objection can be met by giving conscientious objectors the legal right to discharge their obligation in alternative ways. In any event, once again there is no basis for legal distinction between absolute and selective objectors.

Those who argue that it is more difficult to establish working criteria for selective conscientious objectors than for absolute pacifists must prove that this is so. On the face of it, the objection is implausible—as anyone familiar with the arbitrariness of the present system knows. Certainly, at the level of theory it is just as easy to state criteria for selective conscientious objection as it is for absolute pacifism. In both cases the test is the *conscientiousness* of the objection.

Forcing conscientious objectors to fight and kill *may* be justified if there is a clear and present danger to the survival of all national values. The threat must be more than a mere possibility, or even a probability. There must be a very high probability of national destruction. But in these circumstances the mere fact that someone is an absolute pacifist does not give him rights the selective conscientious objector lacks; or at least I can think of no convincing argument why absolute pacifists should receive special consideration in a national emergency. In any event, given a genuine threat to national security, it is unlikely that selective conscientious objectors would become a practical problem. Cowards would find some way of shirking even just wars; conscientious men would not. And few Americans are cowards. Certainly none of the young men who conscientiously seek to escape service in a war they believe to be unjust do so because they are *afraid* to fight. Only those who have no understanding of these young men will regard such a claim as even plausible.

I said only that grounds *may* exist for forcing conscientious objectors to fight and kill. Even a clear and present danger to national security may not be sufficient. A society may be so bad that its destruction would restore, not destroy values. Nazi Germany was a fairly clear case.

Moreover, even when decent societies are threatened with destruction, it may be possible to afford exemptions. For given the changing technology of war, together with population growth, a modern industrial society does not rely as heavily on total manpower as used to be the case.

Yet there may be practical grounds for treating absolute pacifists differently than selective conscientious objectors. Absolute pacifists may, for example, have received the kind of upbringing which makes them unfit to fight. But then the decision to keep them away from the battlefield is a technical decision that ought to be made by military men. *All* ineffective killers ought to be kept away from where the killing is going on; even those who are ineffective for reasons other than their having had a pacifist upbringing.

4. The Alternative of a Volunteer Army

The wrongs of our selective service system cry for correction. Many Americans, disturbed primarily by the system's coercive features, propose that military recruitment be placed on a voluntary basis. They want to use economic incentives to induce people to join the armed forces. Their proposal is entirely practicable. For additional costs and total need for manpower are sufficiently small; and displacing more of the cost of defense from the man who fights to the taxpayer is plainly right. But the idea of a professionalized, voluntary army has at least two fundamental flaws.

First, a military force recruited principally on the basis of economic incentives will simply confirm and legitimize the inherent class bias of the present system. Sloggers who do the dirtiest work, who take the maximum number of casualties, who sacrifice most for "God and country," will come from those with least stake in the *status quo* armies usually protect. Second, any army tends to inculcate the kind of mindless patriotism described in an earlier section. A professionalized, voluntary army would only intensify the problem. In a citizen army whose members are mainly recruited by random selection for short hitches, the rate of reenlistment tends to remain fairly low; fighting men remain reasonably well integrated into the common culture. Under these conditions it is difficult to inculcate in citizen soldiers a thoughtless amoralism. But a professional army that primarily recruits men who pursue military careers is bound to become increasingly separate from the common culture.

One must view a professionalized voluntary army in its larger social context. The threat the military-industrial complex poses to cherished values is due not only to its immense power and ruthless pursuit of special interests, but also to the fact that it tends to be socially autonomous—unresponsive to the general needs and wishes of the larger population. If the pernicious power of the military-industrial complex is ever to be contained, its social isolation must be prevented. Creation of a professional army would increase the difficulties of an already mammoth political task.

If such an army were the *only* alternative to the present system of injustice, however, I should have to favor it. Fortunately it is not the only alternative available to us.

A just selective service system will reduce coercion to a minimum consistent with an equitable distribution of burdens. It will also eliminate any need for the star-chamber proceedings that often occur before draft boards decide whether to exempt someone as a conscientious objector—cumbersome, frequently arbitrary procedures made necessary by the draft board's desire to separate shirkers from authentic objectors. The following system goes some way toward meeting these requirements.

The President's Commission, and all fair-minded men, recognize that those picked from a larger pool of men should be randomly selected. As a Harvard Study Group recently put it,

> The means of determining who serves and who does not serve . . . must be fair and nondiscriminatory and must appear fair and nondiscriminatory both to those who are selected and to those who are not.[9]

Both the Harvard Group and the Commission agree that a lottery can alone fill the bill.

Except in obvious cases of hardship and national need, no exemptions from the obligation to perform service should be permitted once the pool of draft eligibles is established. To make sure that there is compliance with this requirement, clear and precise federal standards should be specified and the draft board system should be reformed so as to make it both more representative and less arbitrary. In these respects the Presidential Commission's proposals are excellent.

Everyone within the proper age range not entitled to exemption from service will have an absolute obligation to serve. But no one should be obligated to perform *military* service. Each individual should be free to choose some form of alternative public service. An adequate range of choices would make it possible for most individuals to do something with which they can identify. Following the model adopted by the Swedish Government, the length of alternative service should be slightly longer than the requirement imposed on those who choose military duty.

The foregoing proposal not only eliminates the need for cumbersome administrative arrangements; it also eliminates forcing any individual to kill. Having the free choice between military and alternative service, those who choose the former can be said to have given a form of tacit consent to the military option. Admittedly, this consent will not be given without that element of coercion involved in the forced choice. Yet I believe that if we are to have an armed force at all, this proposal gives one the maximum amount of freedom consistent with justice.

The Commission majority offers one argument against the policy of alternative service which deserves consideration. They argue that they were

> unable to see the morality of a proposition which would permit the selective pacifist to avoid combat service by performing noncombatant service in support of a war which he had theoretically concluded to be unjust.

The point they seem to be making is that if the selective pacifist is morally sincere, then he ought to refuse all complicity in the system which generally supports the war effort he opposes. This is a curious argument. Taken literally it seems to imply that the selective pacifist should emigrate to a country that does not support the war effort in any way. For to do anything less would implicate him in the system, hence would be morally insincere. But there surely is a difference between complicity that might lead to one becoming a killer, and complicity that does not involve this extreme form of involvement. Once again, a distinction that seems dim to the majority seems to others as clear as a floodlight on a moonless night.

Moreover, the majority seems again to want to set the Government up as a moral authority. Its argument presupposes that the state is a better judge of the morality of choosing noncombatant service than the individual concerned. But in a free society the dimness or clarity of moral distinctions that shape individual judgments ought to be left to the individual when considerations weigh heavily in favor of doing so. And the general case for granting the option between military and alternative service is very strong indeed.

Given the arrangements described above, the use of economic incentives as a partial means of inducing enlistments can be defended. First, adequate pay for military service will insure that those who are willing to make the greatest sacrifice by putting themselves in the greatest jeopardy will not be made to bear the additional burden of subsidizing the taxpayer. Second, by maintaining higher pay rates for military than for alternative service the incentive effect on those who are not genuine conscientious objectors can be strengthened. While the result might be a somewhat higher proportion of recruits from society's lower strata, this evil consequence will be mitigated by the recommendation that there be universal service for those selected by lottery.

A basic objection to the proposed alternative must be considered before concluding. Some may argue that the alternative service arrangement will enable many who are not genuine conscientious objectors to slip through the sieve. No doubt. But they do anyway. And permitting some who are not conscientious objectors to avoid military service is a small price to pay for avoiding administrative inequities, for guaranteeing that all who are conscientious objectors will gain exempt status—always provided that circumstances are such as to make the exemption of any conscientious objector morally justifiable. Too often we become so preoccupied with stopping transgression that we violate the rights of those who do not transgress. Despite some progress, our penal and compulsory psychiatric arrangements tend to result in violation of the rights of many in order to prevent recidivism and insure punishment of the few. The principle of making the "innocent" pay to guarantee that the "guilty" do not escape should not be extended to the selective service system.

In any event, the extent of the problem can be easily exaggerated. First, those who presently avoid conscription by feigning conscientious objection would not, as they presently do, avoid public service altogether. This would provide a disincentive that might actually reduce the size of the problem. Secondly, the tendency to take advantage of alternative service would be lessened by the fact that a certain social opprobrium inevitably attaches to those perceived as "shirkers." Third, during time of international conflict, if the war is just and is perceived as just, most Americans will be strongly motivated to fight. On the other hand, if the justice of the war is problematic, then, under conditions of open debate, the reluctance of men to serve would provide a very useful brake on those who seek to commit bodies other than their own to the cause. And in time of peace, there is unlikely to be any problem. Fourth, the fact that alternative service would involve lower pay and a longer duration of service would increase the likelihood that those who are not genuine conscientious objectors will choose the military alternative.

For those who, in conscience, are altogether unwilling to implicate themselves in the military system, there would still be an honorable alternative. They could refuse and accept the legal consequences of that refusal.

The ultimate test of a free society is the extent to which individuals are able to carve out their own destiny on the basis of reflective choice. In shaping one's destiny, few options are more fundamental than the choice between killing and not killing. Even when policies affecting war and peace are especially bad, a society in which the burdens of military service are distributed equitably and with a minimum of coercion reveals a certain integrity. People who loathe the evil policies will be less reluctant to pursue change within the frame of existing political structures than would otherwise be the case. This point has important application to an America in which intense opposition to the Vietnam war and racial injustice is eroding faith in our form of political democracy.

I have argued that the present selective service system is unjust; that if we are betraying our ideals in Vietnam, it is at least open to Americans to mitigate the wrong by remedying the injustices of the conscription system; that the Presidential Commission's majority offers appallingly bad arguments against legal recognition of selective pacifism; and that there is no basis for moral distinction between absolute pacifists and selective conscientious objectors. One thing is certain: failure to change our present system will intensify the alienation that has afflicted millions of our most conscientious Americans since the Vietnam escalation began.

NOTES

[1] *Report of the National Advisory Commission on Selective Service,* Chairman, Burke Marshall (U.S. Government Printing Office, 1967).
[2] *The Ann Arbor News,* August 28, 1967, p. 19.
[3] *The New York Times,* May 5, 1967.
[4] *The Ann Arbor News,* August 28, 1967.
[5] Unless otherwise indicated, all quotes are from pp. 50–51 of the *Report.*
[6] In my book, *The Radical Liberal: New Man in American Politics* (New York: Atherton, 1968), Chapter 3, pp. 32–43.
[7] From *The Red and Black* (University of Georgia student newspaper), October 24, 1967.
[8] *The Structure of Freedom* (Stanford, California, 1958), p. 110.
[9] "On the Draft" (in *The Public Interest,* no. 9, Fall 1967), p. 95.

Conscientious Objection and Moral Agency

JEROME M. SEGAL

1

I WANT to discuss my own actions. I have filed for the I–0 exemption. I do not see this as heroic; I do not see the legal CO as a hero. In fact, I am not even sure that I have met the minimal demands of morality. I will not fight in Vietnam; if necessary I will go to jail. This much I have made clear. I filed for an exemption I will not get. I said I was conscientiously opposed to participation in war in any form, but my explanation of my beliefs makes clear that I do not neatly fit into the conventional category. My position may be summarized as follows:

(1) There is such a thing as a moral life. The overriding duty which is constitutive of the moral life is to act on one's beliefs as to what is right.

(2) There are true statements about what is right, good, correct, dutiful, etc.

(3) The answers to ethical questions (e.g., "What is the right course of action to follow here?") are non-subjective. Thinking that such and such is right does not make it so. Ethics is never merely personal. If something is wrong for some individuals it is wrong for all individuals in similar circumstances.

(4) The moral self forms the core of the moral life. The moral self is a reflective self, the individual engaged in the constant process of evaluation and reevaluation of past and future conduct.

(5) There is an essential unity of the self and its actions. Only that self is good which strives for consequences which promote the well-being of those affected by it.

(6) There are better and worse ways of conducting the evaluation of actions. In forming an assessment one should bring to bear as much information as possible.

(7) In general, communal values and principles represent the crystallized results of centuries of moral experience and evaluation. All such principles have a tentative status. Ultimately they are subject to the test of future experience. They are *prima facie* true. In general, proper evaluations will be in terms of these principles. They serve to structure the ethical problem.

(8) It is *prima facie* true that war is unjustified, that killing is unjustified, and that any participation in these activities is unjustified.

(9) As the core of the moral life is reflection, investigation, and action based thereupon, it is *prima facie* true that situations which restrict the possibility of so living restrict to that extent the possibility of a moral existence.

(10) Membership in the Armed Forces places restrictions which tend to exclude the possibility of a moral existence.

(11) When the military is engaged in a war, it is *prima facie* true that membership in the Armed Forces not only eliminates the possibility of a moral life but is itself immoral.

I am conscientiously opposed to participation in war in any form because all wars involve the participants in acts which are inherently wrong. And to deny that one is opposed to committing such acts would be to adjust oneself to them in a way which denies one's agency. It is important for people like myself to remember that we oppose all wars, for only then are we least ready to dodge our responsibility for their occurrence. We must not forget that in doing what is in balance justified, we often do much that is inherently wrong. It is only by maintaining a moral tension and conflict that we will keep ourselves from seeing war as righteous. And only if the soldier maintains this tension will he be as he should be, sick at himself for what he does. He must never forget that he kills those who are not morally guilty, that the enemy always believes that he, too, is doing what is right. Because being in the army involves military training and discipline designed to produce a capitulation of moral agency, because it commits one to a *program* of violence or a *program of training* which will lead one to regard violence as a commendable solution to problems, I have opposed it in peace time as well as in war time. Nonetheless, because I believe that it is possible for such circumstances to exist that one is justified in participating in war, I will not be granted the exemption. I will be regarded as an objector to specific wars, not all wars.

I applied for the exemption in the hope that if I was denied it, I could then challenge the constitutionality of the exemption provision in the courts. I believe that, as written, the provision is unconstitutionally discriminatory. But this is of little import. If the courts agreed that people like myself were entitled to an exemption, it would not be long before the Constitution was amended; there are too many of us. In short, I registered in order to file a small, quiet protest and to slightly raise my chances of not going to jail.

I have avoided confrontation; so long as I have a student deferment or an occupational deferment, my case will not come up. I have not given up my student deferment. In so doing, I have done what all those who get the exemption have done. I have participated in a system which rests on the premise that, by and large, people will act for their own self-interest. Like the CO who has his exemption and performs his alternative service, I have participated in a system which exists because if it were otherwise there might be "considerable opposition to Selective Service operations and a lessening of national unity."[1] Given the situation in Vietnam, this is less than heroic.

2

Some people are exempt from military service because they are "conscientiously opposed to participation in war in any form and [are] further conscientiously opposed to participation in noncombatant training and service in the Armed Forces." These people are in a draft classification called I–0. If you are conscientiously opposed in the above way, then you are *entitled* to an exemption from service in the Armed Forces. You do not ask to be exempted, you do not beg to have your conscience respected. You claim an exemption. That is the law. As a social fact, the exemption stands right in the middle of the experience of conscientious objection. It is around the exemption that the notion of conscientious objection takes its substance. If you claim the exemption, you say, "I applied for CO." If you get it, you say, "I'm a conscientious objector." If you want to raise an issue in the courts, you must first go through the system, claim I–0 status, and appeal when it is refused. More than anything else, the exemption involves you in seeing yourself as someone presenting himself to others as an object that meets a certain description. You can begin to think of yourself increasingly in terms of the image of a conscientous objector, an image taken over from others.

The exemption procedure becomes a danger. It is a corrupting force. The individual is involved in obtaining for himself a favored position. More and more his attention turns away from the war. More and more the war is a given and his relationship to it becomes not so much opposition as avoidance. His activity is one of finding his place in terms of the war and the society. He works his way out of a dangerous situation. Once again tension is eased, it is possible to relax. The war is bad. He has opposed the war. The society is wrong; he has dissented. He will not have to participate in the war. He will remain one unit. His actions will not belie his judgments. Yet he will remain at one with the society. Non-participation is provided for by law. He will not become an outcast, he will not have to emigrate, he will not have to go to prison. Somehow, he has been provided for. There exists a special draft category for those in his position. Given all this, it is hard not to be thankful; it is hard not to be grateful. One almost marvels at the greatness of the society, at the wisdom of the legislation. It has done so much for him. He is told, "If you volunteer for alternative service before the draft board decides on your claim for CO status, this will go a long way toward establishing your sincerity and good faith." Giving the alternative service becomes something one wants to do, almost out of gratitude, out of love for the society. All in all the exemption mellows the objector. It turns him away from the war, away from opposition to social policies and structures, it turns him toward himself. It is important to stop thinking of yourself from an external point of view. It is important to stop asking the societal questions: "Does the law entitle me to an exemption on the basis of opposition to particular wars? Can the society afford to permit this as a basis for an exemption?" We must also stop asking the personal questions: "Why am I doing this? Am I sincere? Am I trying to avoid the draft? Am I a CO?" Both sorts of questions are traps. I am glad to be free of them. Only one question is really relevant: "What should I do; which course of action is right?"

Arguing that one of the basic reasons why the colonies joined together was to "provide for the common defense," the courts have rejected the claim that there is a constitutional right to conscientious objection:

> There is no such principle of the Constitution, fixed or otherwise. The conscientious objector is relieved from the obligation to bear arms in obedience to no Constitutional provision, express or implied; but because and only because, it has accorded with the policy of Congress thus to relieve him.[2]

If the exemption exists only because of Congressional action, why was the exemption provided? Without doubt it is relevant that there is a felt respect for the man of strict religious scruples, but a more fundamental understanding is provided on page 1 of the Selective Service volume on conscientious objection:

> If no consideration at all had been given to those objecting on the grounds of conscience, the result might have been considerable opposition to Selective Service operations and a lessening of national unity. On the other hand, if the treatment of individuals who claimed to have scruples against service had been liberal enough to allow them freedom of action, the other and vastly larger group of

citizens, willing to make sacrifices, would have been antagonized to the point where unity would also have been impaired.

. . . The soundness of this approach was demonstrated in the contributions to the war effort and to national welfare by the different classes of conscientious objectors, and by the fact that such contributions were made without lowering the morale of the armed forces or other groups.

If Congress passes a law which will not be obeyed by a group of basically law-abiding citizens, it is sometimes in the national interest to exempt these individuals from the duties they reject, provided that the form of the exemption does not seem unfair to most people. In terms of the conscientious objector, alternative service accomplishes part of this and restricting the exemption to those who are religiously opposed to all wars does the rest.

It would never do to exempt, in the midst of war, all those who think that the war is wrong. The exemption would defeat its purpose. For such a policy would, in itself, greatly increase the number of people who would declare that they judged the war to be wrong. To the man in the army, the man with the exemption would not seem to be a different sort of person but only a man with a different opinion. He, too, would be tempted to develop a different opinion. It would be far better if those exempted were members of a group that seemed to deserve special treatment. They should be above suspicion of faking; they should be members of a group that could be respected by the society, and yet seen as importantly different from the society.

Partly because both the government and the objector need to build a certain image of the exempted objector, and partly because there were many who fitted the image, there has developed a somewhat mythological notion of what it means to *be* a conscientious objector. The conscientious objector is seen not just as someone with certain beliefs and intentions, but as someone with a radically different kind of moral experience than most of us. As things stand now, only those who maintain an absolutist position are able to qualify for an exemption. Indeed, the more inflexible the position, the greater the likelihood of obtaining an exemption. Thus, even in the Seeger case, which greatly expanded the religious bases of the exemption, the Court of Appeals tells us:

> When Daniel Seeger insists that he is *obeying* the dictates of his conscience or the imperatives of an *absolute* morality, it would seem impossible to say with assurance that he is not *bowing* to "*external commands.*" . . .

Implicit in our notion of "conscientiously objecting" is our idea of conscience. If the voice of God coming from the burning bush no longer grips modern man, it is not because there are no voices to listen to. The voice has been internalized, but it still commands; it still tries to be the master. We are presented with Luther's words as a paradigm: "Here I stand, I can do no other!" No one turns to Luther and asks why it is that he "can do no other," or how that is relevant. No one asks if it is right to obey an "inner command." Nowhere is the immorality of blind obedience recognized. Man is still not seen in his full freedom, a freedom to mold his "inner voice" and to reject it if it deserves rejection. The choice facing the individual is construed as a choice of masters. Either to God or Caesar, State or Conscience, man must be obedient. It is almost as if one were saying to the state, "I can do no other, I can't help it, I must do this. Threats and sanctions will be to no avail." And it tends to work both ways, for one does not deserve to be punished if one can do no other, and it is just those who will do no other that the State wants to identify.

Given this image of the conscientious objector, who am I to claim an exemption from military service? I have yet to encounter a command from my conscience. I have yet to encounter something I could call a conscience. I do not experience compulsions to goodness, and if I did, that would still not be a reason for doing anything. At best, one's compulsions can *account* for behavior; they do not serve as a basis for decision-making.

I tend to see war as something that is not a fitting practice for man, as something beneath my dignity as a person. Nations at war take on the look of insect colonies, strange colonies which seek to destroy their own kind, anxious to seek out the members of the other colonies and poke holes in their bodies. I have no such desire. I feel friendly toward the members of other societies. Without knowing them, I know that they are people. I feel close to them. Like myself, they are trapped within the practices of their own colony. Like myself, they do not know why the world is the way it is. Like myself, they do not understand why we are at war. Given all this, I ask myself, "Can I participate in this horror, this insanity? Can I submit to training; to an attempt to relieve me of these perceptions; to turn me into a purely functional being, a part of the war machine?"

Can I let this happen to me? Taken literally, the answer must be yes, I can. I could probably become a good soldier. I have that in me too. If I refuse to participate, it isn't because I can do no other. I'm a free agent. To a large extent I make my own personality, and I can let myself be made into a soldier. I can sit and watch TV as the war news comes through and discover to my shock and bewilderment that I have been rooting—even believing what I do about the current war—I have been rooting for our team. As the death figures come in, I have been awaiting a higher number for "the enemy." (Some days I root for them.) Can there be any question that I could be a soldier? How well prepared I am for that.

But I do not want to be this way. I will not let myself be this way. The shock of what I am like is so great that I can only deal with it by taking it lightly. Only in this way can I gain the upper hand. I tell myself, "These thoughts are reactions, I have been conditioned." They are so remote from me that I treat them as foreign elements. I declare, "They have been planted in me—they are not *my* reactions or thoughts—I have just served as a screen for them—just a mechanism for their presentation. They are the traces of the inroads the society has made—of how deeply it has conquered." I scoff at them. At will, I perform a deeply personal surgery. "These thoughts do *not* reveal my attitudes—they do *not* form my sympathies, they do *not* reflect my views—and they will *not* mold my actions—they are flukes—isolated freaks of the society." My being is complex and discordant. I seize one part of it and say, "This is me." I fence part of myself away. I discard it as so much rubbish. Perhaps I can make myself into a CO.

The setup is such that I do not know what happens if I am honest, if I stop trying to see myself as a CO. Being honest means admitting much, admitting that there is much you could do that is inconsistent with the image you want to put forward, with the image you want to cloak yourself in. It means admitting that you don't experience inner commands. Being honest means facing the question of sincerity, of trying to discover why it is that you do what you do—admitting that you never wanted to go into the army—that there is something pleasurable about objecting—that it is gratifying to take a stand and no longer be accommodating. And it means trying to decide whether you are a coward or a liar; it means saying something like: "Yes, it's true. I don't want to die, or fight, or be pushed around. Yes, these beliefs are convenient for me and, yes, it's true that it is probably the case that being what I am, if these beliefs had not been convenient, I might not have come to them." Being honest means admitting all of this while trying not to smile knowingly. That is the trap, this social smile, thinking that admitting all of this amounts to something, thinking that these admissions can serve as a basis for one's actions, thinking that this is the kind of knowledge that is important.

The simple fact is that I believe it would be wrong for me to allow myself to be inducted into the army. Everything else is beside the point—it would be wrong to participate in the war and I will not. Anything else about me is relevant to my conduct only if it gives reason to doubt the *correctness* of my beliefs about the rightness of my actions. What is relevant to the policymakers or the courts depends on *their* enterprise. I must not confuse myself with them. I must not accept their image of a conscientious objector. I must focus on my future actions.

There are radically different ways of going through the world. Sometimes we just go along doing what's expected. This is not because we are concerned about what would happen if we did something unexpected, it is not because we fear some sanction. It is not that rational. Other people, social codes, habits, and our own past gently guide us forward. We experience no constraints.

We continue to glide, action flowing naturally from the past to the future. Most of us who have been in the Selective Service maze have operated this way.

Focusing on one's future actions, taking them fully seriously, is not easy. When we break with a pattern of doing the expected, of accommodating ourselves within the structure, the world suddenly becomes confusing, it becomes problematic in a way that it never had been. Action becomes a way of cutting one's path through a resisting world. When we act, we bring into being some situations and remove from being other situations. After I have acted, things are different. What was true is no longer true. What was not the case now is.

But how are we to harness our own energy, how are we to order our own action? There are so many alternatives which are equally rational. There are so many things about which we may be concerned. There are so many different persons we can become. Perhaps there is no method for deciding how to make decisions. Perhaps every method employs a method. . . .

The problem of how to act is not solved. It is never solved. There is no formula for determining what one should do. There are only general principles, guiding rules which tell you what to look for, what to pay attention to. The actual situations we face are often bewildering. We can get into a morass of considerations where one is no more certain of the correctness of the abstract principles or reasonings one is employing than one is of the conclusions one reaches. A moral life involves doing the best one can to determine what is right. One hobbles along hoping he is right, knowing that he knows far less than he needs to know.

If one hobbles honestly, he must admit that, as a unique faculty of knowing, as a special power which informs us on moral matters, there simply is no such thing as a conscience. We must not pretend to have resources we lack. Our faculties of perception, our normal intelligence are all we have. Sometimes they are adequate; sometimes they are not. In order to discover what is right, economic, sociological, and political data are needed. Nor should we leave out psychological, biological, historical, and geographical factors. When one objects on grounds of conscience, one is objecting on moral grounds. The old conception, which limited conscientious objection to those areas where a given law conflicts with a particular tenet of a religious faith, severely circumscribed the area of possible objections and severely restricted the number of potential objectors. In recognizing that an objection of conscience is merely an objection based on a judgment that something is morally wrong, one recognizes that all human action is subject to moral judgment and that all members of the society are potential objectors.

3

There are a number of difficulties in trying to deal with the question of war from within the moral life. In particular, there is the problem of how political obligations enter into the determination of the right action, and how one ought to acquire the beliefs he uses to guide his actions. Before discussing these difficulties, however, I will defend the basic contention that there *are* difficulties in dealing with war from within the moral life.

If the moral life is a struggle to discover which courses of action are right, it is also the case that some questions are more difficult to answer than others. *Sometimes the question, "Should I participate in this war?" is more difficult to answer than at other times.* Implicit in this claim is the belief that it is logically possible that the answer to the question will sometimes be "yes." That is, it is possible to envision a war in which one's participation would be justified. In the view of many people, including many conscientious objectors themselves, the conscientious objector is a person who does not believe that there are any considerations which could justify his participation in a war. I want to put forward the following theses: (1) There are considerations which could justify participation in war. (2) Many of those people who are recognized as conscientious objectors to all wars would, if pressed, have to admit that there are such considerations. (3) Those few with a truly absolute position, a position which admits of no such considerations, have a morally irresponsible position (and such positions are not deserving of special respect by the society).

The second contention is important because it suggests that there are broad similarities between the position of the objector to a particular war and the position of the standard, government-approved CO. I am not maintaining that the objectors themselves are similar, but rather that their *positions* are similar.

In general, it seems to be that any position which is not ultimately grounded in a concern for human beings is morally irresponsible. It is easy to go from a concern for human life to an opposition to war. It is because war destroys what is human, what is valuable, that it is wrong. Yet, hypothetically, what if a given war could do more good than harm? What if it were really true of a war that unless it were fought, there would be at some later point a nuclear war which would destroy all life? Of course the real problem is in coming to know that this is true of any restricted war. But if it were true, then would not a concern for human well-being justify for almost anyone—including the CO— participation in that war? This is an extreme case, but not an unrealistic one. The argument has already been put forward with regard to Vietnam. We will hear it again, and every position deserving of respect will have to deal with it in one way or another.

I am not suggesting that all those who claim to be "opposed to all wars" are misstating their beliefs, but rather that, as often used, the phrase "opposed to all wars" does not mean that the person described believes that participation is unjustified in all logically possible war. It may mean that the person is opposed to participation in all the wars he can imagine occurring, or would have been opposed to all those in the past, or is opposed to war in itself, but nevertheless feels that participation could be justified. Thus when someone thinks of himself as being opposed to participation in all wars, he is generally working with some rather implicit but perhaps unrecognized assumptions about wars. Needless to point out, any objection which is implicitly based on the belief that failure to participate in the war would not lead to the destruction of all life is an objection implicitly based on a political belief, that is, a belief about the behavior of nations and the effects of their weapons. Prior to the development of nuclear weapons, one could quite reasonably feel that his opposition was justified without dealing explicitly with this issue. Now, this is no longer true.

I believe, therefore, that there is no clear distinction between most of the positions opposing all wars and those opposing particular wars, *and* no clear difference between those positions based on beliefs about the political behavior of nations and those that are not. Almost all objectors have the same *kind* of background assumptions. Some have been more explicit than others in recognizing the substance of and the evidence for these background beliefs. It makes sense, therefore, to deal with specific difficulties encountered in justifying one's participation in actual wars.

4

"Moral life," "Moral agency," the words themselves take on an ideal quality. It is as if there were far off in the distance a pure state of being that one has dedicated oneself to becoming. But there is something false about this image; it's too untainted, too far removed from the world to actually have the quality that such a way of being has when one acts in the real world. Pure moral agents could only exist in a far more perfect world than this. The moral agent "acts on his beliefs as to what is right." But how can this be pure when what is right is often also horrible, when so much that is not beautiful enters into the determination of "the right."

Operating from within the moral life there is only one ultimate question: "What should I do; what is the morally justified course of action?" There is no question that war, all war, is in itself horrible, and that, in isolation, one never ought to participate in any war. But we have seen that the world is such that one is rarely able to act in isolation. Thus, a war that is in itself wrong might have the consequence of preventing world destruction. Given that one lives in a society which requires its members to participate in warfare, the refusal to participate involves one in more than simply declining to take part. In refusing to participate one does other things, one violates the law, one fails to keep a political obligation, one breaks faith with the society. The moral agent is also a member of society. And while it is true that in being a member of a society, one does not cease to be a moral agent, is it not possible that one's political obligations determine, in part, one's moral obligation?

The fact that a refusal to participate in a war may violate the laws of one's society should be taken into account in deciding if it is right to refuse. The force this consideration adds to the argument that we ought to obey the law is twofold. Not carrying out a political obligation is *prima facie* wrong and also tends to produce situations which are harmful. These bad effects are things such as the increase of general lawlessness and disorder that is encouraged in the society when any significant group does not obey the laws. I'm not sure that all the effects are bad-in-themselves. Some effects, such as encouraging others to reflect on the morality of their acts, may be beneficial, but I do not want to dwell on these issues. Of far more significance is the claim that it is wrong-in-itself to break a political obligation. Is this so? And if it is wrong, how much weight should we give it as a consideration? (Killing is also wrong-in-itself; we are involved in balancing considerations.)

The decision to object breaks a person's identification with his society. At this point in my life, the political obligation feels artificial. Once, I felt it. I will try to reconstruct it.

We are members of a community. True, there was no original contract, but we have operated in certain ways, sharing certain procedures for determining what will be done, and expecting the others to go along with the group's determinations even when they disagreed or were adversely affected. We can vote, and dissent and try to alter policy; we can enter into the determination of it, into the determination of legal duties and obligations. There is no contract on our part, but then our fellow citizens, likewise, never explicitly bound themselves to us. Yet we work to alter the laws and policies, and we make demands on others, and they keep faith. Is it not a part of what holds us together that we even agreed not to act on our own judgment as to what is best for the group if this violates the law? Of course, we are not absolutely bound by this, but does it not lay some claim on us? I am not suggesting that one has a moral obligation to do what is wrong. The point is that one's political obligations enter into the determination of what is wrong.

I'll build the case against refusal even stronger than it is. Let us assume a few things. First, that in refusing to enter the army the person is breaking faith with the society, that he is really failing to obey legitimate commands. More specifically, let us assume that the war is lawful even without a declaration of war. Let us further assume that restricting the exemption for CO so that it does not apply to all objectors is constitutional, and finally let us assume that the relations between international law and domestic law are such that we really *do* have a legal obligation to submit to induction. Again let us assume that somehow those who are called to fight have really entered into the determination of policy. Let us assume it is not the case that the society promotes its interests by sacrificing its children, by sacrificing those who have least entered into decision-making. Let us build the obligation to mythical proportions.

Let us remember that the issue is the war. This is crucial, for the war goes beyond my relations with my community. I am quite prepared to admit the political obligation into the determination of the moral course of action. But what kind of weight should it have? Perhaps an analogy will help. Consider: I agree to meet a friend at four o'clock. At 3 o'clock I no longer wish to. I realize that it will cause him some discomfort, but judge that mine would be greater than his. Considering only the total well-being of all concerned, I would not go. But this is not right, for I have agreed. I have an obligation to him. I cannot go ahead and pretend that I never agreed to meet him. By agreeing to meet him, I have, within reason, restricted my right to consider my well-being. He has a claim on me. This is largely the force of the political obligation. By entering into the decision-making processes of the society, to a large extent, we give up the right to enter our well-being into the picture when determining if it would be morally justifiable to break the law. Furthermore, in part, we agree not to act freely on our own judgment of what is in the interests of the society once a law has been passed. We adopt a group process for determining how each will act for the group interest.

But the war goes beyond the community. It involves doing harm to people who were not party to our tacit agreements and understandings. The fact that I have certain agreements with one section of humanity cannot justify my doing harm to another. My communal obligations have moral force only on internal communal matters. Consider a band of criminals: Because of their agreements and relations to one another they may have many obligations to each other. Yet no one would argue that their obligations to one another, derived from their oaths and agreements, could justify their doing harm to someone outside their group. Similarly, if participation in a war is not justified on the basis of factors other than communal agreements, then my agreement or contract cannot justify that participation. It carries no weight. (This does not mean that we have no obligation to obey laws which harm those outside the society, but rather that whatever force this obligation has, it does not derive from contract or agreement. It must be based on extrinsic considerations such as the bad effects of general lawlessness.)

Perhaps it will be said that as a member of this society I have no right to consider the well-being of outsiders, or at least no right to consider that their well-being is as important as that of my countrymen. And thus all that is important is that the war be in the national interest. Indeed, this is how some people reason. It is a discriminatory way of deciding what to do. It is halfway between the egoistic and the moral in that it cuts out a segment of humanity from consideration. It is a view that does not truly deal with the moral question.

5

I have said that a person participates in a moral form of life when he acts on his belief that certain actions are morally right. We have seen that it is not always easy to know which action is right. In coming to a moral judgment we are especially concerned with much we do not observe, such as the motives of different parties—how they see their own actions, what they are trying to do, what they believe to be true about their situation. Certainly, before we run off to destroy the V.C., a moral inquiry would lead one to ask how fifteen-year-old guerrillas see what they are doing, whether they believe themselves to be fighting a just cause, whether they are trying to impose a tyranny on others, etc. But furthermore, our concern is with consequences, in particular the basically subjective experiences of other human beings. It is the experience of human beings that is the primary bearer of value. It is their experience of pain, hunger, terror, injustice, freedom, and dignity that we are concerned with. These constitute the bulk of those situations which are important-in-themselves. And by and large our knowledge of motives and experiences of others is dependent on testimony, on what others can tell us. We believe what they say about themselves when we believe them to be speaking in good faith, because they are authorities on the subject. Thus, at this basic level and all along the line we form our beliefs by accepting as true or probably true what others have told us.

The point is that the moral life, doing what one believes is right, is not incompatible with believing others, or with accepting the pronouncement of others as authoritative. Of necessity we do this all the time, and *on this score* the difference between the most skeptical of us and those who believe they have access to the revealed knowledge of God is only a matter of degree. However, there are more or less reasonable grounds for believing that someone who claims to speak authoritatively really is an authority. There are more or less responsible ways of conducting inquiry even on the secondary level, or levels even more removed from the actual situation. And it is possible to treat a given source as an authority for other reasons than that we believe him to know or probably know the truth. When we begin to act on the beliefs of others for reasons other than our belief that they are wise, it is then that we are no longer moral agents.

There is nothing in the notion of a moral agent which rules out looking to laws and government policies as guides to discovering what one ought to do. There is nothing which rules out believing that the men who make government policy are far wiser, more experienced, and far more familiar with the actual facts of the situation, and that we *ought*, therefore, to accept their judgments about what we should do (e.g., participate in a war). But does it make sense to see the government as a source for the beliefs one should act on? Is it reasonable? Is it responsible?

At first the questions seem silly. Is it not obvious that governments have often had people do much that was immoral? Perhaps it is on this issue that Americans divide. Yet it seems amazing. Is there anyone who really believes, looking back at history, that those who have obeyed the law have done no wrong, that obedience to law is the surest guide to right conduct? Was it true of the Germans? Was it true of those who reported (in accordance with the law) the hiding places of Jews?

Does it make any sense to see a legislative directive, a law, a command to perform a particular act—as a command to perform that act which is an answer to the moral question: what ought I to do? Can anyone really believe that laws have contained the answer to this question? We must remember that, in trying to discover what act is right, we must pay attention to the experiences of all people. The leaders of nation-states have special obligations to their own people and their nation; they have been placed in office to promote the *national* well-being, the *national* interest. All the mechanisms for control of leaders are national mechanisms. In short, officials are, at best, responsible to a national constituency. This idea is at the heart of the concept of a nation-state. That national policies have no ultimate concern with the well-being of those outside its borders is so "natural" that we hardly ever make it explicit.

Some policies that are in the national interest are also in the world interest, for instance, avoiding a global nuclear war. Assume that the government claims that a given war is necessary because it will check a flow of events which will otherwise lead to nuclear war. When a government says something of this sort, is it to be believed? *Is believing the government the best way to acquire true beliefs in this area?*

Given the situation in Vietnam, the question seems like nonsense. But we should remember that there was a time when most of us knew absolutely nothing about Vietnam, and it is often the case that we have to act without having the time to learn very much. For many this is the general situation. We go along unaware. Suddenly the situation breaks. Something has happened in Asia, Latin America, or Africa. Events are upon us. We need guidelines for dealing with government assertions from a position of ignorance and limited time. We need to choose between a stance of general confidence and a stance of general skepticism. We need to define our relationship with our nation-state.

Make no mistake about the significance of the issue. If it is reasonable to regard the government as an authority on matters of this sort, then the moral agent is not really autonomous. A person concerned with the war's justification might reason as follows:

1) The war is justified if it will prevent a nuclear war. (Or do a, b, and c.)

2) The government said that the war will prevent a nuclear war. (Or do a, b, and c.)

3) The government is the best authority we have on this matter.

4) It is probably the case that the war will prevent a nuclear war. (Or will do a, b, c.)

5) Therefore, it is probably the case that the war is justified.

It is distressing to see that being a moral agent may be compatible with simply accepting what we are told by the government, with simply going along with government policy. It is distressing to see that, in substance, the moral life might not differ, in this area, from an unreflective reliance on the commands or expectations of others. It may not differ from an abdication of agency. This possibility exists.

Granting that the government has at its disposal great resources of information, intelligence, and experience, granting that the average individual cannot match these resources, we should note: (1) Despite its resources, the government is often ignorant of important matters of fact. This is especially true in the higher circles of decision-making. (2) The government is a partisan to a debate. It is attempting to justify its own policies which, even when they correspond with a world interest, were intended to promote a much more limited interest. Its spokesmen sometimes unconsciously view the world in ways which would justify those policies. Sometimes there is no real concern with the truth of statements offered as justifications. (3) Often there are other authorities that disagree with the government. The universities can provide non-governmental expertise. Other nations should be seen as being at least as great an authority as our own government. Thus, if the relevant factual issue in the Vietnam debate is the effect of U.S. withdrawal on China's foreign policy, we should look at the views of China's neighbors: India, Burma, Russia, Japan, Pakistan, Nepal, Thailand, North and South Vietnam, and North and South Korea. (Of course, some, like ourselves, are far too involved to be considered objective.) (4) On the specific issue of nuclear war, we may assume that those whose actions our government feels must be stopped, in order to avoid nuclear war, do not themselves believe that their unchecked actions will lead to world destruction. Often, they should know at least as well as our government (assuming that our government does not intend to start a nuclear war). (5) And finally, we should note that any conclusion to the effect that the government should be seen as an authority on factual matters would, if widely believed, be self-defeating. For, without independent evaluation of the government's claims, those in power would soon put forth their claims with less and less warrant.

All this places the moral agent in a very difficult position. He must concern himself with political questions about which he has no great knowledge. He can never be fully certain of his conclusions. He will be making personally momentous decisions on the basis of judgments about which the courts have said, "These judgments have historically been reserved for the government, and in matters which can be said to fall within these areas, the conviction of the individual has never been permitted to override that of the state." (The Seeger case.) Perhaps the wisest stance is one of critical doubt: "All wars are unjustifiable until proven otherwise." Yet it is hard to be sure. It is hard to predict what would happen if many people did this. It is hard to say what a wise social policy would be. We cannot know for sure that a time will not come when there will be a war which should be fought in order to prevent the destruction of all life. We cannot be sure that such a war would be fought if dubious potential soldiers have to be convinced.

Ultimately, events press in on us. Acting or refraining from acting become equally significant. The moral agent can proceed only by knowing about the world. Yet he must operate in far greater ignorance than he might wish. Often the conscientious objector maintains a Luther-like style and image which reassures and comforts him and protects him from the society. He does this by deluding himself about how much he knows.

APPENDIX

Because they may be of some interest to those who are considering applying for the I-0 exemption, I have included the actual answers I gave to the two main questions on the Selective Service forms.

QUESTION 2: *Describe the nature of your belief which is the basis of your claim made in series I. . . .*

The single overarching duty upon man is to be a moral agent. This duty can be expressed in terms of an absolute injunction to live the moral life, the life of the moral self. As such it is the only absolute injunction or imperative, all others are contextual. At best they are quasi-absolute. They cannot be fully absolute in that they may conflict with one another or with the overriding injunction. That is, in a specific situation it may be impossible to satisfy all of our duties and obligations. For instance, we all agree that a man has an obligation to keep his promises. We also recognize that a father has an obligation to promote the well-being of his children. Suppose that a man promises to take his son swimming on a certain day, but when the day comes the temperature is fifty-five degrees. The father fears that his son will catch a cold if he swims in such weather. It does not matter which he decides to do, keep his promise or act for his son's welfare. The point is that he has two obligations, yet in the actual situation he can fulfill only one. The obligation which is not fulfilled, even though the man acts as he should, is sometimes said to have been *merely prima facie*. Because there is always a logically possible situation such that any obligation will be *merely prima facie*, we may say that all obligations are only relatively absolute. There is one obligation or duty which is an exception; this is the injunction to moral agency. Only this duty to be a moral agent is fully absolute. One may ask if it is not possible for there to be a situation in which the obligation to be a moral agent is *merely prima facie*. The answer is, "NO." Whatever reason one could provide to show that one should act in fashion X instead of fashion Y (the course of action in accordance with moral agency) would also show that we were mistaken in supposing that action Y really was the moral course. It is part of the meaning of "moral agency" that one can never be said to be a moral agent when one is acting in a fashion he knows is wrong. The injunction to moral agency is thus absolute in that it can never be overridden; it is constitutive of the moral life, part of what it means to be a moral individual.

The above statements are not put forward as my beliefs only, or as statements which are in some sense "true for myself alone." They are neither personal nor subjective. The injunction to moral agency is incumbent upon all men. Furthermore, I do not mean by the use of the terms "imperative" or "injunction" to suggest that I am referring to some command issued by some commander to whom we owe an absolute duty of obedience. There can be no absolute duty of obedience, because it is always possible to be ordered to act contrary to what is consistent with moral agency. But since the injunction to moral agency is absolute, any order, duty, or obligation which was inconsistent with it would be, at best, *merely prima facie*. Thus, all duties that arise from human contracts and associations, tacit or otherwise, are subordinate to the injunction to moral agency. Since all obligations are subordinate to that of moral agency, any particular obligation is subordinate (e.g., obligations to one's government). It is my belief that membership in the armed forces is contrary to what is moral. This I hope to make clear in what follows.

The injunction to moral agency is formal in that even after one knows that he must be a moral agent he does not yet know what the moral course of action is in a given specific situation. He must relate the specifics of the actual situation to the formal injunction. The meaning of the injunction to moral agency may be explicated in terms of the following components:

—Action in accord with one's beliefs as to what is right. The individual must be an agent in the sense that he guides his own conduct. In this sense he retains the ultimate authority over his own activity.

—His beliefs as to what is right and wrong are *ultimately* based on his own evaluation and reflection. This, too, is implicit in the notion of agency. *Ultimately* each person must reject all others as authoritative sources of knowledge as to what is right or wrong.

—The evaluation of actions must be made with close attention to the consequences of those actions. In assessing the consequences of actions we must treat all persons equally. (Thus in evaluating a foreign policy, reference to national interest is not a suitable guide if it means that the well-being of foreigners is counted as less important than that of nationals.)

I have referred to the above as formal constituents of moral agency in that they provide a form or framework for decision-making. But prior to an investigation of the specific case there is no way of telling which of two incompatible actions is moral (e.g., should I break my promise or keep it?). Knowledge of what is right in a specific situation is generally guided by the lessons of past experience, often found embodied in the customary codes of the community. In dealing with a specific case, all relevant knowledge should be brought to bear. The following considerations serve to link the formal aspects of moral agency or selfhood with the present question of military service:

—membership in the armed forces involves placing oneself in a situation where proper reflection over the rightness of one's action is impossible.

—membership involves placing oneself in a situation where one is not free to act in accordance with whatever beliefs one might have about the rightness of a course of action. It is an abdication of agency.

—membership, in any capacity, involves participation, directly or indirectly, in specific acts of violence and killing, presently in Vietnam, where such acts cannot be, and have not been, justified. In time of peace, membership involves one in preparation and readiness to perform such acts should you be ordered to.

—membership in the armed forces not only denies the possibility of moral agency and involves one in immoral activities; in addition, military training and discipline is designed to produce a capitulation of moral selfhood which cannot but bring into being patterns of action and thought which will have detrimental effects on the character of the future self and on future lines of conduct.

QUESTION 5: *Under what circumstances do you believe in force?*

If we distinguish force from violence, then I believe in the use of force in all sorts of situations; particularly, the force of reasoned argument and moral appeal and testimony. As to violence, I feel that it is, in general, unjustified, and any purported justification would have to be consistent with moral agency. Thus, each individual act of violence must be justified. If one is a moral agent, he cannot commit himself to a *program* of violence or a *program of training* which will lead him to regard violence as a commendable solution to problems.

One key factor in attempting to justify some act of violence is guilt. For a person to be morally guilty, in the fullest sense, he must know that what he is doing is wrong. Needless to say, this condition is never met in time of war.

Of most importance in justifying an act of violence is that it be necessary. I mean more than that the act appears necessary within the given context. I mean that there is nothing that could have been done, or could still be done so as to make violence unnecessary. In this sense, acts of violence are almost never truly necessary. What I am suggesting, then, is that we should not regard a contest as fixed and ask questions of a static nature. We must always consider our obligation to work for social reconstruction. Thus, we might say that in a given context (preventing a rape) violence is *excusable*, but this does not mean that it is *right*.

It is essential that we come to see violence as, at best, excusable in certain situations. For the claim that violence is right, or fully justified, is a way of denying one's agency. It is a way of denying that it was in one's power to have avoided that situation. It is a way of avoiding responsibility for future changes. In short, it is a way of adjusting oneself to that which is inherently wrong.

NOTES

[1] *Conscientious Objection*, published by the U.S. Government, p. 1.
[2] *U.S. vs. Macintosh*, 283 U.S. 605.

ST. PAUL SEMINARY LIBRARY
ST. PAUL, MINN. 55101

DATE DUE